The Naval & Military Press Ltd

Published by

The Naval & Military Press Ltd
Unit 10 Ridgewood Industrial Park,
Uckfield, East Sussex,
TN22 5QE England

Tel: +44 (0) 1825 749494
Fax: +44 (0) 1825 765701

www.naval-military-press.com
www.military-genealogy.com
www.militarymaproom.com

Prepared by
The Commander Submarine Force
U .S. Pacific Fleet
1946

TABLE OF CONTENTS

INTRODUCTION

TO THOSE whose contribution meant the loss of sons, brothers or husbands in this war, I pay my most humble respect and extend my deepest sympathy. As to the 374 officers and 3131 men of the Submarine Force who gave their lives in the winning of this war, I can assure you that they went down fighting and that their brothers who survived them took a grim toll of our savage enemy to avenge their deaths.

MAY GOD REST THEIR GALLANT SOULS.

From speech given in Cleveland, Navy Day 1945 by Vice Admiral C. A. Lockwood, Jr., Commander Submarine Force, U. S .Pacific Fleet, January 1943 - January 1946.

INTRODUCTION

The submarines paid heavily for their successes in World War II. A total of 52 submarines were lost, with 374 officers and 3,131 enlisted men. These personnel losses represented 16% of the officer and 13% of the enlisted operational personnel. Of the 52 losses, two submarines, DORADO and R-12, were lost in the Atlantic, S-26 was sunk in a collision off Panama and S-28 was an operational loss in training at Pearl Harbor. The remaining 48 were lost either directly or indirectly as the result of enemy action, or due to stranding on reefs during combat operations. S-39, S-36, S-27 and DARTER were lost as the result of such strandings. In all these strandings all personnel were rescued.

In the cases of the losses due to enemy action, three officers and five men from FLIER and all but four men from SEALION were saved. The remaining submarines were lost with all hands, though some personnel from GRENADIER, PERCH, SCULPIN, TANG, two men from S-44 and one from TULLIBEE were repatriated at the end of hostilities, having been held as prisoners of war by the enemy. Four men are said to have survived ROBALO's sinking but they have not been recovered following the end of the war, and it is assumed that they perished as prisoners of the enemy.

The 52 submarines represent approximately 18% of all submarines which saw combat duty. This loss of 18%, while high in comparision to the losses sustained by other types of ships of the Allied Forces, is considered remarkably low when considered in relation to the results achieved, or when compared with the losses sustained by enemy submarine forces. The Germans, in World War I, lost 178 submarines of a total of 272 submarines in commission during that war, and in World War II they lost between 700 and 800 submarines. With but meagre results to show for their submarine effort, the Japanese in World War II lost 128 submarines and had but 58 remaining at the end of hostilities, and many of the remaining 58 were non-operational.

In analyzing our losses, the following factors are considered as having been responsible for the low figure as compared to those of our enemies:

(1) Excellent mental and physical condition of our submarine personnel, and their high state of training.

(2) Superiority of our radar over that of the Japanese.

(3) Weakness of Japanese anti-submarine measures.

Submarine crews, upon their return from a war patrol, were transferred to a Rest and Recuperation Camp for a period of two weeks while their submarine was being refitted by a relief crew. During this two week period the regular crew had no official

duties to perform other than to rest and relax and divorce their minds from all thoughts of war and combat. There were some who criticized this practice as being in the nature of pampering. The submarine force commanders vigorously defended it as being not a luxury but a vital part of submarine warfare. War patrols, normally lasting from 45 to 60 days, introduced a protracted mental tension unknown to other types of warfare. Without the rest periods to ease this tension the personnel would soon have cracked up under the strain. As a result of the rest and recuperation policy submarine crews went to sea mentally and physically alert and it is considered that this was the primary factor in keeping our losses to a minimum. Hand in hand with the excellent mental and physical condition of our personnel, was the high state of training in which they departed on patrol. Prior to a submarine's first patrol she was given an extensive training period, either on the east coast or at Panama, followed by advanced training in the Pearl Harbor area. Immediately preceding the departure upon subsequent patrols, the submarine was given an intensive refresher training period, lasting from four to eight days. Training kept pace with enemy anti-submarine measures, new training methods being introduced to counter the latest trends in enemy offensive or defensive measures.

The superiority of submarine radar, as compared to that of the Japanese anti-submarine forces, was another factor contributing much to keeping our losses low. Submarines started the war without radar, but within a few months all were equipped with the SD (aircraft warning) radar. The SD, by giving early warning of the approach of planes, did much to prevent surprise air attacks on surfaced submarines.

The installation of the SJ (surface search) radar a few months later did the same to prevent the undetected approach of enemy surface craft during darkness and low visibility. When it became apparent that enemy electronic science had progressed to the point where they were able to produce efficient radars, the APR was developed to warn of their presence, and later, the ST and SV radars, using shorter waves than the SD and SJ, were installed to combat the enemy's quite successful efforts to detect our own radars.

At the start of the war, enemy anti-submarine materiel was comparable with our own; their listening and echo ranging gear were practically duplications of that installed in our own anti-submarine vessels. The Japanese are notoriously poor inventors but great copyists, and with their espionage services cut off during the war, they rapidly fell behind in the development of anti-submarine measures. And although their original equipment was good, their technique of employing it was faulty. They seemed to have little trouble in locating a submarine with their listening gear following a torpedo attack, but having located her, they failed miserably in the solution of the mathematical problem of where to drop their depth charges. Their attacks were characterized by a consistent lack of persistence. They were prone to accept the most nebulous evidence as positive proof of a sinking, and being sure of a kill, they were off about their business, to let the submarine surface and thank God for the Japanese superiority complex. While only 48 submarines were lost in combat operations, and of these, not more than 41 were directly due to enemy action, the Japanese, at the end of hostilities, furnished us with information which showed a total of 468 positive sinkings of our submarines. The U. S. Navy, by a wise policy of total censorship of submarine operations, encouraged the enemy in their belief of their anti-submarine sucesses. When we failed to announce the successful attacks of our submarines, the enemy naturally assumed that the submarines never got home to report them.

The chart on the following page shows the known or estimated positions of all submarine losses in the Pacific. The estimated positions must be accepted with caution - at best they are only fair guesses. In several cases submarines departed from their bases for patrol and were never heard from again. In such cases the estimated position is given as inside the area to which the submarine was assigned but the loss might have occurred anywhere between that area and the base. In general, solid dots have been placed on the chart where the position of the loss is known with reasonable certainty to have occurred within the area covered by the dot. Open dots have been used where positions are not certain, due to circumstances explained in the text.

A study of the chart will reveal some amazing facts, as for example:

(a) Not a single submarine was lost in the Central Pacific waters until the loss of PICKEREL in April 1943, sixteen months after the start of the war.

(b) The area south of Honshu, at the entrance to Toyko Bay, and at the Kii Suido and Bungo Suido entrances to the Inland Sea, would normally be considered the areas where enemy anti-submarine measures would be most intense. Yet, although these areas were constantly and heavily patrolled during the entire war, not a single submarine was ever lost along the southern coast of Honshu.

(c) Next to the southern Honshu areas, the most intense enemy anti-submarine measures could be expected at his strongest outposts - Truk and Palau. Yet the war was two years old before the first of two submarines was lost near Truk, and information indicates that the only loss near Palau - TULLIBEE in March 1944 - was caused by a circular run of one of her own torpedoes.

(d) The shallow waters of the Yellow Sea made submarine evasive tactics difficult, and permitted extensive defensive mining by the enemy, yet only two submarines were lost in that area, and none during the last ten months of the war when the greater part or all submarine offensive patrols were concentrated therein.

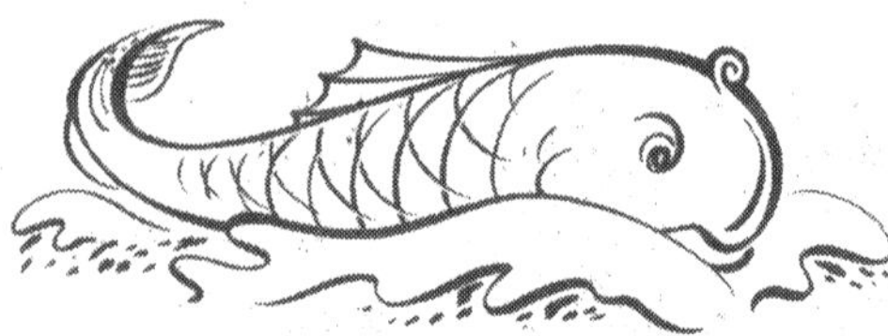

CHART

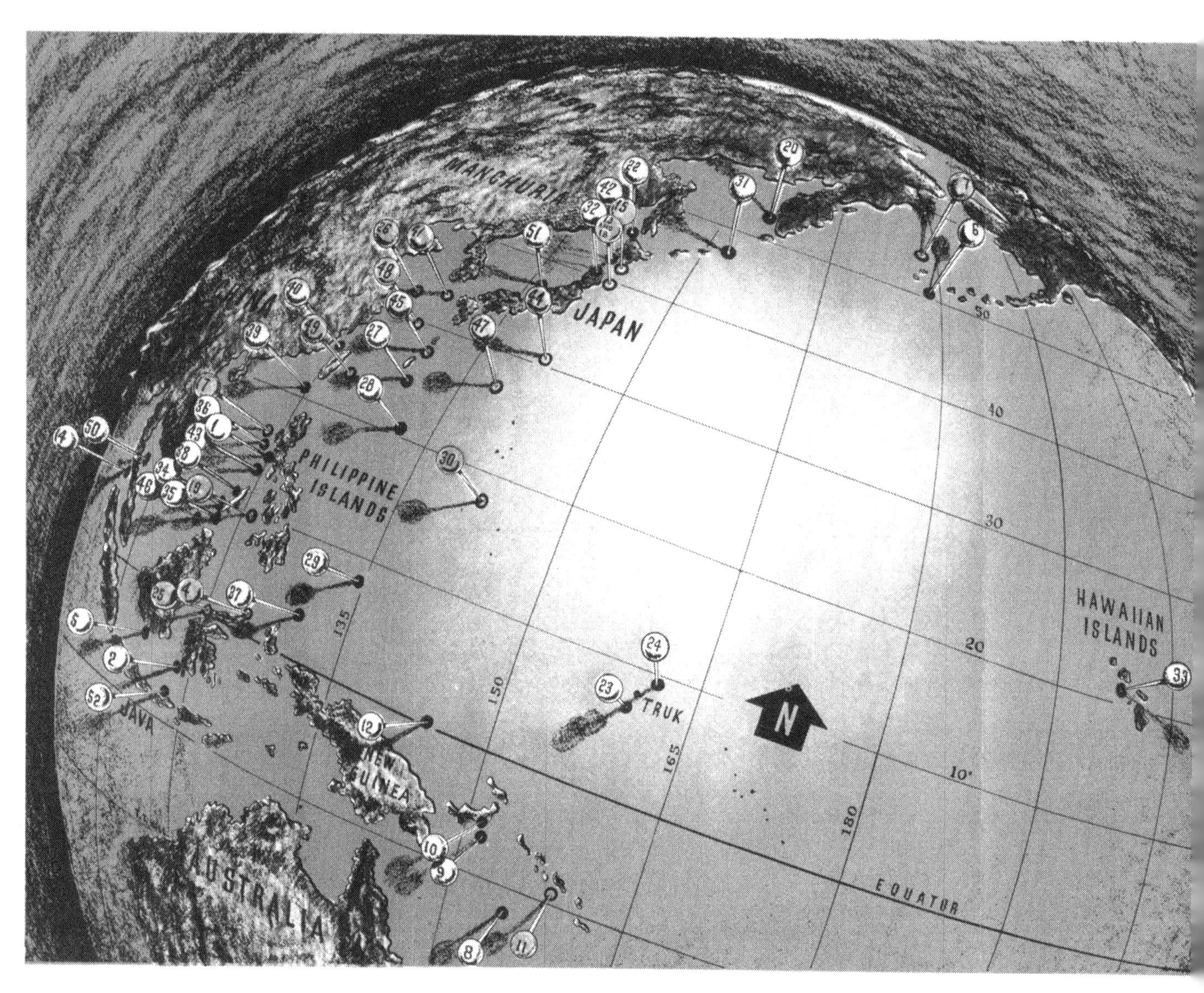

POSITIONS OF SUBMARINE LOSSES

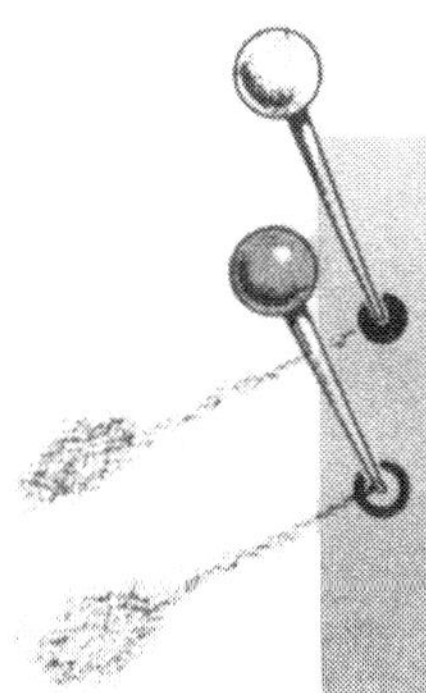

INDICATES KNOWN POSITION

INDICATES ESTIMATED POSITION

1.	SEALION	12-10-41
2.	S-36	1-20-42
3. ●	S-26	1-24-42
4.	SHARK 1	2-11,21-42
5.	PERCH	3-3-42
6.	S-27	6-19-42
7.	GRUNION	7-30,8-6-42
8.	S-39	8-13,14-42
9.	ARGONAUT	1-10-43
10.	AMBERJACK	2-16-43
11.	GRAMPUS	3-5,6-43
12.	TRITON	3-15-43
13.	PICKEREL	4-3-43
14.	GRENADIER	4-22-43
15.	RUNNER	5-28,7-4-43
16. ●	R-12	6-12-43
17.	GRAYLING	9-9,9-12-43
18.	POMPANO	8-29,9-27-43
19.	CISCO	9-28-43
20.	S-44	10-7-43
21. ●	DORADO	10-12-43
22.	WAHOO	10-11-43
23.	CORVINA	11-16-43
24.	SCULPIN	11-19-43
25.	CAPELIN	11-23,12-9-43
26.	SCORPION	1-5,2-24-44
27.	GRAYBACK	2-26-44
28.	TROUT	2-29-44
29.	TULLIBEE	3-26,27-44
30.	GUDGEON	4-7,5-11-44
31.	HERRING	6-1-44
32.	GOLET	6-14-44
33.	S-28	7-4-44
34.	ROBALO	7-26-44
35.	FLIER	8-13-44
36.	HARDER	8-24-44
37.	SEAWOLF	10-3-44
38.	DARTER	10-24-44
39.	SHARK 11	10-24-44
40.	TANG	10-24-44
41.	ESCOLAR	10-17,11-3-44
42.	ALBACORE	11-7-44
43.	GROWLER	11-8-44
44.	SCAMP	11-9,16-44
45.	SWORDFISH	1-12-45
46.	BARBEL	2-4-45
47.	KETE	3-20,31-45
48.	TRIGGER	3-26,28-45
49.	SNOOK	4-8,20-45
50.	LAGARTO	5-3-45
51.	BONEFISH	6-18-45
52.	BULLHEAD	8-6-45

● Losses not shown on chart: DORADO, en route New London to Panama, October 1943. S-26, at Panama, January 1942. R-12 at Key West, Florida, June 1943.

In the pages which follow, the circumstances surrounding the loss of each submarine, so far as they can be ascertained, are given. In each case, all evidence available at the time of this writing has been adduced in seeking to assign a specific cause for each loss, and to establish a definite position where the loss occurred. With the war so recently over, it will be obvious to every one that all returns are not in - that the coming years may be expected to divulge further information bearing on our submarine losses, and that the conclusions presented here will have to be modified as these data come to light. So for the benefit of future researchers, an outline of the data and methods used is in order .

The table which follows gives a condensed summary of the causes for the loss of each of our submarines which did not return, and an estimate as to the accuracy of the analysis. In preparing this summary and the descriptive matter covering the loss of each ship, the first source utilized was the operation order delineating her area and the despatches sent to her and received from her during the patrol on which she was lost. Due to the necessity for submarines to maintain radio silence during their operations, information gleaned from incoming messages was usually sketchy. Any reports of enemy aircraft or surface craft in the vicinity of losses were taken into account; reports by other submarines of

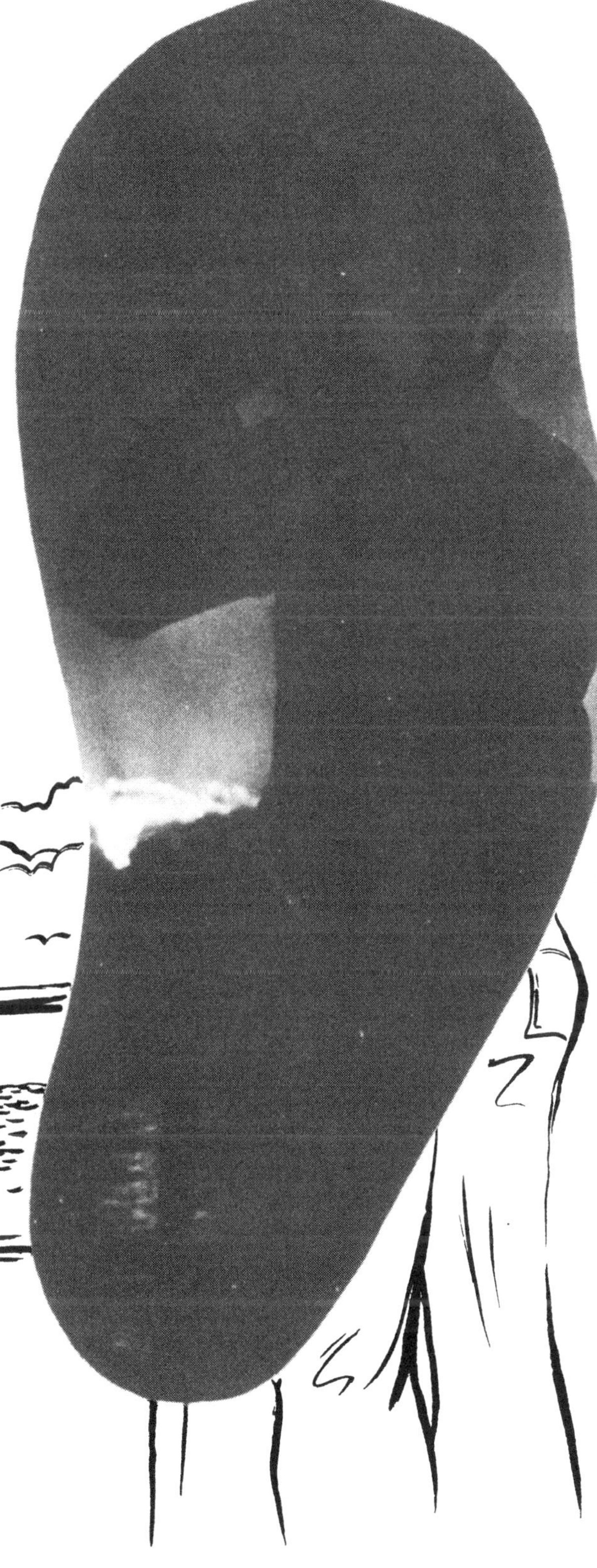

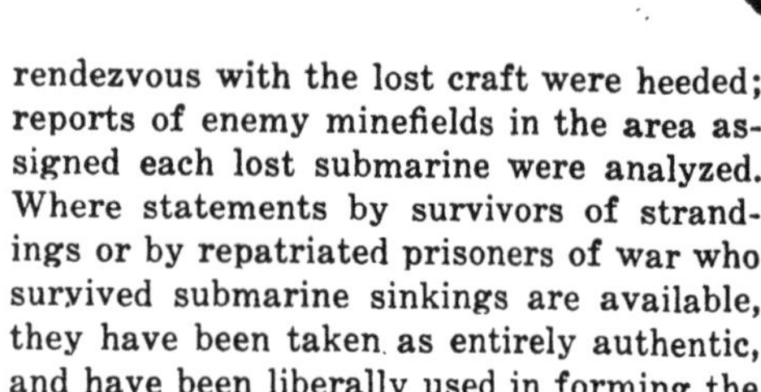

rendezvous with the lost craft were heeded; reports of enemy minefields in the area assigned each lost submarine were analyzed. Where statements by survivors of strandings or by repatriated prisoners of war who survived submarine sinkings are available, they have been taken as entirely authentic, and have been liberally used in forming the story of the loss.

When the war began, submarines operated alone and in far flung areas. The paucity of contacts with them by other ships and their operational commanders makes it difficult to establish definitely small areas, both in time and in position, where their loss occurred. As the war progressed and wolfpacks came into being, the frequent exchange of information among members of the pack gives much more material concerning ships lost while patroling as members of packs.

The chief source of information as to attacks made on U. S. submarines by the enemy has been provided by the Japanese since war's end. The list consists of two parts, both exact translations, and purports to be a list of positive sinkings. The first part gives the date and place of attacks made on U. S. submarines; the second is an amplifying report which gives further information on each attack. An attached note states that those attacks whose dates or locations are uncertain have been eliminated by the Japanese. The enemy was prone to accept the most inconclusive evidence as proof that a submarine was sunk, and, from that point of view, it would seem that the list should be fairly complete. Yet the definite possibility exists that one or more of the attacks not reported because it was thought to be ineffective or because the date or position was garbled might explain the loss of one of our submarines whose end is now only a matter for conjecture. Furthermore, the report states that the record of April 1943 is imperfect

and that "since about July 1943 more strict investigations have been gradually instigated to confirm the sinkings, but the reports of the sinkings prior to this date are listed here without further investigations." In the cases of a great many attacks made before July 1943, only positions and dates are given - no information is available even as to whether the attacks were by surface ships, planes or submarines, much less concerning evidence to confirm sinkings. Moreover, Japanese records are notoriously ill kept, and several instances where the descriptive matter concerning an attack has been linked with the wrong item in the date - position list have been discovered. Although seven submarines gave up prisoners of war to the Japanese, only four attacks in which American prisoners were taken are listed in the report. The number of anti-submarine attacks which, for one reason or another, never were reported to any central Japanese agency will probably never be known. Excellent circumstantial evidence indicates that at least one of our submarines, GRAMPUS, was lost as the result of an attack by two enemy destroyers who were themselves sunk shortly thereafter and thus never reported the attack. Also the poor coordination evident in the Japanese military and naval organizations may mean that records of attacks made in outlying places received poor handling.

A SUMMARY OF

		ACCURACY OF ANALYSIS		ENEMY ACTION			FRIENDLY FORCES		OTHER					
		PROBABLE TO POSSIBLE	CERTAIN TO PROBABLE	SURFACE CRAFT	AIR CRAFT	SUBMARINE	SURFACE CRAFT	AIR CRAFT	MINES	CIRCULAR RUNS	OPERATIONAL	STRANDING	UNKNOWN	
1.	SEALION		X		X									12-10-41
2.	S-36		X									X		1-20-42
3.	S-26		X								X			1-24-42
4.	SHARK 1	X		X										2-11,21-42
5.	PERCH		X	X										3-3-42
6.	S-27		X									X		6-19-42
7.	GRUNION												X	7-30,8-6-42
8.	S-39		X									X		8-13,14-42
9.	ARGONAUT		X	X										1-10-43
10.	AMBERJACK		X	X	X									2-16-43
11.	GRAMPUS	X		X										3-5,6-43
12.	TRITON		X	X										3-15-43
13.	PICKEREL	X		X										4-3-43
14.	GRENADIER		X		X									4-22-43
15.	RUNNER	X							X					5-28,7-4-43
16.	R-12		X								X			6-12-43
17.	GRAYLING												X	9-9,9-12-43
18.	POMPANO	X							X					8-29,9-27-43
19.	CISCO	X		X	X									9-28-43
20.	S-44		X	X										10-7-43
21.	DORADO		X					X						10-12-43
22.	WAHOO	X			X									10-11-43
23.	CORVINA		X			X								11-16-43
24.	SCULPIN		X	X										11-19-43
25.	CAPELIN	X		X										11-23,12-9-43
26.	SCORPION	X							X					1-5,2-24-44

SUBMARINE LOSSES

		ACCURACY OF ANALYSIS		ENEMY ACTION			FRIENDLY FORCES		OTHER					
		PROBABLE TO POSSIBLE	CERTAIN TO PROBABLE	SURFACE CRAFT	AIR CRAFT	SUBMARINE	SURFACE CRAFT	AIR CRAFT	MINES	CIRCULAR RUNS	OPERATIONAL	STRANDING	UNKNOWN	
27.	GRAYBACK		X	X	X									2-26-44
28.	TROUT		X	X										2-29-44
29.	TULLIBEE		X							X				3-26,27-44
30.	GUDGEON	X		X	X									4-7,5-11-44
31.	HERRING		X	X										6-1-44
32.	GOLET		X	X										6-14-44
33.	S-28		X								X			7-4-44
34.	ROBALO		X						X					7-26-44
35.	FLIER		X						X					8-13-44
36.	HARDER		X	X										8-24-44
37.	SEAWOLF		X				X							10-3-44
38.	DARTER		X									X		10-24-44
39.	SHARK 11		X	X										10-24-44
40.	TANG		X							X				10-24-44
41.	ESCOLAR	X							X					10-17,11-3-44
42.	ALBACORE		X						X					11-7-44
43.	GROWLER												X	11-8-44
44.	SCAMP		X	X	X									11-9,16-44
45.	SWORDFISH	X		X					X					1-12-45
46.	BARBEL		X		X									2-4-45
47.	KETE												X	3-20,31-45
48.	TRIGGER		X	X	X									3-26,28-45
49.	SNOOK												X	4-8,20-45
50.	LAGARTO		X	X										5-3-45
51.	BONEFISH		X	X										6-18-45
52.	BULLHEAD		X		X									8-6-45

For purposes of the summary table, the category "Probable to Certain" conveys that the evidence at hand is deemed at least complete enough to present a reasonably strong case for the analysis presented; "Possible to Probable" implies that no specific information can be adduced to support any conclusion as to the cause of the loss, but one particular cause seems a great deal more likely than any other; "unknown" covers a multiplicity of indeterminable causes, none of which can be chosen as any more likely than the others. Throughout, it must be kept in mind that Japanese claims and reports are considered by no means complete or accurate. "Operational" losses are those caused by errors of personnel incorrectly handling the ship, by fatal breakdown of the ship itself, or by any other accident short of direct enemy action or stranding which might cause the ship and personnel to be lost. The term "circular run" refers to the tragic phenomenon in which a submarine's torpedo, due to some defect, runs in a circle and shortly arrives at the point from which it was fired.

In the summaries of patrol results, the figures for ships sunk and damaged are the officially credited ones, except in the cases of major combatant vessels. These latter have been correlated with official Japanese lists of combat ship losses, and only those ships actually confirmed as sunk are mentioned here. In the cases of small combat ships and merchant ships, the officially accredited results are based on the Commanding Officer's own estimates of results achieved during the patrol, modified as deemed necessary by higher authorities. It is apparent therefore, that such figures are subject to normal human error, and may not be completely correct. As yet, no official attempt has been made to correlate every submarine sinking with an official Japanese list of merchant ships sunk.

Lastly, it must be mentioned that in searching Japanese records to locate attacks which might have spelled doom for our lost submarines, a great many assumptions have been made. Where only one attack can be tied in with a loss, it has been designated the most probable cause of the loss. This, it is realized, may be leaving out much of the story, for, while it is perfectly possible the story, for, while it is perfectly possible for an accurately placed depth charge or bomb to sink a submarine immediately, the amount of damage sustained and survived by U. S. submarines during this war is nothing short of amazing. Undoubtedly, many stories of heroic fights to control damage are locked forever in the depths beneath the waves. Many submarines probably lasted for some time beyond the attack which was the primary agent causing the loss. That these stories cannot be told can only be lamented as one of the minor tragedies of war.

SUMMARY - CAUSES OF SUBMARINE LOSSES

	Certain To Probable	Probable To Possible	Total
ENEMY SURFACE SHIP ATTACKS	12	4.5	16.5
ENEMY AIRCRAFT ATTACKS	4	1	5
ENEMY COOPERATIVE AIRCRAFT-SURFACE SHIP ATTACKS	4	2	6
ENEMY SUBMARINES	1	0	1
FRIENDLY SURFACE FORCES	1	0	1
FRIENDLY AIRCRAFT	1	0	1
ENEMY MINES	3	4.5	7.5
CIRCULAR RUNS	2	0	2
OPERATIONAL	3	0	3
STRANDING	4	0	4
UNKNOWN	—	—	5
TOTAL	35	12	52

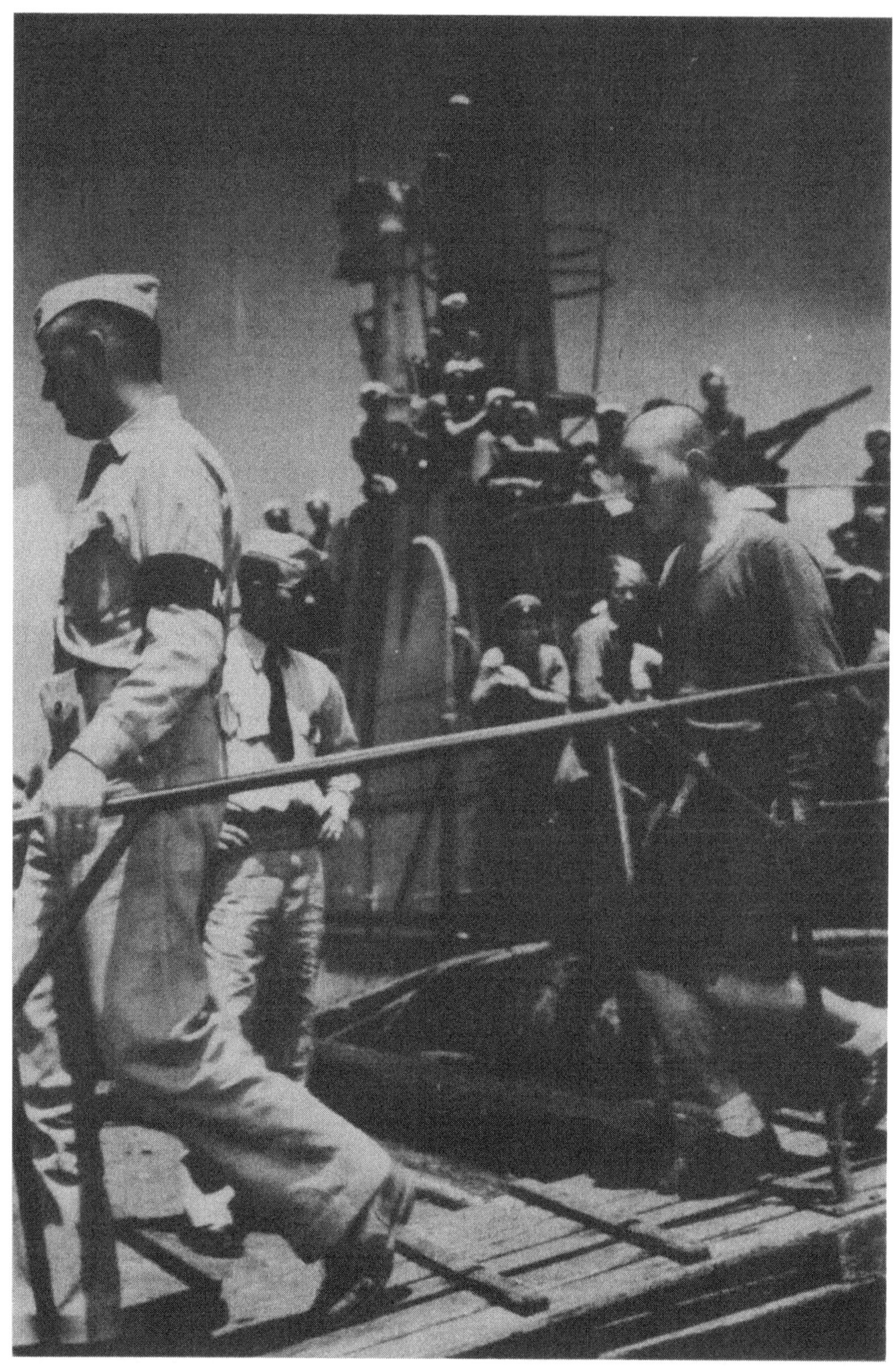

SEALION (SS195)

The first submarine victim of enemy action was SEALION (Lt. Cdr. R. G. Voge). The start of the war on December 8 (east longitude date) found her, along with SEADRAGON, in the last stages of overhaul at the Navy Yard, Cavite, P. I. Both were scheduled for completion on December 12th.

Although there were frequent air raids in the Manila area during the first two days of the war, no enemy planes visited the Navy Yard Cavite until the afternoon of the 3rd day, December 10th. On that day the air raid alarm sounded about half hour after noon, and shortly thereafter 54 planes, in two groups of 27 each, were sighted heading for the Navy Yard. SEALION was nested at Machina Wharf with SEADRAGON inboard and the minesweeper BITTERN outboard. With the exception of the Commanding Officer, the Executive Officer (Lieut. A. Raborn) and three men, all personnel were below decks. The first stick of bombs landed from 100 to 200 yards astern of SEALION, and at that time, Voge, seeing that the planes were going to bomb from high altitude where machine gun fire could not reach them, ordered all hands below. It was a most fortunate decision. [illegible] the next bombing run, but a few min[illegible] later, two bombs hit SEALION al[illegible] simultaneously. One struck the after [illegible] of the conning tower fairwater, complete[illegible] demolishing the machine gun mount whic[illegible] had just been vacated, the main induction, the battery ventilation and the after conning lower bulkhead. It exploded outside the hull a few feet above the control room. Had it entered the hull before exploding, the majority of SEALION's crew would have been lost, as most of the personnel were in that room. A fragment from this bomb pierced the conning tower of SEADRAGON, killing instantly Ensign Sam Hunter who was stationed therein, the first submarine casualty of the war. Other fragments from this bomb pierced the pressure hull, inflicting minor wounds on three SEALION men in the control room.

R. G. Voge

A. Raborn

At almost the same instant another bomb, passing through the main ballast tank and the pressure hull, exploded in the maneuvering space in the after end of the after engine room, killing four men who were working in that compartment - Electrician Mates Foster, O'Connell and Paul, and Machinist Mate Ogilvie.

With this explosion in the maneuvering space, the after engine room flooded immediately and SEALION settled in the mud aft. The forward engine room and the after torpedo room flooded slowly through bomb fragment holes in the bulkheads. Personnel in these compartments, as well as in the other parts of the ship, made their escape through the hatches which, were all still above water. SEALION finally settled down by the stern with about 40% of the main deck underwater and with about 15° list to starboard.

The bomb which exploded above the control room, while doing great superficial damage, did little harm to the pressure hull other than piercing it with numerous bomb fragments. The bomb which exploded aft did the major damage. A more vital spot than the maneuvering space could not possibly have been found. All motor controls, reduction gears, and main motors were wrecked, totally immobilizing the ship. However, the damage would have been considered non-fatal had there been overhaul facilities available for repairs. But such was not the case; the bombing which wrecked SEALION also demolished the Navy Yard Cavite, and the closest repair facilities were at Pearl Harbor, 5000 miles away. The war situation being what it was, it was impossible to tow SEALION that distance, and after removing all gear of value, such as gyro, radio and sound equipment, she was destroyed to prevent her from falling into enemy hands. Three depth charges were exploded inside SEALION on Christmas Day, 1941.

S-36 (SS141)

On her second patrol starting on 30 December 1941, S 36 had completed one daring successful attack, on a small transport moored in Calapan Harbor, Mindoro, P. I. She was proceeding to Surabaya, Java, N. E. I. in accordance with instructions received from ComSubAf, when, at 0404 on 20 January 1942, S-36 grounded on Taka Bakang in Reef Makassar Strait west of Southern Celebes. Her forward battery flooded and appeared to be generating chlorine gas, and the situation seemed grave enough to Lieut. J. R. McKnight, Jr., Commanding Officer, to necessitate sending out a plain language message that she was aground and sinking, SARGO, nearing Surabaya, received the message and tried to relay it, but after five hours of unsuccessful trying she turned back to help S-36.

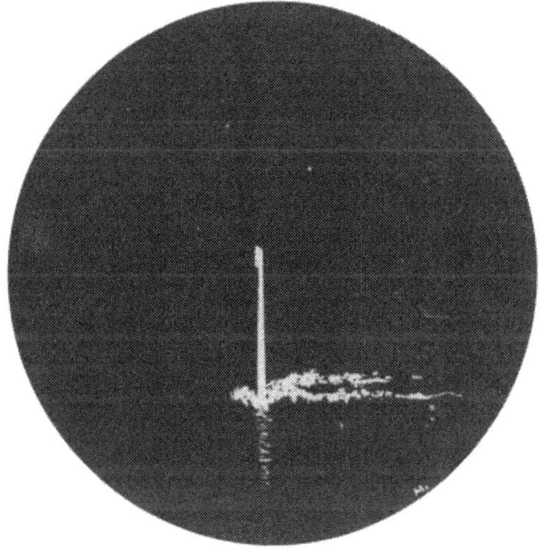

When headquarters at Surabaya finally received the message, SARGO returned there, and a PBY plane was sent to ascertain conditions. By the time the plane arrived the Commanding Officer felt that, with assistance, he could salvage his ship; none of the crew were transferred to the plane at this time, and it went to Makassar City to request assistance from Dutch authorities. The next morning a launch arrived from Makassar, and two officers and 28 men were transferred to her, the remainder of the crew staying on board in the hope that S-36 might be hauled clear.

Conditions became progressively worse, and when the Dutch ship S. S. SIBEROTE arrived on the afternoon of 21 January 1942, the Commanding Officer decided to abandon his ship and destroy her. All officers and men were saved and arrived at Surabaya on 25 February in SIBEROTE.

The first patrol of S-36 had been productive of no sinkings, but for the patrol on which she was lost, she was credited with a 5,000 ton ship sunk.

A LONG AWAITED MAIL CALL

S-26 (SS131)

S-26 (Lt. Cdr. E. C. Hawk) was lost at 2223 on 24 January 1942 in the Gulf of Panama about fourteen miles west of San Jose Light in three hundred feet of water. There were three survivors, two officers, one of whom was the Commanding Officer, and one enlisted man. These people were on the bridge at the time of the collision; the fourth person on the bridge, an enlisted man, was lost.

S-26 was proceeding from Balboa, C. Z. to its patrol station in company with S-21, S-29 and S-44 and an escort vessel, PC-460, at the time of the disaster. At 2210 the escort vessel sent a visual message to the submarines that she was leaving the formation and that they could proceed on the duty assigned. S-21 was the only submarine to receive this message. Shortly thereafter PC-460 struck S-26 on the starboard side of the torpedo room and the submarine sank within a few seconds.

E. C. Hawk

Salvage operations were started immediately under Captain T. J. Doyle, USN, Commander Submarine Squadron Three and Submarine Base, Coco Solo, Canal Zone, and attempts at rescue were made but without success. The submarine was not raised. She had previously made one war patrol but had inflicted no damage on the enemy.

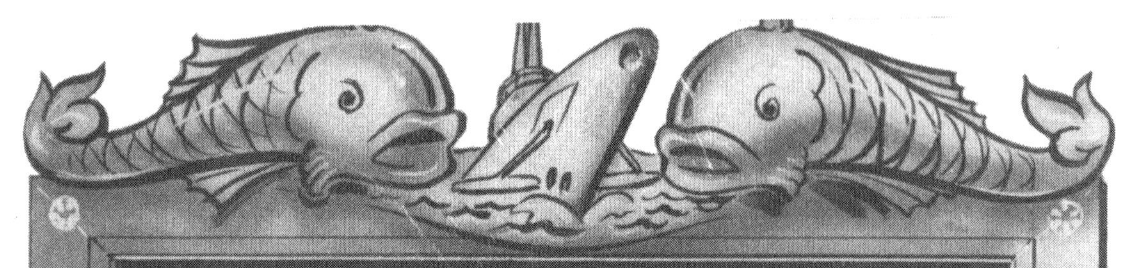

U.S.S. S-26

ADAMS, L.W............MM1c
AMICK, L.A.............S2c
ANDERSON, G.W.........EM2c
BARANICK, G............F2c
BAUER, C.A............MM1c
BAUMBACH, A.C..........S2c
BIEBUYCK, W.P..........S1c
BROWN, H.A.............Y1c
BURCHART, E.B.........MM1c
BURROUGHS, G.O.........F2c
CLAFLIN, C.R...........F2c
CLARK, C.C............MM2c
CLOUGH, R.K...........MM2c
CRABTREE, E.O..........S1c
CRUMBLEY, B........CMM(PA)
DAWSON, J.D...........RM3c
EHRLE, E..............GM3c
EVANS, D.B.........CMM(PA)
FREEMAN, R.A..........MM2c
GAMBLE, R.F...........MM2c
GILL, J.M..........CTM(AA)
*HAWK, E.C........LT.CDR.CO
HOLT, R.E.............QM2c
HOMIC, B.S............MM1c
*HURST, J."B"...........S1c
JOHNSON, N.N........Matt1c
KASSEBAUM, H.J........MM1c
LORENTE, W.G..........EM1c
LOVE, L.M...............S1c
MAC LACHLAN, R.W......RM1c
MATTES, R.C...........TM3c
NELSON, R.E..............AS
O'BRIEN, J.P..........SM3c
PETERS, T.V.............LT.
PETERSON, A.B..........F1c
PYLER, H."B"..........MM2c
RAMSEY, C.R...........GM2c
RIFKIN, S.S............F1c
RUSSELL, G.G..........EM2c
RUSSLER, C.E..........SM1c
SCHMUTZ, J.M.......CRM(PA)
SIEBERT, W.C..........TM2c
SHATTUCK, H.F......CTM(PA)
STUBBINS, J.B..........Ens.
TAYLOR, H.L............Ens.
THOMPSON, T.C.........SC2c
TOW, P.H..............TM2c
*WARD R.E.M.........LT.Exec
VEZINA, R.D............F2c

*- SURVIVORS

SHARK 1 (SS174)

After having transported Admiral Hart and other officials from Manila to Surabaya on her first patrol, SHARK, commanded by Lt. Cdr. L. Shane, Jr. departed on 5 January 1942 for her second war patrol. She saw a torpedo, fired at her by an enemy submarine on 6 January, miss.

In anticipation of a possible enemy attack at Ambon Island, ComSubsAsiatic told SHARK to contact Dutch submarines at the harbor entrance of that island. On 25 January, SHARK was advised that heavy air raids on Ambon might indicate that an enemy landing force was moving toward the island.

Two days later SHARK was ordered to take station as part of a submarine group performing reconnaissance of a major enemy move south through Molukka passage. On 29 January, because another move toward Ambon was indicated, SHARK was ordered to cover the passage to the east of Lifometola. The next day this was enlarged to include the area to Banka Passage. On 2 February SHARK reported to Surabaya that she had been depth charged 10 miles off Tifore Island and that she had missed on one torpedo attack.

Five days later SHARK reported an empty enemy cargo ship heading northeast. In answer to these messages, Surabaya pointed out that such transmissions contained little information of use in appraising the situation, and that they might very possibly reveal to the enemy a position to avoid. No further messages were received from SHARK.

She was told on 8 February to proceed to Makassar Strait via the north coast of Celebes, and later was told to report information. Nothing further was heard from SHARK and on 7 March she was reported as presumed lost.

A Japanese report of anti-submarine attacks available now records at least three attacks which might have been on SHARK. One was east of Menado on northern Celebes on 11 February 1942; the second was north of Kendari on the southeast coast of Celebes on 17 February 1942; the third was east of Kendari on 21 February 1942. Also, in 1944, a Japanese press release claimed that an enemy sub chaser rammed a U. S. submarine in Manipa Strait in February 1942. No mention is made of this attack in official Japanese reports, but their reports are notoriously inaccurate and incomplete, especially during the early part of the war. Since Dutch and English submarines were operating in the area patrolled by SHARK, it is impossible at this time to determine whether any or all of the above mentioned attacks were survived by submarines operating with our Asiatic Fleet. Loss of SHARK to an enemy minefield is deemed improbable, since the enemy was on the offensive at this time, and would naturally hesitate to lay mines in the path of his advance down the Strait of Makassar. Thus indications point to the probability that SHARK was lost through enemy depth charge attack; however, the specific attack responsible for the loss cannot be determined. The one on 11 February off Menado is thought most likely, since SHARK had been ordered to northern Celebes.

U.S.S. SHARK I

BELLARD, T.A.........MM1c
BLANCHARD, W.R....CTM(PA)
BOLTON, J.A...........RM1c
BRANNAN, T.L..........S1c
RYUS, G."G"..........MM1c
CASSIDY, E........LT.(JG)
COOLEY, J.P..........MM2c
CRAWFORD, B.B.........F3c
CROFT, A.E...........EM2c
DAWSON, W.T..........EM2c
DENBY, E.Jr.......LT.(JG)
DILLEN, R.F. Jr.LT.(JG)Exec.
EJAYPE, P........OffStd3c
ESTES, R.A...........EM1c
EVANS, F.A...........MM2c
EVANS, T.F...........TM1c
FABRA, A.........OffStd3c
FARRELL, F.H.........TM1c
FRUIT, A.D...........MM1c
GILMAN, M.R.......CMM(AA)
GIMENEZ, P...........SC1c
GLASS, L.C............S1c
IVERSON, J.A..........F1c
JEFFREYS, R.L.....CMM(AA)
JOHNSTON, J.E.........F2c
JONES, C.E...........TM1c
LESTER, J.A.........PhM2c
LIDGERDING, W.C......RM2c
LOUGHLIN, T.P........TM2c
LUND, A.R............MM1c
MARKIN, L.R...........F2c
McELROY, R.E.........EM2c
McKINNEY, K.E........EM2c
MILLER, R.F...........F2c
MORAN, A.P........CMM(AA)
MORRIS, F.J..........SM1c
MYER, W.H............MM2c
PECHACEK, E.J........SM2c
PERKINS, A.E..........S1c
PETTIT, R.L.......CMM(AA)
PHILABERT, F.F.......ENS.
PILGRAM, W.E......CEM(PA)
POLIDORI, B.J........EM1c
SANDMANN, K.L.........Y2c
SCHMITT, H.L.........MM2c
SHANE, L.Jr....LT.CDR.C.O.
SMITH, J.H........CEM(PA)
SMITH, T.C...........TM2c
SPILMAN, T.P.........RM3c
STEPHENS, R.H.........S1c
STRIEGLER, H.F.......EM1c
THEW, R.R............FC1c
TUBRE, H.O............S1c
TUROCZY, J.A.........SC1c
WARREN, R.H..........MM2c
WHITE, J.K...........GM1c
WORSHAM, J.M.........TM3c
YANKS, C.R...........SM2c
ZEORLIN, H...........TM2c

PERCH (SS176)

Having been serviced at Port Darwin, Australia, PERCH (Lt. Cdr. D. A. Hurt) departed on 3 February 1942 for her second patrol, in the Java Sea. At this time the Japanese campaign to secure the Netherlands East Indies was at its height. The Philippines had been effectively neutralized by them, and their fall was only a matter of time. The Japanese were forcing their way down the Strait of Makassar, and an invasion of Borneo or Java was imminent.

From 8 February to 23 February PERCH was sent several reports concerning enemy concentrations near her area, and was directed to patrol or perform reconnaissance in various positions near the islands of the Java Sea. On 25 February she was directed to go through Sallier Strait and patrol along the 100 fathom curve northeast of the Kangean Islands as part of the force then attempting to defend Java.

On 25 February she reported two previous attacks with negative results, and stated that she had received a shell hit in her conning tower, which, damaging the antenna trunk, made transmissions uncertain, but she could receive. On 27 February, she sent a contact report on two cruisers and three destroyers at 6°-08'S, 116°-34'E. No further reports were received from her and she failed to arrive in Fremantle where she had been ordered by despatch.

The following account of what happened to PERCH is taken from a statement made by her surviving Commanding Officer, who was repatriated at the end of hostilities, having been held by the enemy. The last station assignment was given PERCH on 28 February 1942, in the Java Sea. A large enemy convoy had been cruising about for several days, waiting to land at Java, and now the landing point had been discovered and submarines were to disregard areas and attack at the landing point.

Shortly after surfacing on the night of

D. A. Hurt

1 March, PERCH sighted two destroyers, and dove. After the destroyers had passed well clear, they came back and one came near PERCH. Hurt prepared to attack with torpedoes, but at 800 to 1000 yards, the destroyer turned straight toward him. The Commanding Officer ordered 180 feet. At 90 to 100 feet, the destroyer passed over and dropped a string of depth charges, and shortly thereafter PERCH hit bottom at 147 feet.

During the depth charge attacks which followed, the ship lost power on her port screw, but she managed to pull clear of the bottom and surface when depth charging had ceased. Shortly before dawn two Japanese destroyers again were sighted, and once more PERCH went to the bottom, this time at 200 feet. Efforts to move from the bottom were unsuccessful, and the attackers continued depth charging until after daylight.

At dusk on 2 March PERCH again surfaced, after an hour of effort. There was no enemy in sight. Reduction gears were in bad shape, there were serious electrical grounds and broken battery jars, and the engine room hatch leaked badly, so arrangements were made to scuttle if necessary.

On trying to dive before sunrise 3 March 1942, it was found that, due to damage sustained in the severe depth charge attacks she had been through, water poured in from the conning tower hatch, the engine room hatch, the three inch circulating water line and leaks in the hull. Nothing the crew did seemed to help the leakage and while further attempts were being made to repair the ship, three enemy destroyers came in sight and opened fire. The submarine's gun was inoperative, and torpedoes could not be fired. Enemy depth charges had caused three of PERCH's torpedoes to run in their tubes, and the heat, exhaust gases and nervous tention resulting therefrom had aggravated the already extremely difficult conditions. The decision was made to abandon and scuttle her. The entire crew was gotten into the water safely, and all were picked up by the Japanese ships. The significant statement of Japanese anti-submarine capabilities is made by Lt. K. G. Schacht, a survivor of PERCH, that, "loss of air and oil during attacks caused both previous enemy groups to believe their target had been destroyed".

Personnel of PERCH were taken to the illegal questioning camp at Ofuna, Japan, and then to the Ashio mines, where they were forced to work until the close of the war. Twenty-seven of their number have been received from the Japanese since the war's end. PERCH was credited with sinkink a 5000 ton enemy freighter on her first patrol, conducted west of the Philippines.

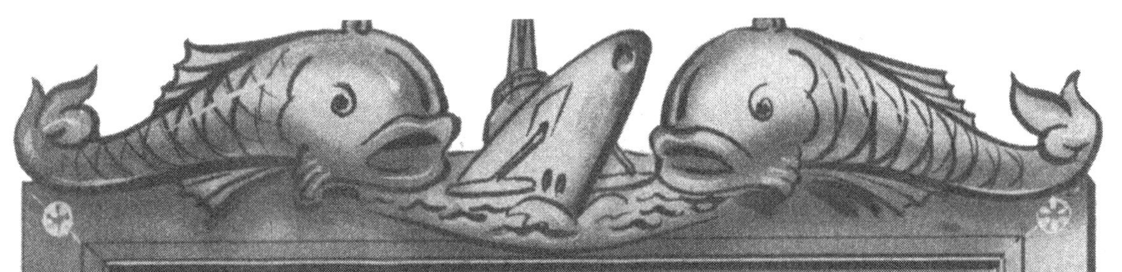

U.S.S. PERCH

ALBONEY, F............TM3c
ARNETTE, E.H..........F1c
ATKEISON, W.I.........TM3c
BERRIDGE, R.C.........RM3c
BOERSMA, S.H.......CQM(AA)
BOLDEN, S.............SC3c
BOLTON, V.............SC2c
*BROWN, C.N...........MM1c
BYRNES, T.F.Jr........MM1c
CLEVINGER, G.B.........S1c
CRIST, D..............EM3c
CROSS, C.L.Jr.........TM1c
DAGUE, L.W............MM2c
DELEMAN, B............MM2c
*DEWES, P.J........CPhM(PA)
EARLYWINE, R.I.........Y1c
EARLYWINE, V.E........GM1c
*EDWARDS, H.E.......CEM(PA)
EVANS, R.W............TM3c
FAJOTINA, A...........OC3c
FOLEY, J.A............MM1c
GILL, B.S..............F2c
GOODWINE, C.E.........MM1c
*GRECO, J.............TM3c
HARPER, E.R............S1c
HURT, D.A......LT.CDR.C.O.
*KERICH, T.L...........F3c
KLECKY, R.............MM2c
LENTS, R.W............TM2c
McCRAY, J.G...........MM1c
*McCREARY, F.E........MM1c

MONROE, E.P...........EM2c
MOORE, T...............S1c
*NEWSOME, A.K.......CMM(AA)
NORMAND, J.R..........RM2c
ORLYK, S.M............MM1c
*OSBORN, R.W...........S1c
PEDERSEN, V.S.......CEM(AA)
PETERS, O.V............F2c
PLANTZ, E.V............S1c
REH, T.J..............RM1c
RICHTER, P.R.Jr.......EM2c
ROBINSON, J.H.........EM2c
RYDER, J.F.............LT.
SARMIENTO, M..........OC2c
SCHAEFER, G.E..........S1c
SCHACHT, K.G...........LT.
SIMPSON, S.F..........TM1c
STAFFORD, F.F.Jr......SM3c
TAYLOR, G.E...........TM1c
TURNER, M.M...........EM2c
VAN BUSKIRK, B.R.LT.Exec.
VAN HORN, E...........EM1c
VANDERGRIFT, I.J.Jr.LT.(JG)
WALTON, F.B...........MM2c
WEBB, J.F.............QM1c
WELCH, F..............TM3c
WILCOX, M.O............Y1c
*WILSON, R.A..........FC1c
WINGER, A.W...........EM3c
WRIGHT, R.N............S1c
YATES, H.S.........CMM(PA)

*- Died as prisoners of war.

LOADING TORPEDOES - Painting By Vandis

S-27 (SS132)

In June of 1942, the enemy landed on Kiska Island in the Aleutians and the U. S. Fleet was interested in Amchitka Island, 60 miles east of Kiska. S-27, on her first patrol, with Lt. H. L. Jukes in command, was sent to make a reconnaissance of Constantine Harbor, at Amchitka, and then to go around the island and patrol off Kiska. By 19 June 1942, the reconnaissance was completed, and S-27 started for her area.

In the Aleutian area at that time of year there is daylight eighteen hours of the twenty-four, and when S-27 surfaced at 2200 on the night of 19 June, after the necessarily prolonged submergence during daylight hours, her batteries were badly in need of charging. Navigating only by DR since she had no radar or fathometer, S-27 gained a position well off the land, and hove to in order to charge batteries. While she was lying to, currents took her about five miles from her DR position, although fog prevented knowledge of it at the time. At about 2240 on 19 June, S-27 was able to go ahead on one engine while charging on the other. Almost immediately, she struck a reef about 400 yards from Amchitka Island and rolled over into a rocky basin.

H. L. Jukes

All efforts to get off the rocks were futile, and of six despatches sent telling her plight, only one, which did not give her position, was picked up. The torpedo room was flooding, the after battery was getting wet and generating chlorine, and the boat had an eight to twelve degree down angle. The ship was abandoned, and all hands were taken ashore in a rubber lifeboat. They spent the night huddled around fires, and the next morning set out for the village at Constantine Harbor, across the island. There they found a church and two buildings, the Japs having bombed the rest, but no inhabitants. Food, guns, and ammunition had been salvaged from the ship and the men were organized by the Commanding Officer into a regular military camp.

On the sixth day a PBY flew over, sighted the men, and landed. He took 12 men and an officer back to Dutch Harbor and the next morning three other PBY's flew out for the rest of the men. The crew survived this disaster without a single injury or case of illness.

S-39 (SS144)

After having started twice for her fifth patrol, and been forced to return to Brisbane because of major breakdowns, S-39, under Lt. F. E. Brown, once more was faced on 7 August 1942 with the necessity for heading toward land. Her Executive Officer was put on the sick list on 5 August, and two days later his condition warned of the development of pneumonia, so Brown asked for instructions and was directed to proceed to Townsville, on the northeast coast of Australia. On 10 August in the smooth waters of Townsville harbor, the officer was transferred for further medical treatment, and S-39 once more got underway for her patrol area off the southeast coast of New Ireland.

In the night of 13-14 August 1942, S-39 struck a submerged reef off Rossel Island, in the Louisade Archipelago. The ship took a list of 30 to 35 degrees port and was jolting heavily due to heavy following seas breaking over the deck. Backing the screws had little effect, even after all possible fuel and ballast tanks had been blown dry. The ship began swinging broadside to the sea and was being washed farther up on the rocks, so all fuel and ballast tanks were again flooded to hold her steady.

At high tide on the morning of 14 August the screws were backed and twisted until the low voltage limit on the batteries was reached. The ship backed about fifty feet, but again listed about 30 degrees to port and pounded heavily on the rocks. Ballast tanks were ruptured by the rocks and they were again flooded in an effort to ease the pounding. In the afternoon word came from Australia that HMAS KATOOMBA would arrive on the following morning to lend aid.

Throughout the day breakers 15 to 20 feet high broke over the ship. Efforts were made to charge the batteries, but several cells had been reversed and only the after battery could be charged. Shortly after dawn on the 15th, the torpedoes were inactivated and fired. Again Brown tried backing on the after battery, but the screws were too high; they had little effect. With the termination of backing efforts, the ship rapidly rolled over until the list was 60 degrees port. Fearing that the seas would roll the ship entirely over, the Commanding Officer gave permission for anyone who desired to swim to a nearby reef, although he was not ready to abandon the ship. No one ventured into the water, but Lt. C. N. G. Hendrix volunteered to swim to the reef with a line and then to haul the two mooring lines to the reef as a riding line for the rest of the crew.

When Hendrix had gained the reef and was having a difficult time with the lines, due to the seas, W. L. Schoenrock, CCStd(PA), offered to swim ashore and help. The two men pulled in the lines and secured them to one of the torpedoes, which was resting on the reef. Thirty-two men reached the reef via the line, and twelve remained aboard when HMAS KATOOMBA arrived shortly after noon.

By 1000 on 16 August KATOOMBA's boats had made three trips to shore and all hands were safely aboard the ship. It was felt that S-39 would soon be broken up by the pounding seas, and no attempt was made to shell her from KATOOMBA. The S-39 crew members arrived in Townsville, Australia on 19 August 1942, and were assigned further duty on other submarines.

S-39's first war patrol was conducted east of the Philippines and resulted in the loss to the enemy of a 5,000 ton freighter.

On her second patrol, she reconnoitered Tablas Strait and Verde Island, in the Philippines group, but made no successful attacks. During February and March 1942, S-39 patrolled an area in the South China Sea, and sank a 5,000 ton tanker. Her fourth patrol, made in the Solomons, resulted in no enemy contacts for S-39.

GRUNION (SS216)

The submarine GRUNION arrived at Pearl Harbor on 20 June 1942, reporting for duty from the west coast. This vessel engaged in the pre-patrol training given to all submarines reporting from new construction yards, and on 30 June, left for patrol.

M. L. Abele

Lt. Cdr. M. L. Abele, in command, was ordered to proceed to the Aleutian theater and patrol westward from Attu on routes between the Aleutians and the Japanese Empire. On 10 July GRUNION was reassigned to the area north of Kiska. GRUNION made her first report on 15 July Dutch Harbor received her message telling that she had been attacked by an enemy destroyer. She had fired three torpedoes at it, and missed with all.

Shortly after this message was received, GRUNION sent another relating that she had sunk three destroyer type vessels on 15 July. This message was garbled to the extent that details of the attacks were never learned, (Japanese information reveals that GRUNION sank patrol boats 25 and 27 and damaged a third patrol vessel). On 19 July GRUNION, S-32, TRITON and TUNA were assigned areas in the approaches to Kiska, all to be there by daylight 22 July.

There was a strong concentration of enemy vessels at Kiska, this time being only

a month and half after the enemy had taken that island. The vessels patrolling there were told to watch particularly on the afternoon of 22 July 1942 for departing enemy naval vessels, since our own surface forces were scheduled to bombard Kiska on that afternoon. The bombardment did not take place in accordance with the original plans, but our forces did stage the operation on 28 July and GRUNION was told to guard the exits from Kiska during darkness on this date. On this day GRUNION reported an attack on unidentified enemy ships six miles southeast of Sirius Point, Kiska. She had fired two torpedoes, made no hits, and been depth charged, but sustained no damage.

GRUNION's last transmission was received on 30 July 1942. She reported heavy anti-submarine activity at the entrance to Kiska, and that she had ten torpedoes remaining. On the same day, GRUNION was directed to return to Dutch Harbor. She was not contacted or sighted after 30 July, despite every effort to do so, and on 16 August, she was reported lost. Planes observing the approaches to Kiska for indications of enemy salvage operations in connection with GRUNION reported negatively.

Japanese anti-submarine attack data available now records no attack in the Aleutian area at this time, and GRUNION's fate remains an unsolved mystery. We know of no enemy minefields which were in her area; thus her loss may be presumed to have been operational or as a result of an unrecorded enemy attack.

U.S.S. GRUNION

ABELE, M.L....LT.CDR.C.O.
ALEXANDER, F.E.......SM3c
ALLEN, D.E..........SM3c
ARVAN, H.J.........Matt2c
BANES, P.E.....CMoMM(AA)
BEDARD, L.J.I...CMoMM(AA)
BLINSTON, W.H........RM3c
BONADIES, N.R.........S1c
BOO, R.T............RM3c
BOUVIA, C.L..........MM1c
CALDWELL, G.E..........EM
CARROLL, R.H..........S2c
CLIFT, J.S...........TM2c
COLLINS, M.F..........F2c
COOKSEY, L.D.......MoMM1c
CULLINANE, D....CMoMM(AA)
CUTHBERTSON, W.H.Jr..ENS.
DEATON, L.D..........S2c
DE STOOP, A.E.....CTM(AA)
DIGHTON, S.R......LT.(JG)
DEVANEY, W.P.Jr.......S2c
DOELL, L.H.Jr........RM2c
FRANCK, L.H...........S1c
GRAHAM, M.D.......CTM(PA)
HALL, K.E.............S2c
HELENSMITH, E.G......EM2c
HENDERSON, H.B.....MoMM2c
HUTCHINSON, C.R......TM3c
KENNEDY, S.J.......MoMM2c
KNOWLES, E.E.Jr.......S2c
KOCKLER, L.R.........TM1c
KORNAHRENS, W.G...LT.(JG)
LEDFORD, J.J.......CY(AA)
LEHMAN, W.W..........EM1c
LOE, S.A...........MoMM2c

LUNSFORD, S.Jr.......EM2c
LYON, J.W.............F1c
MARTIN, C.R....CMoMM(PA)
MARTIN, T.E.........EM1c
MATHISON, R.........EM1c
McCUTCHEON, R.G.....TM3c
McMAHON, J.M.........LT.
MILLER, E.C..........F2c
MYERS, D.O...........F1c
NAVE, F.T.........MoMM2c
NEWCOMB, A."G".......RM1c
NOBLES, J.W.......MoMM1c
PANCOAST, J.E.....MoMM3c
PARZIALE, C.A.......TM3c
PAUL, C.Jr.........Matt2c
PICKEL, B.J..........S1c
POST, A.C............S2c
RANDALL, W.H.........RM2c
RYAN, L.Jr...........S2c
SANDERS, H.A.......MoMM1c
SCHUMANN, E.T.....CQM(PA)
SULLIVAN, P.P.......PhM1c
SUROFCHEK, S.........SC1c
SWARTWOOD, D.N........S2c
TEMPLETON, S.A.......GM1c
THOMAS, M.W........LT.Exec
TRAVISS, B.A..........S2c
ULLMANN, A............S1c
VAN WOGGELUM, M.F.....F3c
WALTER, M.H...........F3c
WEBSTER, R.E.........EM2c
WELCH, D.F...........FC2c
WELLS, J.H...........TM2c
WILSON, J.E.Jr.......SC3c
YOUNGMAN, R.J.........F2c

GUN BATTLE - Painting By Vandis

ARGONAUT (SS166)

While operating in the area southeast of New Britain between 5°-15'S and 6°-00'S and west of 153°-50'E during her third patrol, ARGONAUT, (Lt. Cdr. J. R. Pierce) intercepted a Jap convoy returning to Rabaul from Lae, on 10 January 1943. A U. S. Army plane which was out of bombs saw one destroyer hit by a torpedo, saw the explosion of two other destroyers, and reported that there were five other vessels in the group.

After a severe depth charge attack ARGONAUT was forced to surface and the destroyers, according to the plane's report, circled and pumped shells into her bow, which was sticking up at a considerable angle. This action took place in 5°-40'S, 152°-02'E, and further efforts to contact ARGONAUT by radio were fruitless. It is quite certain, then, that ARGONAUT met her end in this action. Japanese reports made available since the end of the war record this attack as a depth charge attack followed by artillery fire, at which time the "destroyed top of the sub floated".

ARGONAUT's first patrol near Midway had resulted in no damage to enemy ships, but her second was a most successful one. It was conducted following a complete modernization. at Mare Island. Her mission on this one had been to cooperate with NAUTILUS in transporting 252 Marine officers and men to Makin Island for a diversionary raid against enemy shore installations. In the early morning of 17 August 1942, the raiders were debarked in boats. After nearly two days ashore, the Marines returned, and the submarines transported them back to Pearl Harbor, ARGONAUT arriving on 26 August.

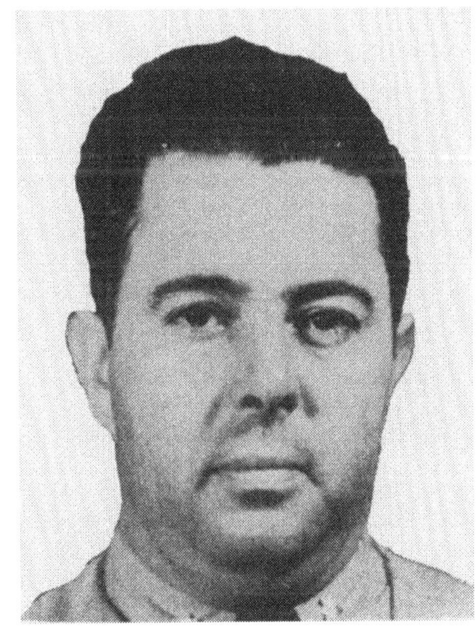

J. R. Pierce

On the basis of the report given by the Army flier who witnessed the attack in which ARGONAUT perished, this ship was credited with having damaged one Japanese destroyer on her last patrol.

U.S.S. ARGONAUT

ALEXANDER, C.H...........Y1c
ALEXANDER, R.D.........QM2c
ALLEN, R.W..............LT.
BAKER, C.H........CMoMM(AA)
BALL, R.N...............S1c
BEECHAM, T.W........CEM(PA)
BERGADO, M.T...........MA1c
BODAK, J.B...........MoMM2c
BOWERS, F.H.............F1c
BOWKER, G.A.............LT.
BOYT, R.H.........CMoMM(PA)
BROOKS, M.M..........MoMM2c
BROWN, V.M...........MoMM2c
CAMPBELL, C.K........MoMM2c
CARLISLE, S.H........MoMM1c
CARTMELL, W.A.....CMoMM(PA)
CERRINACK, C.J.......CGM(PA)
CORBIN, I.B.............RM1c
COX, A...................F2c
DAVIDSON, R.C...........GM3c
DAVIS, W.W...............S2c
DEGUZMAN, J..........OCC(AA)
DISCHNER, D.H........MoMM2c
EVERETT, J.L.Jr..........LT,
FACCHINI, D.F........MoMM2c
FERENTZ, J...............S2c
FERGUSON, C.V............S1c
FINELY, G.W.............BM2c
FITGERALD, W.D..........GM1c
GASKO, J................BM2c
GILLILAND, J.A.Jr........S1c
GOSHORN, R.L............GM2c
HALL, V.E................S2c
HANSEN, E.J.............EM2c
HARBISON, R.N...........TM3c
HARRISON, E.H...........SC3c
HARTMAN, D.R.........MoMM2c
HUDSON, B.J.............RM1c
HOGG, F.M............MoMM2c
HUNTER, R................S2c
JENKINS, G.S.........CQM(PA)
KAPLAN, G................S2c
KAYLOR, F.G............PhM1c
KELLEY, J.A..........MoMM1c
KESSINGER, H............SC1c
KNAPP, A.L..............QM3c
KOCIS, G.N...............ENS.
KOLLER, F.M.............TM3c
LAUDER, G.E.............TM2c
LAY, G.E.............MoMM2c
LEAVERTON C.C...........EM1c
LEGLER, K.R.............RM3c
LELAND, L.D..........CRM(PA)

LEWIS, F.H..............EM3c
LOGAN, H.L........CMoMM(PA)
LOKEY, G.A..............EM2c
LOS BANES, Z.L..........MA2c
MALONEY, R.M.Jr.........TM1c
MARTIN, P.P.............MA2c
McCLELLAND, E............F2c
MILLER, R.H.............EM2c
MILLER, W.F..............S1c
MILTNER, B.C.........LT.(JG)
MORGAN, T.M..........FC(M)3c
MYERS, W.H.Jr............S1c
NARROW, T.A.Jr...........S1c
NICHOLS, F.R............EM3c
OLDS, P.J...............OC2c
PARKER, B.B..............S1c
PARKER, T............MoMM2c
PARSONS, R.Jr...........BM2c
PEEVEY, J.W.............EM3c
PIERCE, J.R........LT.CDR.C.O
PRITCHARD, W.L...........F1c
RAMOS, M.Jr.............OS1c
RASIMAS, A.J.........CEM(AA)
REMILLARD, P.B..........SM2c
ROBERTSONS, R.N.....LT.Exec.
ROLLAND, H.L.........CGM(PA)
ROLLINS, G.M.............S1c
ROMERO, L..........CCStd(PA)
ROUP, M.F............MoMM1c
RULE, J..............MoMM2c
SCHEMPP, F.E............TM3c
SEIDMAN, W.F............RM3c
SERAFINI, H.J........MoMM2c
SHEEKS, D.C..............Y2c
SIGLER, E.W..........MoMM1c
SIMONEAU, F.W............LT.
SMITH, T.L...........CBM(AA)
SPAETH, J.R..........MoMM2c
STANLEY, J..............GM2c
THOMAS, W.D.............OC2c
TINLING, H.J.............S1c
VESMAN, J...............GM1c
VIERLING, W.E........MoMM1c
WAGNER, E.J..........MoMM2c
WEHNER, W.G..............F1c
WHITE, C.C.Jr...........TM2c
WHITE, T.A...............S1c
WIDENER, H.R..........CY(AA)
WILLIAMS, R.W...........TM3c
WINSOR, W.D.............GM1c
WYLIE, R.D...............F1c
ZINTZ, E.L..............SC3c

AMBERJACK (SS 219)

Following her second patrol, AMBERJACK's period of refit, rest and recuperation was cut to twelve days, due to the urgent necessity for submarines in the operating areas. She started out on 24 January, but was forced to return to port for the repair of minor leaks experienced during a deep dive.

J. A. Bole, Jr.

Again departing Brisbane on 26 January 1943, AMBERJACK, under Lt. Cdr. J. A. Bole, Jr., started her third war patrol in the Solomons area. On 29 January she was directed to pass close to Tetipari Island and then proceed to the northwest and patrol the approaches to Shortland Basin. Orders were radioed on 1 February for her to move north and patrol the western approaches to Buka Passage. Having complied with these orders, AMBERJACK made her first radio report, on 3 February, telling of contact with an enemy submarine 14 miles southeast of Treasury Island on 1 February, and of sinking a two-masted schooner by gunfire twenty miles from Buka the afternoon of 3 February 1943. At this time she was ordered to move south along the Buka-Shortland traffic lane and patrol east of Vella Lavella Island.

Making a second radio transmission on 4 Febraury, AMBERJACK reported having sunk a 5,000 ton freighter laden with explosives in a two-hour night surface attack on 4 February in which five torpedoes were fired. During this engagement Chief Pharmacist's Mate Arthur C. Beeman was killed by machine gun fire, and an officer was slightly wounded in the hand. On 8 February, AMBERJACK was ordered to move to the west side of Canongga Island and on the 10th, she was directed to keep south of Latitude 7°-30'S, and to cover the traffic routes from Rabaul and Buka to Shortland Basin. On 13 February AMBERJACK was assigned the entire Rabaul-Buka-Shortland Sea area, and told to hunt for traffic.

The last radio transmission received from AMBERJACK was made on 14 February 1943. She related having been forced down the night before by two destroyers, and that she had recovered from the water and taken prisoner an enemy aviator on 13 February. She was ordered north of Latitude 6°-30'S, and told to keep hunting for Rabaul traffic.

All further messages to AMBERJACK remained unanswered, and when, by March 10, she had failed to make her routine re port estimating the time of her arrival at base, she was ordered to do so. No reply was received, and she was reported as presumed lost on 22 March 1943.

Reports received from the enemy since the end of the war record an attack which probably sunk AMBERJACK. On 16 February 1943, the torpedo boat HAYODORI and subchaser number 18 attacked a U. S. submarine with nine depth charges in 5°-05'S, 152°-37'E. An escorting patrol plane had previously attacked the submarine. A large amount of heavy oil and "parts of the hull" came to the surface. This attack is believed to have sunk AMBERJACK. However, no really conclusive conclusions can be drawn, since GRAMPUS was lost in the same area at about the same time. From the evidence available, it is considered most likely that the attack of 16 February sunk AMBERJACK, but if she did survive this attack, any one of the attacks and sightings thought to have been made on GRAMPUS (see section on GRAMPUS' loss) might have been made on AMBERJACK.

This vessel was credited with sinking three ships, for a total of 28,600 tons, and damaging two more ships for 14,000 tons damaged. AMBERJACK's first patrol was made in the Shortland-Rabaul-Buka area, as her last was. During this first patrol conducted during the last half of September and the first half of October 1942, she sank a freighter, a transport and a large tanker of 19,600 tons. In addition she damaged a freighter and a transport, and made a valuable reconnaissance of several islands in her area. The second patrol of this vessel was in the area west of Bougainville. Although several attacks were made, no damage was done to the enemy. On the basis of her radio report, AMBERJACK was credited with having sunk a 5,000 ton freighter on her final patrol. The enlisted men's recreation center at the Submarine Base, Pearl Harbor is named for Chief Pharmacist's Mate Arthur C. Beeman, who was killed in the gun battle of 4 February.

U.S.S. AMBERJACK

ALLMON, M.W.........MoMM1c
BAKER, W.A.Jr.........RM3c
BANISTER, P.B.......MoMM2c
BARR, L.V..............F1c
BARTOLI, R.............S1c
BEEMAN, A.C..........PhM1c
BLAUVELT, R.P..........LT.
BOLE, J.A......LT.CDR.C.O.
BOLZE, J.F............FC1c
BRANT, H.J............SC2c
BROSSY, H.E...LT.CDR.Exec.
BROUSSEAU, M.J.........S2c
BUCHAN, W.N...........EM1c
CALDWELL, L.J.D........S2c
CHAFFIN, E.E...........F2c
CHENEY, J.F............LT.
CHRZAN, R.J...........TM3c
CLARK, B.L............TM1c
COLEMAN, J.L..........GM2c
COULTAS, W.E........MoMM2c
DAVIS, E.S.............S1c
DAVIS, L C............EM3c
DE GROOT, J............F2c
DEMLER, A.M...........ENS.
DUCHARME, D...........QM3c
EASTMAN, A.G.H........TM2c
EVERETT, E.J..........RT1c
GILLARD, G.H...........S2c
GOSCINIAK, T........MoMM2c
HAMILTON, J.W.......MoMM2c
HENDERSON, L.G........RM2c
HAITT, D.L............EM3c
HILL, W.M.O............F2c
JACKSON, V.T........MoMM2c
JAMES, H.E............EM2c
JETER, W.L............SM3c
JEWELL, T.E........CSM(PA)
KINGSTON, F.P.......MoMM2c
KOREYVA, V.J........MoMM2c
LESTER, R.L............S2c
LEVESQUE, R.A.........EM2c
LEWELLYN, J.E.........ENS.
LORD, H.S..........LT.(JG)
LUCAS, J.B.Jr.......MoMM2c
MACY, M.R.............RM2c
MASSEY, A.R...........MA2c
MCDANIELL, R...........S1c
MC LEAN, R.A..........TM1c
MONTAGUE, W...........MA1c
MUIR, C.R..........CTM(PA)
OGILVIE, H.R..........TM2c
OUZTS, C.M.Jr.......MoMM1c
PAVLIN, B.F...........EM2c
PISARSKI, H............F1c
RANGER, J.A...........RM2c
RAKYTA, J.G............S1c
RUNKOWSKI, C.L........TM3c
RYALL, L.R..........MoMM1c
SALLNE, C.K...........SC1c
SEIDELL, D.R..........ENS.
SMOROL, P.P............F2c
SPIERER, E.F...........S1c
SPRINGSTEEN, C.A.......S1c
ST. JOHN, F.T..........Y1c
STERN, R.G.........LT.(JG)
TAYLOR, H.A...........TM2c
THURMAN, I.H...........F1c
TRASK, P.B............TM2c
TOBIN, W.J............EM2c
ULLSTROM, J.H..........S2c
WARD, A.G.............EM3c
WILSON, E.I............F3c
WINQUIST, H.C.A..CMoMM(AA)

GRAMPUS (SS 207)

After starting on the 9th and being ordered to return on the 10th, GRAMPUS Lt. Cdr. J. A. Craig) departed Brisbane on 11 February to make her sixth patrol in the Solomon area, having made two successful previous patrols under Craig. After leaving her exercise target on 12 February 1943, she never was heard from again.

She was directed, during the period from 14 February to 20 February, to patrol successively the area west of Shortland and south of latitude 6°-30'S, the entire Buka-Shortland-Rabaul Sea area, and to leave the southern part to TRITON, which subsequently was lost in this general area.

On 20 February, GRAMPUS was ordered to patrol north of 4°-30'S, until dawn on 21 February, and then to patrol east of Buka and Bougainville. On 2 March she was told to round Cape Henpan, proceed down the west coast of Bougainville, south of Treasury Island, north of Vella Lavella and into Vella Gulf on the afternoon of 5 March. She was to sink enemy ships trying to pass westward through Blackett Strait in attempting to escape our surface ships scheduled to bombard Vila and Stanmore on 6 March. GRAYBACK was teamed with GRAMPUS in the above operation, and each was informed of the other's assignment.

The evening of 5 March, GRAYBACK and GRAMPUS were warned that two destroyers were proceeding from Faisi (off southeastern Bougainville) toward Wilson Strait (between Vella Lavella and Cannongga). These destroyers later went through Blackett Strait and into Kula Gulf, where they were sunk by our surface forces, but GRAYBACK did not report having seen or heard them. Shortly after the report concerning these destroyers was sent, GRAYBACK heard and saw a ship in the part of Vella Gulf assigned to GRAMPUS, and, assuming it was she, maneuvered to avoid. She was unable to track it or ex-

J. A. Craig

change recognition signals by radar, since her SJ radar was not functioning. When GRAMPUS made no radio transmission up to 6 March, she was ordered by ComTaskFor 72 on 7 March to do so. No transmission was received, and on 8 March she was ordered again to make one, again without results. She was reported lost on 22 March, 1943.

Since the war's end, the following facts have been culled from the enemy sources. On 17 February 1943, the enemy claims to have sighted one of our submarines at 5°-35'S, 152°-18'E and later that day in 4°55'S, 152°-30'E. In the afternoon of the 18th, a submarine torpedo attack was delivered on enemy ships at 4°55'S, 152°-18'E and a freighter of 6,400 tons was damaged. An enemy counterattack was made. All of these positions were in GRAMPUS' area.

On the afternoon of 19 February, enemy seaplanes claim to have sighted and attacked a U. S. submarine at 5°-04'S, 152°-18'E. The next day, two patrol boats found a large amount of oil on the surface in this position, and the enemy believed that the submarine had been sunk. However, another enemy report states that a submarine was sighted on 24 February in 6°-15'S, 156°-35'E. Since no other U. S. submarine could have been in this position at this time, it may be assumed that GRAMPUS escaped serious injury on 19 February, or that AMBERJACK was the victim of the attack of 19 February.

Whether the ship GRAYBACK saw and heard in Vella Gulf on the night of 5-6 March 1943 was GRAMPUS is impossible to determine, since she was unable to identify it. However, if it was GRAMPUS and she did survive the enemy attack of 19 February, the only other possibility, so far as is now known, is that GRAMPUS was sunk by the destroyers passing through Blackett Strait on the night of 5-6 March, 1943. From the information at hand, it appears that GRAMPUS could have been no more than 15 miles from GRAYBACK on that night, yet GRAYBACK reported hearing no depth charges. In view of this, it seems likely that GRAMPUS was caught on the surface by the destroyers and sunk by gunfire. Since the enemy ships were themselves destroyed subsequently, no mention of any attack by them is made in Japanese reports. A large oil slick was reported in Blackett Strait on 6 March.

In the five patrols made before her fatal one, this ship sank six ships, for a total of 45,400 tons, and damaged two more, for 3,000 tons.

On her first patrol, conducted in February and March 1942 in the Caroline Islands, GRAMPUS sank two 10,000 ton tankers and reconnoitered Wotje and Kwajalein atolls. Her second patrol was a passage from Pearl Harbor to Fremantle, Western Australia, and no sinkings were made. Going to the area west of Luzon and Mindoro, P. I., for her third patrol, GRAMPUS was again unsuccessful in her attempts to sink enemy ships. She conducted her fourth patrol in the Solomons. Here she landed coast watchers on Vella Lavella and Choiseul Islands, and was credited with one escort type vessel sunk and another damaged. GRAMPUS's fifth patrol was made in the Solomons also. She sank a large transport, a medium transport, a freighter and damaged a destroyer.

U.S.S. GRAMPUS

BALL, L.D...........MoMM2c
BASEL, J.............EM2c
BATHGATE, W.K.W......TM1c
BELEY, M.Jr...........S2c
BENTON, J.L.......LT.(JG)
BERRESFORD, N.T......TM1c
BIGGY, V.T.........MoMM1c
BLACK, C.............OC3c
BOHLER, F.J..........TM3c
BOWLBY, D.W..........FM3c
BRUNNER, F.L.........GM2c
BRUNS, W.A............CRM
BURDETTE, W.E.........F1c
CHAFFIN, K.L..........S1c
COLLINS, T.R.........QM3c
CONLEY, C.J..........EM1c
CORDER, E.F...........S1c
CORUM, R.E.........MoMM2c
CRAIG, J.R........LT.CDR.
DEXTER, R.L...........F1c
DUNNAVANT,. J.H....MoMM1c
FANNING, O.F.........SC3c
FENNER, D.M..........MA1c
GONZALES, E..........SC3c
GOODRUM, H.C.......MoMM1c
GRIFFITH, A.M........RM1c
GUILER, R.P........3rdLT.
HANDY, W..............S1c
HAUPT, E.P.............LT.
HENDRY, W.............F3c
HERRIN, H.E...........S1c
JOYCE, M.P............F1c
KANE, S...............F1c
KILPATRICK, D........SM1c
LARSON, H.R..........EM1c

LAW, B.W.............GM3c
MC CLURE, W.J.........S1c
MICHAEL, R.G.........SC1c
MITCHELL, G.W......MoMM1c
MOELLER, W............CEM
NASH, J.H..........MoMM1c
O'CONNOR, E.R.....LT.(JG)
OLEXA, D.E.........MoMM2c
O'NEAL, J.W..........CPhM
PATRICK, C.W........CMoMM
PHELPS, G.F..........EM3c
PILLSBURY, G.C........Y1c
POYNER, T.E...........F2c
PRESLEY, L.E..........CGM
PURDOM, V.M..........TM3c
ROBERTS, L.H.........TM3c
RUDD, C.E............TM3c
SAGER, R.V.........MoMM1c
SANDELL, I.J...........LT.
SBISA, A.F.........LT.Exec
SCHMIDT, W.B.........EM1c
SHAFRANSKI, F.........S1c
SHEPARD, M.W.........TM2c
TAGESEN, A.R..........S1c
TEVIS, A.............SM3c
THOMAS, G.L..........EM2c
THOMAS, J.H..........RM2c
THRASHER, R.T........TM1c
TOWNLEY, M.C.........FC1c
TREGO, R.V............F2c
TREMMEL, L.E.........MM1c
TUTTLE, M.P..........EM2c
VANDER REYDEN, R.....EM2c
VEDDER, G.A..........TM1c
WALTERS, W.M.......MoMM2c
WILSON, N.E........MoMM1c

TRITON (SS 201)

The fourth of our submarines lost in the Solomons-Bismarck area in the early part of 1943, TRITON, commanded by Lt. Cdr. G. K. MacKenzie, Jr., left Brisbane on 16 February 1943 to begin her sixth patrol in that area. She hunted for traffic between Rabaul and Shortland Basin on her way north, and began to patrol the equator between 154°E, and 156°E, on 23 February.

G. K. MacKenzie, Jr.

She reported on 26 February of having seen smoke on 22 February, and that she obtained evidence of enemy radar on Buka. Moving westward, she patrolled areas northwest of SNAPPER and southeast of TRIGGER from 26 February to 6 March, when she left her area to attack a convoy in TRIGGER's area. Her report on 7 March, amended by another 8 March, stated that the convoy had been composed of 5 ships and 1 DD escort. She reported their speed and course and the fact that she had sunk two AK's of the convoy and damaged another, claiming 3 hits out of 6 torpedoes fired at noon 6 March. A circular torpedo run forced her deep, where she was depth-charged by the destroyer. She had later tried two night attacks, one dawn attack, and one afternoon attack, all without success, and was returning to her area at the time she sent the message. About eight hours after this message came, TRITON transmitted another telling of another night attack on the convoy. She claimed 5 hits of 8 torpedoes fired, and, although she could not observe results due to gunfire and attack by the escorting destroyer, she believed two more freighters to be sunk.

The last word received from TRITON came on 11 March 1943 when she reported, "Two groups of smokes, 5 or more ships each, plus escorts. . . Am chasing". She was ordered to stay south of the Equator, and was informed of the area (an adjacent one) assigned TRIGGER.

On the morning of 13 March TRITON was told that three enemy destroyers had been sighted at 2°-00'S, 145°-44'E on a northerly course. She was informed that they were probably on a submarine hunt or were a convoy cover and had missed contact.

TRITON, on 16 March, was ordered to change her area slightly to the east. TUNA and GREENLING were placed in adjacent areas (to the south and west, respectively) on 22 March, and all were to disregard areas when on the chase, and to avoid when encountering a submarine. TRITON was told to clear her area on 25 March 1943, and return to Brisbane. When she failed to make her report of position, new results, and estimated time of arrival when it was expected, she was ordered to do so. No report was received and she was reported as lost on 10 April 1943.

Information available now that the war is over shows that TRITON was, without a doubt, sunk by the enemy destroyers of which she was given information on 13 March. Enemy reports show that these ships made an attack on 15 March at 0°-09'N, 144°-55'E. This position was slightly north and west of TRITON's area, but she undoubtedly left her area to attack the destroyers or the convoy they were escorting. The report of the attack by the destroyers leaves little doubt as to whether a kill was made, since they saw "a great quantity of oil, pieces of wood, corks and manfactured goods bearing the mark 'Made in U. S. A'." In addition, TRIGGER, in whose area this attack occurred, reported that on 15 March she made two attacks on a convoy of five freighters with two escorts at 0°N, 145°E. At this time she was depth charged, but not seriously, and she heard distant depth charging for an hour after the escorts had stopped attacking her. Since she was only about ten miles from the reported Japanese attack cited above, it is presumed that she heard the attack which sank TRITON. Apparently by this time the destroyers had joined their convoy.

TRITON was a most active and valuable member of the Submarine Force prior to her loss. In total, she is credited with sinking 16 ships, totaling 64,600 tons, and damaging 4 ships, of 29,200 total tons. Her first patrol, conducted around Wake Island, resulted in no damage to the enemy, but her second, in the northern part of the East China Sea, was very productive. In ten days she sank two freighters and damaged a freighter-transport and another freighter. She went back to the East China Sea for her third patrol, and again was most successful. She sank a trawler, two freighters, a freighter-transport, two sampans, and a submarine. The latter was I-164, and was torpedoed south of Kyushu on 17 May. TRITON's fourth patrol was made in the Aleutians. During it, she is credited with sinking two escort type vessels.

On her fifth patrol, TRITON went into the Solomon area. She sank a tanker, and two freighters, in addition damaging a tanker of 10,200 tons and a freighter. She was credited with having sunk two medium freighters on her last patrol.

U.S.S. TRITON

ALDRICH, R.E. F2c
ASHTON, T.E.Jr. EM3c
BALLOU, W.E. .... CEM
BARNES, F.K. S1c
BARTON, E.J. .... CTM
BASSO, L.D. F1c
BOOTH, W.L. FC1c
BOYD, S.S. EM2c
BRUDERER, W.L. MoMM1c
BUSH, A. F1c
CHRISTY, F.H. SC2c
CLEMENT, V.C. S1c
COLEY, H.P. MoMM1c
COOPER, J.W. S1c
COTTON, C. .... CCStd
CRUTCHFIELD, J.R. ...... LT.
DABNEY, J.D. OC3c
DOTSON, L.D. EM1c
EICHMANN, J.H. .... LT.Exec.
FEDORCHAK, J. S1c
FIELDS, H.S. EM3c
FIELITZ, R.D. TM2c
FORD, G. TM3c
GEORGE, D.R. TM3c
GROOMS, B.J. PhM1c
HALE, D.E. S1c
HALL, D.G. .... CMoMM
HARBOLD, R.L. S1c
HARMON, F.R. S1c
HERSTICH, M.L.Jr. TM1c
HOBBS, L.H. EM3c
HOGG, J.T.Jr. GM3c
HOLLAND, C.Jr. MoMM2c
HOLQUIST, D.E.W. .... CMoMM
HOWIE, G.J.Jr. RT1c
ISOM, L.L. F1c
JONES, M. .... CQM
KLEKOTKA, A. MoMM1c
KLIMOSEWSKI, J.P. MoMM1c
LANDERS, C.W. F1c
LARKINS, W.H. EM1c
LAWLER, J.W. F3c
LINES, W.E. MoMM2c
LONG, P.E. TM2c
MARTIN, W.B.Jr. S1c
McCALOP, H.T. MA1c
MC CLURE, K.G. S1c
McKENZIE, G.K.Jr. LT CDR.C.O.
MC KENZIE, L.C. TM1c
MEADE, J. RM2c
NIXSON, R.B. S1c
OLVEY, R.B. Y2c
O'SULLIVAN, C.D. .... LT.(JG)
OTTERSEN, R.O. TM1c
PAGE, R.E. RM3c
PARKS, E.S.Jr. .... LT.(JG)
PEELER, W.L. F3c
PETRUN, J. MoMM2c
POYNEER, C.F. RM2c
ROSS, B.C. S1c
SCHLABECKER, H.R. TM1c
SCHNEIDER, L.M. F2c
SEVERANCE, E.S. .... CMoMM
SHANNON, J.F. F2c
SHEPHERD, L. F1c
SORENSEN, V.F. .... LT.
THOMPSON, T.C. EM1c
TROWBRIDGE, R.E. EM2c
VAN ROOSEN, H.C. .... LT.(JG)
VISNICH, G. SM2c
WARD, W.A. MoMM1c
WHITE, F.B. QM2c
WYCOFF, D.E. MoMM2c

The USS TRITON (SS 201) photographed from a U.S. Navy blimp

PICKEREL (SS177)

PICKEREL commanded by Lt. Comdr. A. H. Alston, Jr., the first submarine to be lost in the Central Pacific area, set out from Pearl Harbor on 18 March 1943 and, after topping off with fuel at Midway on 22 March, began her seventh war patrol off the eastern coast of northern Honshu. She was never heard from after her departure from Midway.

She was ordered to remain in her area until sunset 1 May 1943 and then to return to Midway. Standing orders required her to transmit by radio prior to entering a circle of radius 500 miles from Midway, and this report was expected by 6 May. When it was not received, a message ordering an immediate reply was repeatedly sent. No answer was received, and plane search along her expected course revealed nothing. As a result, she was reported lost on 12 May 1943.

Anti-submarine attack data submitted by the Japanese at the end of the war list one attack which could conceivably have been on PICKEREL. This attack occured on 3 April, 1943, off Shiramuka Lighthouse, on the northern tip of Honshu. This position is outside the area assigned to PICKEREL, but no other submarine was in that area. FLYINGFISH was enroute to the area between Honshu and Hokkaido and arrived there on 6 April, but PICKEREL might well have moved into the northern area for a few days prior to FLYINGFISH's arrival if she found hunting poor in her own area. Indeed, unless the Japanese attacked a submarine which was the product of their own imaginations, they must certainly have attacked PICKEREL on 3 April, since no other of our boats was near the area of the attack.

However, a special notation is made on the Japanese records to the effect that they are inaccurate for the month of April 1943. Thus there is every reason to speculate that, if PICKEREL did survive the attack of 3 April, she may have been attacked later in her own area and the attack may not have been reported. We know that there were Japanese mine plants along the coast of Honshu, but a study of the track chart for PICKEREL's sixth war patrol, conducted in the same area, shows that the Commanding Officer was accustomed to stay outside the 60 fathom curve. Mines are normally ineffective in water that deep.

The probability as to the cause of PICKEREL's loss is that she was sunk by enemy depth charge attack. Operational casualties or mine explosions represent possibilities, but are not thought to be likely.

During the six patrols before her final one, PICKEREL sank five ships totaling 16,100 tons, and damaged 10, totaling 9,100 tons. On her first patrol she did no damage to the enemy. Her second, conducted between Manila and Surabaya, resulted in the sinking of two freighters. PICKEREL's third patrol was conducted along the Malay Barrier and again no successful attacks were made. In her fourth patrol, in the Philippines, six attacks were made, but none resulted in damage to the enemy. PICKEREL's fifth patrol was a passage from Australia to Pearl Harbor for refit, with a short patrol in the Marianas enroute. She damaged a freighter on this run. On her sixth patrol this ship went to the Kuriles to patrol the Toyko-Kiska traffic lanes. In sixteen attacks, she sank a freighter and two sampans, and did damage to another freighter and eight sampans.

U.S.S. PICKEREL

ALSTON, A.H.Jr.LT,CDR.C.O.
APSAY, D...............OC2c
AYER, E.N...........CGM(PA)
BAURMEISTER, K.H........S1c
BAYS, L.D..............EM1c
BEAURECARD, J.A.R...MoMM1c
BECK, F.G...............Y1c
BERGMAN, J.J..........Bkr2c
BLAYLOCK, W.E...........S1c
BROWNELL, R.E..........FC3c
BROWNING, D.L.Jr........S1c
CARROLL, R.C..........CMoMM
CLINE, C.A.............TM1c
COFFEY, T.H.............F2c
CYNEWSKI, P.T.......MoMM2c
DAVIS, G.T.............TM2c
DOWE, H.III..........LT.(JG)
EAGAN, R.E.............TM3c
EVANS, W.E..............S2c
EVIDON, D...............S1c
FEIOCK, T.G............TM3c
FLANDERS, E.T...........F2c
FLOWERS, J.E...........EM1c
FRAZIER, M.B..........PhM2c
GAETANO, N..............F2c
GARNER, A.L............EM3c
GOODIN, L.J.............S2c
GREISIGER, W.R..........F2c
HARRIS, C..............TM2c
HARGET, L.J.Jr.........RM3c
HELM, R.L...............LT.
HERY, F.P...........MoMM2c
HERDA, T.M.............QM2c
HILBERT, H.R...........SM1c
HIRST, H.J..............F1c
HOGE, W.T..............ENS.
HORVATH, A.J............S1c
HUNT, W.B...............F2c
HUTCHENS, F.R..........EM3c
ISLEY, R.L..............S2c
JOHNSON, J.R...........GM3c
KARAUS, E...........MoMM1c
KIMBALL, R.F...........FC1c
LEMKE, W.J.............SC2c
LINDSAY, J.C...........EM3c
LITCHFIELD, R.E........SM1c
LITTLEDAVE, J.B.........S2c
MARKLE, C.O.Jr......MoMM2c
MATTSON, W.T.E..........F2c
MC CORMACK, P.H........EM3c
MC MAHON, J.........CTM(AA)
MEISCHKE, F.L.......CEM(AA)
MITCHELL, H.M...........S2c
MOORE, H.W.Jr...........LT.
MORRISON, G.C.Jr.......RM3c
NOWVIOCK, T.W..........EM1c
OLAGUERA, F............OS2c
OSBORN, B.C............SC3c
PEIFER, W.A.............S1c
PIERCE, "J"."W".W.......S2c
POLK, D.................S1c
PORE, J.W..............EM1c
POWELL, C.A.............CRM
RAY, S.B.............LT.(JG)
RASMUSSEN, S.J......MoMM1c
RUSSELL, E.H S1c
SHAFFER, W.C.Jr.........LT.
SHARP, T.F...........LT.Exec
SHIFFER, D.A........MoMM2c
STANTON, R.W............F1c
STEVENS, W.A...........RM3c
STOCKTON, E.C.......MoMM1c
TAYLOR, L.M.Jr.........RM1c
VAN CLEVE, M.G.........TM2c

GRENADIER (SS 210)

Patrolling in Lem Voalan Strait in the northeast Indian Ocean, on her sixth war patrol, GRENADIER under Lt. Cdr. J. A. Fitzgerald met her end on 22 April 1943. The following account of her fate is taken from statements made by her Commanding Officer and five of her men after they had been recovered from Japanese camps.

On the night of 20 April 1943, having had poor hunting for two or three days in Lem Voalan Strait, (northwest of Penang on the Malay Peninsula) GRENADIER ventured out ten miles west of that place to see what she could find. She found two ships, but before she could attack, they turned away. Figuring that they would come back to their original course in an hour and a half, Fitzgerald planned an attack to meet them on their course at that time. About 15 minutes before time to dive and prepare for the attack, a plane came in on GRENADIER, and she dived. As she was passing 120 feet, a violent explosion shook the ship, and all lights and power were lost. She was brought to rest on the bottom at about 270 feet. The hull and hatches were leaking badly aft, and a fire in the control cubicle kept the ship without propulsion. A bucket brigade kept the motors dry, and later a jury rig pump was called into service to perform the task, while the electricians worked all day to restore propulsion. Several men were prostrated by heat and exertion, but the work went on.

At dusk, GRENADIER surfaced and continued the work of trying to restore herself. Finally, they were able to turn over one shaft very slowly, but everything possible had been done, and no more speed could be expected.

Toward morning what appeared to be a destroyer, but was actually an 1800 ton merchantman, and an escort vessel were seen on the horizon, and a plane was driven away by gunfire. The skipper decided to scuttle the ship then, and it was done, with all hands being taken prisoner by the enemy merchant ship. The statements of the men relate the brutal treatment they received at the hands of the Japs, and of how their spirit was kept up by their Commanding Officer. The enemy gained no information from this gallant crew, despite the worst they could inflict, and all members of the crew were recovered from prison camps at the close of the war.

GRENADIER's record prior to her loss was six ships sunk, for 40,700 tons, and two ships damaged, for 12,000 tons. Her first patrol, beginning in February 1942, was conducted off the coast of Japan, and GRENADIER sank a freighter. Going to the Formosa shipping lanes for her second patrol, GRENADIER sank a large transport and a freighter. On her third patrol, she sank a large tanker. GRENADIER's fourth patrol was a mining mission in the South China Sea, and she damaged no enemy shipping. On her fifth patrol, this vessel patrolled the Java Sea area, and sank two small freighter and a sampan. In addition she damaged a freighter.

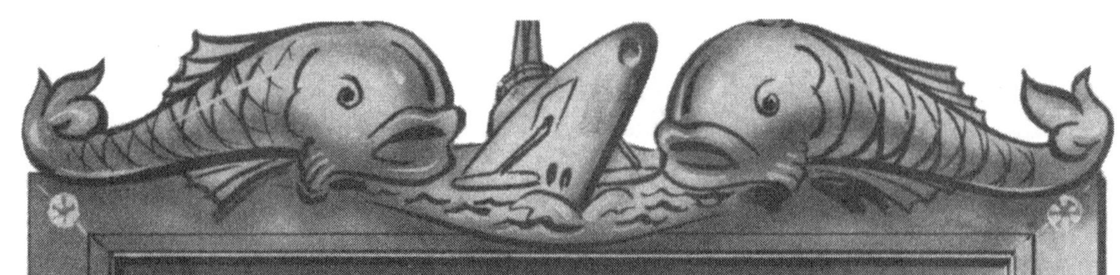

U.S.S. GRENADIER

ADKINS, R.L..............EM1c
ALBERTSEN, N.A..........TM1c
ANDREWS, D.J............TM1c
BARRINGTON, C.W.........TM3c
BARKER, L.L.............EM3c
CLARK, L.R..............SM1c
COURTNEY, T.R...........S2c
COX, G.C................S1c
CRITCHLOW, J.N..........LT.
CUNNINGHAM, W.M.........S2c
*DOYLE, C..............MoMM1c
EMBRY, J.C.............MoMM1c
ERISHMAN, C.A..........CMoMM
EVANS, R.E..............SC3c
EVANS, R.R..............RM3c
FITZGERALD, J.A.LT.CDR.C.O.
FULTON, B.H.............EM2c
FOURRE, G.R.............EM2c
GARRISON, R.J...........SC1c
*GUICO, J.G............Matt1c
GUNDERSON, J.H..........S1c
HARTY, K.D..............LT.
HERBERT, C.W............F2c
HINKSON, R.J............EM2c
INGRAM, J.G.............F1c
JOHNSON, C.E............EM3c
KEEFE, W.H..............RM2c
KEYSOR, R.H.............TM3c
KNUTSON, I.S............RM1c
LANDRUM, J.D............EM2c
LESKOVSKY, J............TM3c
LESLIE, R.G............MoMM1c
*LINDER, C.F...........MoMM2c
LOFTUS, I.C.............S1c
MC BEATH, J.J...........PhM1c
MC COY, C.H.............S1c
MC GOWAN, D.E...........F2c
MC INTYRE, A.G..........LT.
MINTON, J.A.............QM3c
O'BRION, E.A............EM1c
OUILLETTE, V.A..........F2c
PALMER, R.W.............Y1c
PIANKA, J.K............MoMM1c
PIERCE, M.B.............S1c
POSS, E.L...............RM1c
PRICE, J.T..............F1c
QUARTERMAN, C.O.........COM
RAE, T.J................S1c
ROBERTS, W.E............TM2c
ROSKELL, C..............F2c
RUPP, A.J...............S2c
RUSSELL, P.D............F3c
RUTKOWSKI, H.W..........S1c
SAWATZKE, L.L...........F2c
SCHWARTZLY, J.F.........F1c
SHAW, L.C..............MoMM2c
SHOEMAKER, D.B..........TM2c
SHERRY, H.B.............LT.
SIMPSON, J.E............S1c
*SNYDER, G.W.Jr.........MM3c
STAUBER, G.F............MM2c
TAYLOR, O.A.............FC2c
TOULON, A.J.Jr..........LT.
TRIGG, T.J.............Matt1c
VER VALIN, C.H.........MoMM2c
WALDEN, J.S............Gunner
WESTERFIELD, C.W.......CCStd
WHITING, G.H.......LT.Exec.
WHITLOCK, C.H...........CEM
WILSON, C.M............MoMM1c
WISE, W.E...............GM2c
WITHROW, W.C............CTM
WITZKE, B.W.............F1c
YORK, R.F...............EM2c
ZUCCO, P................S1c
ZUFELT, F...............GM1c

*- Died in prison camp.

RUNNER (SS275)

On 28 May 1943 RUNNER (Lt. Cdr. J. H. Bourland) left Midway to proceed to Latitude 48°-30'N, Longitude 154°E and begin her third patrol. She was to patrol south and west from this spot, until she came into the area south of Hokkaido and east of the northern tip of Honshu, where she was to patrol from about 8 June to 4 July 1943. The submarine was never heard from following her departure from Midway.

She was expected at Midway about 11 July, and not later than 15 July, and should have made a transmission when approximately 500 miles from this base. She was ordered on 11 July to make an immediate transmission, but no reply came. A careful lookout was maintained in the hope that RUNNER was safe but without transmission facilities, but the results were negative. On 20 July RUNNER was reported as presumed lost.

A summary of Japanese anti-submarine attacks received since the close of hostilities contains no mention of an attack which could explain the loss of RUNNER. Thus, her loss must be ascribed to an enemy minefield, of which there were at least four in the area to which she was assigned, to an operational casualty, or to an unreported enemy attack. Destruction by a mine is considered the most likely of these possibilities.

J. H. Bourland

This ship sank three ships, totaling 19,800 tons, and damaged three more, for 19,000 tons, on her first two patrols. RUNNER patrolled the Palau area on her first war run in February 1943, and all of her sinkings were made here. She sank three medium freighters, and damaged two more. During her second patrol off Hongkong in the South China Sea, RUNNER damaged a freighter.

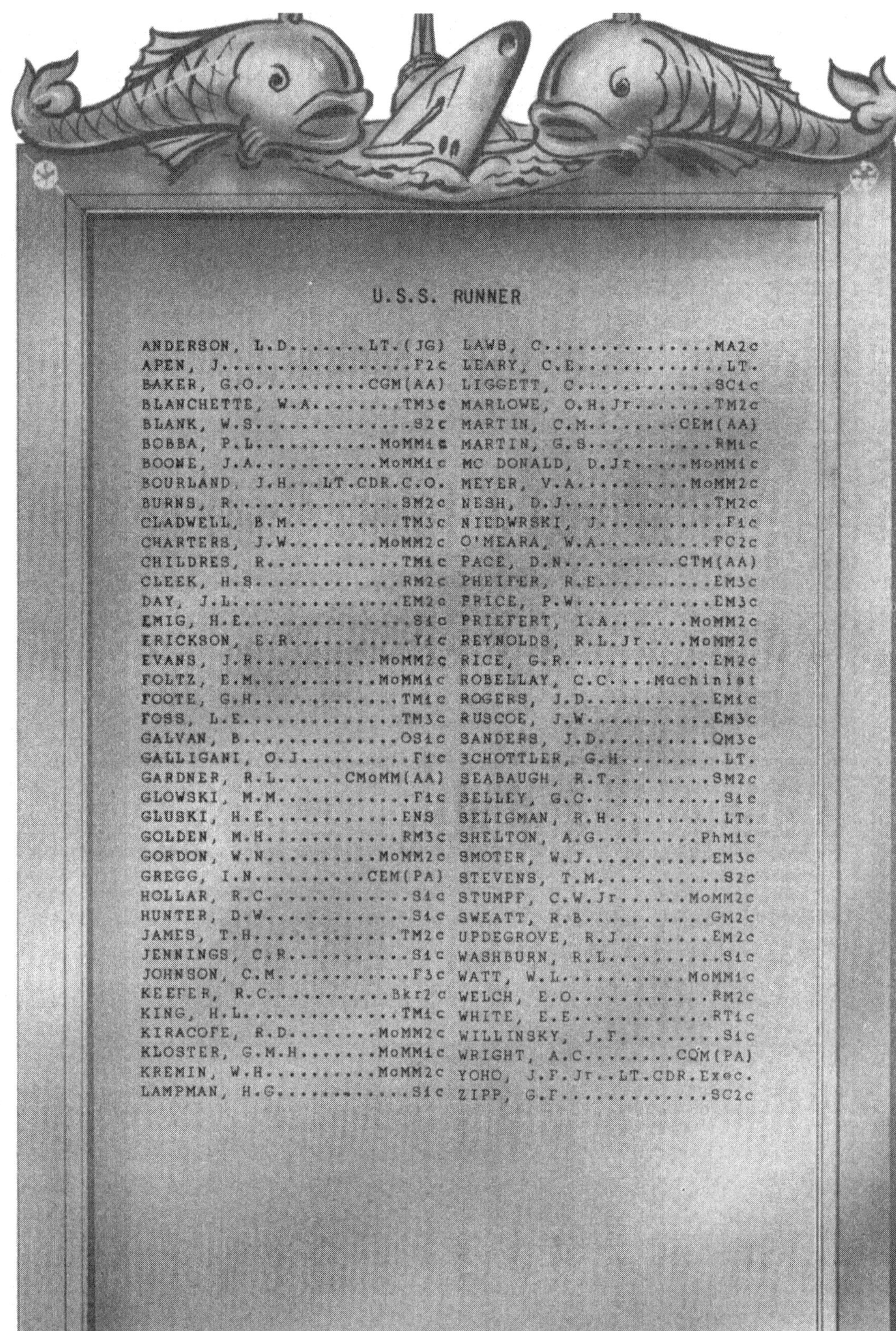
U.S.S. RUNNER
ANDERSON, L.D.......LT.(JG)
APEN, J.................F2c
BAKER, G.O..........CGM(AA)
BLANCHETTE, W.A........TM3c
BLANK, W.S..............S2c
BOBBA, P.L..........MoMM1c
BOONE, J.A..........MoMM1c
BOURLAND, J.H...LT.CDR.C.O.
BURNS, R...............SM2c
CLADWELL, B.M..........TM3c
CHARTERS, J.W.......MoMM2c
CHILDRES, R............TM1c
CLEEK, H.S.............RM2c
DAY, J.L...............EM2c
EMIG, H.E...............S1c
ERICKSON, E.R...........Y1c
EVANS, J.R..........MoMM2c
FOLTZ, E.M..........MoMM1c
FOOTE, G.H.............TM1c
FOSS, L.E..............TM3c
GALVAN, B..............OS1c
GALLIGANI, O.J..........F1c
GARDNER, R.L......CMoMM(AA)
GLOWSKI, M.M............F1c
GLUSKI, H.E............ENS
GOLDEN, M.H............RM3c
GORDON, W.N.........MoMM2c
GREGG, I.N..........CEM(PA)
HOLLAR, R.C.............S1c
HUNTER, D.W.............S1c
JAMES, T.H.............TM2c
JENNINGS, C.R...........S1c
JOHNSON, C.M............F3c
KEEFER, R.C...........Bkr2c
KING, H.L..............TM1c
KIRACOFE, R.D.......MoMM2c
KLOSTER, G.M.H......MoMM1c
KREMIN, W.H.........MoMM2c
LAMPMAN, H.G............S1c
LAWS, C................MA2c
LEARY, C.E..............LT.
LIGGETT, C.............SC1c
MARLOWE, O.H.Jr........TM2c
MARTIN, C.M.........CEM(AA)
MARTIN, G.S............RM1c
MC DONALD, D.Jr.....MoMM1c
MEYER, V.A..........MoMM2c
NESH, D.J..............TM2c
NIEDWRSKI, J............F1c
O'MEARA, W.A...........FC2c
PACE, D.N...........CTM(AA)
PHEIFER, R.E...........EM3c
PRICE, P.W.............EM3c
PRIEFERT, I.A.......MoMM2c
REYNOLDS, R.L.Jr....MoMM2c
RICE, G.R..............EM2c
ROBELLAY, C.C....Machinist
ROGERS, J.D............EM1c
RUSCOE, J.W............EM3c
SANDERS, J.D...........QM3c
SCHOTTLER, G.H..........LT.
SEABAUGH, R.T..........SM2c
SELLEY, G.C.............S1c
SELIGMAN, R.H...........LT.
SHELTON, A.G..........PhM1c
SMOTER, W.J............EM3c
STEVENS, T.M............S2c
STUMPF, C.W.Jr......MoMM2c
SWEATT, R.B............GM2c
UPDEGROVE, R.J.........EM2c
WASHBURN, R.L...........S1c
WATT, W.L...........MoMM1c
WELCH, E.O.............RM2c
WHITE, E.E.............RT1c
WILLINSKY, J.F..........S1c
WRIGHT, A.C.........CQM(PA)
YOHO, J.F.Jr..LT.CDR.Exec.
ZIPP, G.F..............SC2c

R-12 (SS89)

R-12 (Lt. Cdr. E. E. Shelby) was lost between 1220 and 1225 on 12 June 1943 at Latitude 24°24'30" North and Longitude 81°38'30" West in six hundred feet of water with the loss of forty two lives. The personnel on the bridge, two officers including the Commanding Officer, and three enlisted men, were the only survivors. Those missing consisted of four U. S. Naval officers , two Brazilian Naval officers and thirty six U. S. Naval enlisted men.

At the time of the accident R-12 was engaged in normal operations off Key West, Florida, being underway to take up her position for a torpedo practice approach. She was rigged for diving (except main induction was open and batteries were ventilating into the engine room) and riding the vents. The Commanding Officer was on the bridge in the act of turning the Officer of the Deck watch over to another officer when the collision alarm was sounded from below and the report that the forward battery compartment was flooding was passed to the bridge Although the Commanding Officer gave immediate orders to blow main ballast and close the hatches, the ship sank in an estimated fifteen seconds from the time the alarm was sounded until the bridge was completely under water .

E. E. Shelby

It was the opinion of the Court of Inquiry that the cause of the loss of R-12 was unknown but probably was caused by the rapid flooding of the forward part of the ship through a torpedo tube.

U.S.S. R-12

1 ALMEIDA, A.G.D............LT.
BACON, G.W...............EM3c
* BAILEY, E.P..........MoMM1c
* BALFE, R.B..............TM2c
* BARNETT, P.E............RM2c
* BOUCHER, C.A............SM3c
BRONSON, R.B..............F2c
BUCKLEY, J.J..............SM1c
CASHELL, F.E..............ENS.
CLAYTON, H.L.........CSM(A)
* CROSS, J.L...............MM1c
* DAVIS, D.E...........MoMM2c
1 DE MOURA, J.L.............LT.
* DURRENBERGER, R..........F1c
* ENGLAND, R.N..............Y2c
FLISHER, R.F...............F1c
GARBULSKY, L.E............S2c
GRAZIANI, F.P.Jr.........GM1c
HALL, J.C.Jr..............EM3c
HARMAN, E.L.Jr.......CRM(A)
HORTON, J.U..........LT.(JG)
HORVATH, J.S..............TM1c
* KAPRAL, J.................TM3c
KNAPP, H.H.................S2c
KRIGBAUM, E........CMoMM(A)
KYMER, L.V............MoMM2c
LE VAN, C.B................S1c
LOBECK, H.P...............TM3c
MATHIS, C.V...............TM3c
* MAYER, W.W.................F1c
MC KIBBEN, P.T............EM1c
MONCADA, J.................MM1c
MULLIS, A.J.................F2c
NESS, G.W...................S2c
* NILES, G.H...................S1c
NOONAM, P.L................S2c
* OVENSON, L...................F1c
* PINKLEY, J.E..............EM3c
* POOL, S.H....................S2c
RABBIT, J.H................EM3c
RAFFERTY, E.J..............MM2c
SCHNAKE, L.E................F1c
SCOTT, C.R...................F2c
* SCHNEE, A.J...............EM3c
* SCHWATTZ, E.E............GM2c
SECOR, H.R..................RM2c
* SHELBY, E.E....LT,CDR.C.O.
SHELLENBERGER, H.H.....F3c
SMITH G.S...................S2c
STARKS, R.N........LT.Exec.
SULLIVAN, D.C..............RM3c
* SULLIVAN, J.J........CCS(AA)
THOMPSON, R.A.Jr..........S2c
UNGER, J.D.............LT.(JG)
* VAN LEUVEN, F.A............F3c
VINCENT, E.W...........MoMM2c
WALKER, N.W............MoMM1c
WALSH, E.F...............MoMM2c
WHEELER, K.J................SC3c
* WILSON, B.L...............STM3c
* WOOD, J.H................MoMM2c
YOUNG, W.D.................STM2c
ZIMMERMAN, G.A.............F3c
* ZIONS, F.J................MoMM3c

* - Men attached to R-12 who survived the tragedy. It is assumed that 3 enlisted survivors were aboard R-12 at the time of her misshap, the remainder were ashore on liberty. Second officer survivor unidentified, not listed here.

1 - BRAZILIAN NAVY.

GRAYLING (SS 209)

GRAYLING (Lt. Cdr. R. M. Brinker) departed Fremantle on 30 July 1943, for her eighth patrol, going through Makassar Strait and thence to the Philippine area. On 19 August, she reported having damaged a 6,000 ton freighter near Balikpapen, and the following day told of having sunk a 250 ton Taki Maru type pocket tanker by gunfire in Sibutu Passage, taking one man prisoner. This was the last report received direct from GRAYLING. On 23 August, she completed a special mission at Pandan Bay, Panay, delivering cargo to guerrillas. This mission was reported by guerrillas. Then she departed for Tablas Strait, there to reconnoiter until 2 September, when she would patrol approaches to Manila until 10 September. She was to return to Pearl Harbor for refit, passing from SubSoWesPac to Subpac on 13 September.

She was not heard from after 19 August 1943, and on 30 September 1943, GRAYLING was reported as presumed lost.

Following war's end, the Japanese have submitted the following reports which bear on GRAYLING. On 27 August 1943 a torpedo attack was seen by the enemy at 12°-36'N, 121°-33'E, and the next day a surfaced submarine was seen at 12°-50'N, 121°-42'E. Both of these positions are in the Tablas Strait area. On 9 September a surfaced U. S. submarine was seen inside Lingayen Gulf; this ties with GRAYLING's orders to patrol the approaches to Manila. It is said that the freighter-transport HOKUAN MARU was engaged in a submarine action on the 9th in the Philippine area, but no additional data was available, and no known enemy attacks could have sunk GRAYLING. Her loss may have been operational or by an unrecorded enemy attack. At any rate, it is certain that GRAYLING was lost between 9 and 12 September 1943 either in Lingayen Gulf or along the approaches to Manila. ComTaskFor 71 requested a transmission from GRAYLING on the latter date, but did not receive one.

GRAYLING's first patrol, made in January and February 1942, was a reconnaissance of the northern Gilbert Islands. She went to the Japanese homeland for her second patrol, and sank a freighter and damaged a sampan. Truk was the scene of GRAYLING's third patrol; she sank a large freighter. On her fourth patrol, this boat again went to Truk, and sank a medium tanker, while she damaged an aircraft transport. In January and February 1943, she patrolled the approaches to Manila on her fifth patrol. Here she sank two freighters and a medium freighter-transport. GRAYLING patrolled the lesser islands south of the Philippines on her sixth patrol, and sank two freighters, a small freighter-transport and two schooners. Damage was done to a large tanker and two freighters. She went to the area west of Borneo for her seventh patrol, and sank a medium freighter and two sampans. Damage was done to a large tanker. Thus GRAYLING's total record is 16 ships sunk, totalling 61,400 tons, and six ships damaged, for a total of 36,600 tons.

U.S.S. GRAYLING

ARNOLD, D.E.... ....LT.
BAKER, E.N.............TM1c
BEAVERS, A.R..........EM2c
BECKER, J.W........LT.(JG)
BOYNE, G.Jr...........EM1c
BRINKER, R.M...LT.CDR.C.O.
BURCH, J.M............EM2c
BUSH, J.W.Jr.........MoMM2c
CAMPANA, C.J........MoMM2c
CHOCKLEY, J.E........CMoMM
CLARK, B.R............GM1c
CLARK, C.D.............F2c
CORBETT, R.A..........SM2c
CRISWELL, H.W.Jr..LT.Exec.
DALLAIRE, W.J..........CSM
DAY, J.E...............CTM
DILLOW, H.E.........MoMM2c
DONALDSON, F.W.........Cox
ELLIS, W..............EM3c
FONTAINE, D.I........PhM1c
GOODNIGHT, J.C......MoMM1c
GRIMES, C.A.Jr.........S1c
GURASKO, T.J...........S1c
HARBAUER, R.E.........SC1c
HARPER, J.K...........FC2c
HAWKINS, C.H........MoMM1c
HICKCOX, F.J...........S1c
HOFFMAN, E.J...........CTM
HOWARD, R.............GM3c
HOWELL, J.L............S1c
HUNT, C.W.............TM3c
JOHNSON, E.............S1c
KELLEY, W.W............S1c
KELLY, J.E..........MoMM1c
KEPLINGER, D.L........RM3c
KYSAR, C.R.............Y2c
LOUDON, L.E...........QM3c
MABUTI, S.P...........CK2c
MALOY, F.B.........LT.(JG)
MARKS, J.H..........MoMM1c
MATHIS, M.O............F3c
MULVENNA, G.A..........CTM
NICHOLS, C.W..........Bkr1c
NICKOLS, J.T.Jr.........LT.
OELDEMANN, H.C.........F2c
OLIVER, R.G...........EM1c
PARRINO, A.J..........GM2c
PAWLOSKI, J.T.......MoMM1c
QUESENBERRY, M.J......TM1c
RAINAULT, A.L..........F1c
SANTOS, J.C...........St2c
SAWERBREY, A.S.........S2c
SCHMIDT, C.E...........CEM
SCHMIDTMEYER, H.A.....EM3c
SCOTT, G.L............TM3c
SEBOURN, L.E.Jr.......TM3c
SHARROCK, D.P.........RM2c
SHIELDS, W.S..........EM3c
SIMPKINS, J.D.........TM1c
SIMPSON, R.T...........F2c
SMALL, R.E.............CMM
SMITH, J.C.............CRM
SMOAK, H.A............EM1c
SPENCER, D.H..........EM2c
STEVENS, R.F..........TM3c
SULLIVAN, E.F......LT.(JG)
WALLACE, W.L..........SC3c
WALLER, J.J...........QM2c
WELCH, J...........LT.(JG)
WELSH, F............MoMM1c
WETSEL, A.F.........MoMM2c
WHITCOMB, H.O.........EM1c
WILSON, J.H...........TM2c
WOLF, M.A..............F1c
YOUNG, J.H............RM2c
ZABS, R.L..............S1c

POMPANO (SS181)

After leaving Midway on 20 August 1943 to start her seventh war patrol, POMPANO, with Lt. Cdr. W. M. Thomas in command, was never heard from again. Her orders were to patrol off the east coast of Honshu from about 29 August to sunset of 27 September 1943, and then to return to Pearl Harbor for refit, stopping at Midway enroute for fuel.

When no transmission was received from her, especially just prior to her expected arrival at Midway on 5 October, word was sent from Pearl to keep a sharp lookout for her. By 15 October, all hope was abandoned, and POMPANO was reported as presumed lost in enemy waters.

Japanese information available now shows no attack which could conceivably have been on POMPANO. On 6 September POMPANO was informed by despatch that the area to the north of her own was open. Since that area was considered more productive of sinkings than the one she was in, it is quite possible that she moved into it. Both the one between Honshu and Hokkaido, and the one east of northern Honshu are known to have been mined by the enemy, with the greatest concentration of mines in the northern area. In view of the evidence given, it is considered probable that POMPANO met her end by an enemy mine. Operational loss or loss by an unreported attack are alternate possibilities.

In the six patrols completed before her loss, POMPANO sank ten enemy ships for a total of 42,000 tons, and damaged four, totaling 55,300 tons. In the first month of the war, POMPANO patrolled near Wake Island, and sank a large freighter-transport of 16,500 tons. On her second patrol, conducted east of Formosa, she sank a large transport, a tanker, a small freighter, and two patrol boats. POMPANO went to the Empire for her third patrol, from mid-August to mid-September 1942, and sank a freighter and a patrol boat. In the Marshalls area on her fourth patrol, she damaged two tankers. Going to the Empire again for her fifth patrol, POMPANO damaged an aircraft carrier. She went to Japan a third time for her sixth patrol, this time along the coast south of Honshu. There she sank a sampan and damaged a freighter.

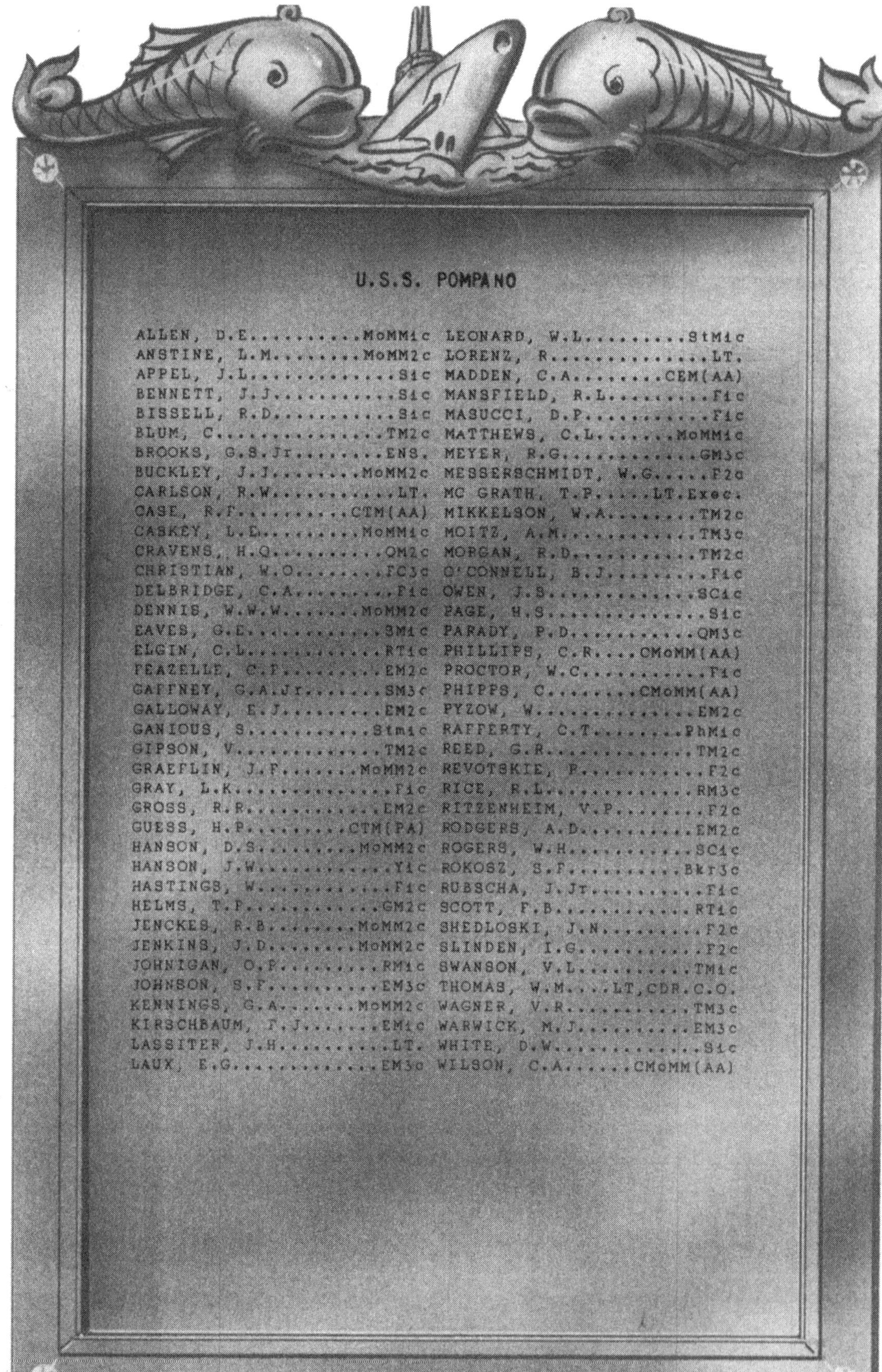
U.S.S. POMPANO
ALLEN, D.E..........MoMM1c
ANSTINE, L.M........MoMM2c
APPEL, J.L.............S1c
BENNETT, J.J...........S1c
BISSELL, R.D...........S1c
BLUM, C...............TM2c
BROOKS, G.S.Jr.........ENS.
BUCKLEY, J.J........MoMM2c
CARLSON, R.W............LT.
CASE, R.F..........CTM(AA)
CASKEY, L.E.........MoMM1c
CRAVENS, H.Q..........QM2c
CHRISTIAN, W.O........FC3c
DELBRIDGE, C.A..........F1c
DENNIS, W.W.W.......MoMM2c
EAVES, G.E............SM1c
ELGIN, C.L............RT1c
FEAZELLE, C.F.........EM2c
GAFFNEY, G.A.Jr.......SM3c
GALLOWAY, E.J.........EM2c
GANIOUS, S...........Stm1c
GIPSON, V.............TM2c
GRAEFLIN, J.F.......MoMM2c
GRAY, L.K..............F1c
GROSS, R.R............EM2c
GUESS, H.P.........CTM(PA)
HANSON, D.S.........MoMM2c
HANSON, J.W............Y1c
HASTINGS, W............F1c
HELMS, T.F............GM2c
JENCKES, R.B........MoMM2c
JENKINS, J.D........MoMM2c
JOHNIGAN, O.F.........RM1c
JOHNSON, S.F..........EM3c
KENNINGS, G.A.......MoMM2c
KIRSCHBAUM, F.J.......EM1c
LASSITER, J.H...........LT.
LAUX, E.G.............EM3c
LEONARD, W.L..........StM1c
LORENZ, R...............LT.
MADDEN, C.A.........CEM(AA)
MANSFIELD, R.L.........F1c
MASUCCI, D.P...........F1c
MATTHEWS, C.L.......MoMM1c
MEYER, R.G............GM3c
MESSERSCHMIDT, W.G.....F2c
MC GRATH, T.P.....LT.Exec.
MIKKELSON, W.A........TM2c
MOITZ, A.M............TM3c
MORGAN, R.D...........TM2c
O'CONNELL, B.J.........F1c
OWEN, J.S.............SC1c
PAGE, H.S..............S1c
PARADY, P.D...........QM3c
PHILLIPS, C.R....CMoMM(AA)
PROCTOR, W.C...........F1c
PHIPPS, C........CMoMM(AA)
PYZOW, W..............EM2c
RAFFERTY, C.T.........PhM1c
REED, G.R.............TM2c
REVOTSKIE, P...........F2c
RICE, R.L.............RM3c
RITZENHEIM, V.P........F2c
RODGERS, A.D..........EM2c
ROGERS, W.H...........SC1c
ROKOSZ, S.F..........Bkr3c
RUBSCHA, J.Jr..........F1c
SCOTT, F.B............RT1c
SHEDLOSKI, J.N.........F2c
SLINDEN, I.G...........F2c
SWANSON, V.L..........TM1c
THOMAS, W.M....LT,CDR.C.O.
WAGNER, V.R...........TM3c
WARWICK, M.J..........EM3c
WHITE, D.W.............S1c
WILSON, C.A......CMoMM(AA)

CISCO (SS290)

Venturing out for her first war patrol, CISCO (Lt. Cdr. J, W. Coe), left Port Darwin, Australia on 18 September 1943. That evening she returned to Darwin due to a derangement of the main hydraulic system which had occurred during the day's operation. The hydraulic system having been repaired to the satisfaction of the Commanding Officer, CISCO once more departed on 19 September.

CISCO's area was a large rectangular one in the South China Sea between Luzon and the coast of French Indo-China. In order to reach it, she was to pass through the Arafoera Sea, the Banda Sea, Manipa Strait, Molukka Passage, the Celebes Sea, Sibutu Passage, the Sulu Sea and Mindoro Strait. On 28 September, CISCO should have been due west of Mindanao in the center of the Sulu Sea. On that day a Japanese anti-submarine attack was made at 9°-47'N, 121°-44'E slightly north and east of CISCO's expected position. In reporting the attack the Japanese state, "Found a

Lt.Cdr. J.W. Coe

sub tailing oil. Bombing. Ships cooperated with us. The oil continued to gush out even on tenth of October." The attack would seem to have been made by planes in co-operation with ships. No submarine which returned from patrol reported having been attacked at this time and position

Nothing has been seen of or heard from CISCO since her departure from Darwin, and on 4 and 5 November 1943, Headquarters Task Force Seventy One was unable to make radio contact with her. At the time of her loss it was considered very unlikelv that a recurrence of trouble with her main hydraulic system could explain her sinking, and the only other possible clue was the fact that a Japanese plane was reported over Darwin at twenty thousand feet on the morning of her second departure. The attack listed above is thought to probably explain this loss. No enemy minefields are known to have been in her area, or enroute to it.

Coe had previously made three war patrols as Commanding Officer of S-39, and three as Commanding Officer of Skipjack. He was considered a most able and sucessful Submarine Officer .

U.S.S. CISCO

ABRAMS, D.B..........FC2c(M)
ANDERSON, D.F....CMoMM(AA)
ANDERSON, J.R.D.........S2c
ARGERSINGER, E.E........S1c
BAKER, W.M..............SC1c
BERRY, H.B.Jr...........LT.
BESNOT, L.R..............S1c
BRIGGS, R.M.............EM2c
BUBP, H.K................F1c
BUCK, J.E.Sr.............F2c
BURATTE, A.O...........TM1c
CANNON, P.J............RM3c
COE, J.E...........CDR.C.O.
COE, W.F...............RT1c
COLE, L.R................S2c
CORKERY, C.R............TM2c
DIERY, R.M..............SC2c
DOHLUS, W.F.Jr.........EM1c
DRAGICH, J.......CMoMM(AA)
EDWARDS, M.J.............S1c
FIPPEN, J.M.............EM3c
FISHER, R.K..........MoMM1c
GENOOZIS, A.M............F2c
GONDORCHIN, G............S2c
GURGANUS, A.A.......CTM(PA)
HAGERDORN, R.J..........MM1c
HALSTEN, D.H.............F2c
HANDREN, W.J.............S1c
HARE, E.N................F2c
HERGOLD, W.B............EM2c
HOOVER, G.P..........LT.(JG)
INTSCHER, M.Jr.......MoMM1c
JOHNSON, D.W.............F2c
JONES, W.F.Jr............F1c
KELLER, A............MoMM2c
KISBAUGH, S.............TM3c
KOVACS, H...............EM2c
KRAUS, H.J...........MoMM1c
LACASSE, D.L............TM3c
LA ROUCHE, R.J...........Cox
LOUNEY, W.H..............LT.
MAIRS, C.H...............S2c
MAZEIDA, J.B.............S2c
MC CARSON, F.B..........EM1c
MENEAR, L.K.............TM3c
MEWBOURN, M.T...........MM1c
MILLARD, L.C............SM2c
MILLER, J.D..........LT.CDR.
MORRISSEY, R.F..........RM3c
NELSON, S................St2c
NICOLL, G.L.............GM2c
NOBLE, C.F...........MoMM2c
PETERSON, C.I............ENS.
PITMAN, R...............TM2c
RAUSCH, R.J..........MoMM1c
RITZLER, A.T............SM1c
SATTERWHITE, M..........TM2c
SERMINI, M.E.............F2c
SWEET, W.W..............EM3c
TEACH, L.E..............TM2c
TIMM, B.C..............PhM2c
TOEBBE, H.E..............CTM
TRAVIS, W.W..............F1c
UPSON, E.R..............GM1c
VILANDRE, R.H............F1c
VITALE, R.J..........MoMM1c
WALTIS, V...............EM1c
WARREN, G.H.............EM3c
WEHR, H.................EM3c
WEINEL, A.F...LT.CDR.Exec.
WETSKY, L.A..........MoMM2c
WILLIAMS, A.W..........Stm1c
WINTER, J.W.............TM2c
ZAR, C..................SC3c
ZEIS, M.J............MoMM1c
ZYWICKI, F.W............QM1c

A TIGHT PLACE–Painting by Vandis

S-44 (SS149)

On 26 September 1943, S-44 (Lt. Cdr. F. E. Brown) departed Attu to begin her fifth war patrol in the Kuriles. She was not heard from again by the shore bases, but the story given here is taken from statements made by her two surviving crewman, E. A. Duva, CTM and W. F. Whitemore, RM3c.

One day out of Attu S-44 was forced down by a plane which dropped several depth charges. Then nothing was seen until 2030 on the night of 7 October, when radar contact was made on what was thought to be a small merchant ship. S-44 went in very close on the surface and started firing her deck gun, and immediately the destroyer they had underrated opened up with all guns.

The Captain ordered, "take her down", and the diving alarm was sounded, but the ship did not submerge, for reasons not made clear in the statements of the survivors. Meanwhile, the destroyer had scored a hit below the water line in the control room, one in the conning tower, and one in the forward battery. The order was given to abandon ship, and a pillow case was waved from the forward room hatch, in the hope that the enemy would cease firing, but they did not. Several more hits were scored by the destroyer.

About eight men got off the ship and into the water before she sank, but only two were picked up by the destroyer. They were taken to the Island of Paramushiru for several days, and then to the Naval Interrogation Camp at Ofuna for a year. Finally, they were forced to work in the copper mines of Ashio until released by Allied forces at the close of the war.

During her first four patrols, all conducted in the Solomon Islands area, S-44 sank three ships and damaged a fourth. Her first patrol was conducted off the east coast of New Britain, and on 12 May 1942 she sank a small freighter. While covering the area west and south of Florida Island on her second patrol, S-44 sank the 1,051 ton converted gunboat KEIJO MARU on 21 July 1942. Her greatest satisfaction and an important contribution to the Allied War Cause came during her third war patrol, conducted on New Hanover. On 10 August 1942, S-44 hit the heavy cruiser KAKO with four torpedoes and sank her. This sinking was particularly opportune as KAKO was one of the four Japanese heavy cruisers of Cruiser Division Six, who at the very time were returning from the first battle of Savo Island. The night before in that battle they had sunk four Allied heavy cruisers without losing any themselves or suffering more than moderate damage. On her fourth patrol, off New Georgia, S-44 damaged a destroyer type vessel.

U.S.S. S-44

BECK, B.M...............S1c
BILLER, T.R.............S1c
BROWN, F.E.....LT.CDR.C.O.
BUTTERS, L.E...........SC1c
CALVERT, C.F.........MoMM2c
CARRIER, P.A...........EM3c
CLEVERDON, T...........CPhM
COOPER, T.O.............S2c
CUTRIGHT, P.P........MoMM1c
DILLOW, W..............CMoMM
*DUVA, E.A...............CTM
ELLIS, W.H..............RM3c
ERHART, W.E..............S1c
ERICO, D.B................BM
FEES, L.R............MoMM1c
FERRELL, E.D.............Y2c
GANDER, D.E..............F1c
GEORGE, F................F1c
GILES, F.Jr..............F1c
GILLEN, F.E.Jr...........S2c
GLENN, C................CK2c
GREEN, L.J...............F3c
GODFREY, E.W.........MoMM2c
GOODIN, T.L..............F3c
HARASIMOWICZ, A..........CEM
HOWARD, H.K..........MoMM2c
HUGYO, N.A...........MoMM1c
JAWORSKI, P.J...........GM2c
JOHNSTON, C.N........MoMM2c
KLINK, L.N...........MoMM2c
MILLER, A.L............CMoMM
MITCHELL, H.M..........StM2c
MORRIS, W.I.Sr...........TM2c
MOSS, C.E...............GM1c
NASH, B.M...............ENS.
PARR, T.S.Jr............SM2c
QUEEN, B.M..............SC2c
QUEEN, F.K.............LT.(JG)
QUINN, R.G.............LT.Exec.
RAUCH, E.M..............EM3c
RODGERS, R.G.........MoMM2c
RODIN, L.J...............S2c
ROSENBERG, H............RM3c
RUBITS, J.V..........MoMM2c
SLOAN, J.H.Jr............F1c
SMITH, A.E..............TM3c
SMITH, C.W..............EM1c
STEPHENS, J.R...........RM1c
STEPHENSON, J.T....LT.(JG)
STROMSOE, H.A...........CTM
THOMPSON, D.R.......MoMM2c
TURNER, F.A.Jr..........QM3c
VELEBNY, J.A............TM1c
WARBURTON, R.L...........S1c
WESTER, G.S..............S1c
*WHITEMORE, W.F.........RM3c
WOOD, J.C................F2c

*- Survivors.

DORADO (SS248)

DORADO, a newly commissioned submarine, under Lieutenant Commander E. C. Schneider, sailed from New London, Connecticut, on 6 October 1943 for Panama. She did not arrive at Panama nor was she heard from at any time after sailing.

The Commander in Chief, United States Fleet in his comments concerning the Court of Inquiry covering the case, lists three possible causes for the loss of DORADO operational casualties, enemy action, and attack by friendly forces.

The standard practice of imposing bombing restrictions within an area of fifteen miles on each side of the course of an unescorted submarine making passage in friendly waters and fifty miles ahead and one hundred miles astern of her scheduled position was carried out and all concerned were notified. A convoy was so routed as to pass through the bombing and attack restriction area surrounding DORADO on the evening of 12 October 1943, assuming correct navigation and adherence to schedule by both.

A patrol plane which was assigned by Commandant, NOB, Guantanamo to furnish air coverage on the evening of 12 October, received faulty instructions as to the location of the bombing and attack restriction area surrounding DORADO and at 2049, local time, the plane delivered a surprise attack of three depth charges on an unidentified submarine. About two hours later, the plane sighted another submarine with which it attempted to exchange recognition signals without success. This submarine fired upon the plane. A German submarine was known to be operating near the scene of these two contacts.

Because of the lack of evidence, the Court of Inquiry was unable to reach definite conclusions as to the cause of the loss of DORADO.

U.S.S. DORADO

ABRUZZIO, L.J..........F2c
ADDY, T.T.............TM2c
ALBRIGHT, V.J..........RM3c
ALLOWAY, T.............S2c
AMAN, P.D GM1c
ANTHONY, B.L...........TM3c
AUSTIN, W L............S2c
BALLMAN, A.F...........ENS.
BECKER, R.H............SM1c
BOYD, J................LT.
BRUBECK, F.L...........TM1c
BURNETT, J.J...........S2c
BURRELL, D.L...........BM1c
CABASE, I..............ST1c
CHANDLER, L.M......CTM(AA)
CILLEY, L.D.........MoMM2c
COELHO, J..............S1c
COSAPTES, T.........MoMM2c
CRISTELLO, D.M.........TM1c
DAVENPORT, D.J..CMoMM(AA)
DIX, H.M...............FC3c
EBERL, E.H.......CMoMM(AA)
FACKRELL, C.E..........SM3c
FISHER, J.B.........MoMM1c
FLOREA, H.C.Jr.........SC3c
FRY, J.W...............F1c
GARDNER, V.E...........F1c
GENDREAU, A.A.Jr.......TM3c
GLASS, D.Jr.........LT.CDR.
GREENLEE, B.B.......MoMM1c
GUIDA, F.F.............EM2c
HARLOCK, R.E...........Y2c
HARRIS, D.............Stm2c
HAUBER, R.L.........CRM(AA)
HINTON, C.C............EM1c
HOLLROCK, G.T......LT.(JG)
HUFFMON, A.V...........EM2c
IRWIN, R.W.............LT.

KAPRAL, J..............TM2c
KLINK, R.L.............MM2c
LEMPER, C.L.........CTM(PA)
LIGGETT, G.W...........TM3c
LOZAW, L.E.............MM3c
LYNCH, M.E..........MoMM1c
MARSH, J.B..........MoMM1c
MAZARI, C.W.........MoMM2c
McBROOME, H,D.......MoMM1c
McCALL, H.E............MM3c
McGRATH, R.M...........QM3c
NELSON, E.W.........CQM(AA)
NILES, R.A.............MM3c
NORMAN, F.B............S1c
NOWACKI, H.A...........EM3c
O DELL, O.F.........CRM(PA)
OHRT, C.N.Jr........CEM(AA)
OTTO, A. J.............TM3c
PERRAULT, J.L..........S2c
POPE, H.I..............S2c
RHODE, E.C.............S2c
ROUTON, P.C............EM2c
SANDERS, L.W...........RM2c
SCHAFER, A.A.Jr.....MoMM2c
SCHNEIDER, E.C.LT CDR C.O.
SINGSCHEIMER, R.K......S2c
SMITH, B.D.............RT2c
SPEIGHT, W.O...........S2c
TALLEY, R.S.........MoMM1c
THOMPSON, D.S..........EM3c
TIPTON, O.P............EM3c
VERNARSKY, J...........F2c
WAGNER, G.A...LT.CDR.Exec.
WHITE, P.B.Jr..........S2c
WILLIAMS, B.T..........SC1c
WILMOTT, L.C...........PhM1c
WILSON, M.H............S2c
WINDFELDT, A.L.........SC1c

WAHOO (SS238)

WAHOO returned to Pearl Harbor from her sixth war patrol on 29 August 1943 with the dejected air peculiar to a highly successful submarine who suddenly could not make her torpedoes run true. In twenty eight days away from port, seven of them spent in her assigned area in the Sea of Japan, WAHOO had expended ten torpedoes in nine attacks without inflicting any damage on the enemy. Her Skipper, Cdr. D. W. Morton, returned to port to have the torpedoes changed or checked, and requested that WAHOO be sent back to the Japan Sea for her seventh patrol.

On 9 September, WAHOO again departed Pearl. She topped off with fuel at Midway and left there on 13 September heading for the dangerous but important Japan Sea. Shortly afterwards, SAWFISH left Midway and also headed for this area. WAHOO was to pass through Etorofu Strait, in the Kurile Islands, and La Perouse Strait, between Hokkaido and Karafuto, and enter the Japan Sea about 20 September. She was to head south and remain below 43 degrees north after 23 September, and below 40 degrees north after 26 September. SAWFISH was to follow WAHOO, entering the Japan Sea about 23 September and patrolling the area north of WAHOO.

D. W. Morton

No transmission was received from WAHOO, either by any shore station or by SAWFISH, nor was she sighted by SAWFISH after she left Midway. She had orders to clear her area not later than sunset 21 October 1943, and to report by radio after passing through the Kurile Island chain

enroute to Midway. This report was expected about 23 October, but Midway waited in vain. By 30 October, apprehension was felt for WAHOO's safety and an aircraft search along her expected course was arranged. When this revealed nothing, WAHOO was reported missing on 9 November 1943.

Although no transmission was received from WAHOO after her departure on patrol, the results of one of her attacks became known to the world via a Toyko broadcast. Domei was quoted as reporting that on 5 October, a "steamer" was sunk by an American submarine off the west coast of Honshu near the Straits of Tsushima. It was said that the ship sank "after several seconds" with 544 people losing their lives. The submarine could have been none other than WAHOO: none other was operating in that area.

In reporting this broadcast, TIME magazine of 18 October 1943 stated:

"KNOCK AT THE DOOR"

"In the rough Tsushima Straits where two decker, train carrying ferries ply between Japan and Korea, an Allied Submarine upped periscope, unleashed a torpedo. The missile stabbed the flank of a Jap steamer. Said the Toyko radio: the steamer went down in "seconds" with loss of 544 persons aboard."

"Fifty miles across at their narrowest, the Tsushima Straits are Japan's historic doors to the Asiatic mainland. Over them centuries ago Regent Hideyoski's armada sailed to battle the Koreans and send home 38,000 enemy ears pickled in wine. Upon them in 1905 Crusty Admiral Togo smashed the Russian Fleet. Presumably the submarine knocking at the door last week was American. It had achieved one of World War II's most daring submarine penetrations of enemy waters, a feat ranking with German Gunther Prien's entry at Scapa Flow, the Jap invasion of Pearl Harbor, the U. S. raid in Toyko Bay."

Information gleaned from Japanese sources since the cessation of hostilities indicates that an anti-submarine attack was made in La Perouse Strait on 11 October 1943. This was two days after SAWFISH went through the Straits. Supplementary data on the attack of 11 October state, "Our plane found a floating sub and attacked it, with 3 depth charges." SAWFISH was attacked here while making her passage, and that attack is not mentioned in Jap records. However the primary attacking agency in that case was a patrol boat, and about five depth charges were dropped. Thus it is safe to assume that the

Fleet Admiral Nimitz Presents Navy Cross to Lt. Comdr. Morton

attack cited here was made on WAHOO, and is not the attack on SAWFISH with an incorrect date. Both Tsushima Straits, where the attack on the steamer was made, and La Perouse Straits, through which WAHOO was to make good her exit from the Japan Sea, are known to have been mined. This despite the fact that SAWFISH transited La Perouse on 9 October and reported no indications of mining. It is felt, however, that WAHOO succumbed to the attack referred to above, and not to a mine.

WAHOO was one of the Submarine Force's most valuable units during her six patrols, and her feats have become submarine legend. She sank 27 ships, totaling 119,100 tons, and damaged two more, making 24,900 tons, in the six patrols completed before her loss. Her patrolling career began in August 1942 in the Carolines. On this patrol WAHOO sank a freighter. Her second patrol was in the Solomons, and she sank a freighter; on 14 December 1942, she sank the enemy submarine I-15 with a single torpedo hit. WAHOO conducted her third patrol in the Palau area. She sank two large freighters, a transport, a tanker, and an escort vessel. In addition, she entered Wewak harbor, on the north coast of New Guinea, seriously damaged a destroyer, which was later found beached there, and obtained reconnaissance data. For her fourth patrol, WAHOO went to the Yellow Sea west of Korea. Here she sank eight freighters, a tanker, a patrol craft and two sampans in March 1943.

Going to the Kurile chain for her fifth patrol, WAHOO sank two freighters and a large tanker, also doing damage to another freighter and a large (15,600 ton) aircraft transport. The sixth patrol of WAHOO was the disappointing one in the Japan Sea due to poor torpedo performance. Not one of the many attacks on merchantmen resulted in a torpedo hit; WAHOO's only sinkings were of three sampans by gunfire. WAHOO was awarded the Presidential Unit Citation for her third patrol. Commander Morton was considered one of the topnotch officers in the Submarine Force, and the loss of this ship was an irreparable blow to the Service.

Japanese records now reveal that the following ships were sunk in the Sea of Japan shortly before WAHOO's loss: TAIKO (AK) 2,958 T. 25 Sept., KONRON (AP) 7,903 T. 1 Oct., KANKO (AK) 1,288 T. 6 Oct., and KANKO (AK) 2,995 T. 9 Oct. WAHOO was the only submarine who could have sunk these ships.

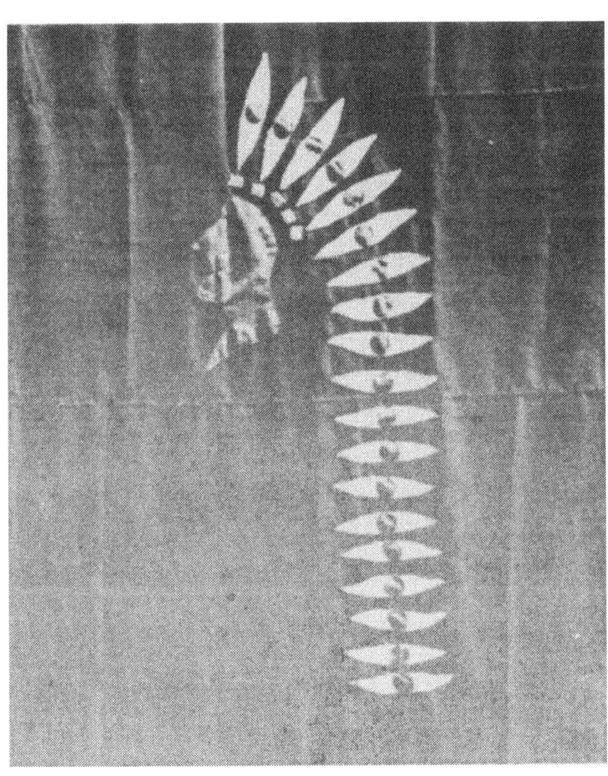

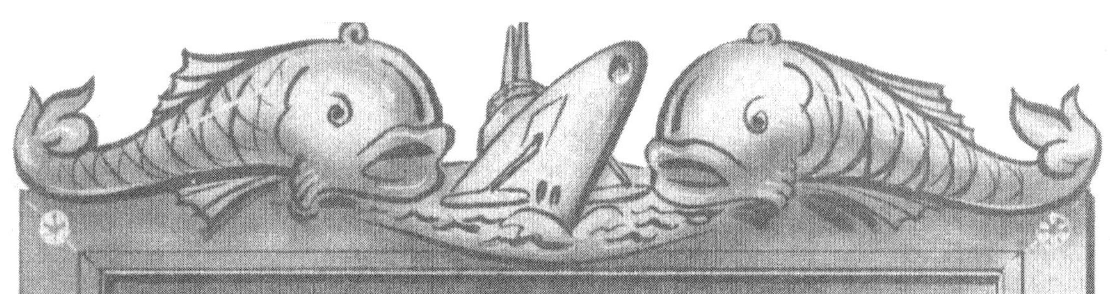

U.S.S. WAHOO

ANDERS, F..............F1c
ANDREWS, J.S...........EM1c
BAILEY, R.E............SC3c
BAIR, A.I..............TM3c
BERG, J.C..............F1c
BROWN, D.R.............ENS.
BROWNING, C.R.........MoMM2c
BRUCE, C.L............MoMM1c
BUCKLEY, J.P...........RM1c
BURGAN, W.W............LT.
CAMPBELL, J.S..........ENS.
CARR, W.J..............CGM
CARTER, J.E............RM2c
DAVISON, W.E..........MoMM1c
DEATON, L.N............TM1c
ERDLEY, J.S............EM3c
FIEDLER, E.F........LT.(JG)
FINKELSTEIN, O.........TM3c
GALLI, W.O.............TM3c
GARMON, C.E...........MoMM2c
GARRETT, G.C..........MoMM2c
GERLACHER, W.L.........S2c
GOSS, R.P.............MoMM1c
GREENE, H.M............LT.
HAND, W.F..............EM2c
HARTMAN, L.M...........F1c
HAYES, D.M.............EM2c
HENDERSON, R,N.........LT.
HOLMES, W.H............EM1c
HOUSE, V.A.............S1c
HOWE, H.J..............EM3c
JACOBS, O.............MoMM1c
JASA, R.L..............F1c
JAYSON, J.O............CK3c
JOHNSON, K.B...........TM1c
KEETER, D.C............CMM
KEMP, W.W..............QM1c
KESSOCK, P.............F2c
KIRK, E.T..............S1c
KREBS, P.H.............SM3c
LAPE, A.D..............F2c
LINDEMANN, C.A.........S1c
LOGUE, R.B.............FC1c
LYNCH, W.L.............F2c
MacALMAN, S.E..........PhM1c
MacGOWEN, T.K.J......MoMM1c
MCGILL, T.J............CMoMM
McGILTON, H.E..........TM3c
McSPADDEN D.J..........TM1c
MAGYAR, A.J............F1c
MANALISAY, J.C.........St3c
MANDJIAK, P.A..........F1c
MASSA, E.E.............S1c
MAULDING. E.C..........SM3c
MAULDING, G.E..........TM3c
MILLS, M.L.............RT1c
MISCH, G.A..........LT.(JG)
MORTON, D.W..........Cdr.CO
NEEL, P................TM2c
ONEAL, F.L.............EM3c
O'BRIEN, F.L...........EM1c
OSTRANDER, E.E.........F1c
PHILLIPS, P.F..........SC1c
RENNELS, J.L...........SC2c
RENNO, H...............S1c
SEAL, E.H.Jr...........TM2c
SIMONETTI, A.R.........SM2c
SKJONSBY, V.L..LT.CDR.Exec
SMITH, D.O.............EM1c
STEVENS, G.V..........MoMM2c
TERRELL, W.C...........QM3c
THOMAS, W..............S1c
TYLER, R.O.............TM3c
WACH, L.J..............Cox
VIDICK, J..............EM2c
WARE, N.C..............CEM
WALDRON, W.E...........RM3c
WHIPP, K.L.............F1c
WITTING, R.L...........F1c
WHITE, W.T.............Y2c

CORVINA (SS226)

Venturing into enemy water for her first time, CORVINA (Cdr. R. S. Rooney) departed from Pearl Harbor on 4 November 1943. After topping off with fuel at Johnston Island she proceeded to an area south of Truk, there to attack enemy naval forces during our surface operations in the Gilbert Islands. She was to patrol as close to Truk as enemy anti-submarine measures would permit. On 14 December, she was to pass to command of Commander Task Force Seventy-Two and proceed to an eastern Australian port for refit and duty in SubSoWestPac.

When the major surface force operations in the Gilberts were finished, CORVINA was directed by despatch on 30 November to pass to command of Commander Task Force Seventy-Two on 2 December 1943. The message was repeated three times on each of two successive nights, and an acknowledgement was directed, but none was received. Because of the difficulty being experienced as a result of Japanese interference, CORVINA was considered to have passed to Commander Task Force Seventy-Two, despite her failure to acknowledge. She was directed to proceed to Tulagi and rendezvous with a surface escort, but she did not appear. Again transmissions directing answer were repeatedly sent, but were not fruitful. Since she had not appeared or been heard from since her departure from Johnston Island on 6 November, CORVINA was reported as presumed lost on 23 December 1943.

Enemy records indicate that CORVINA met her doom on 16 November 1943, by enemy action. An enemy submarine reported having sighted a surfaced submarine in Latitude 5°-50'N, Longitude 151°-10'E, and torpedoed her. Three torpedoes were fired and two were reported to have hit, causing "a great explosion sound."

CORVINA Down the Ways 9 May 1943 at Groton Connecticut

U.S.S. CORVINA

Name	Rating
ALLISON, D.	QM3c
ATWOOD, J.D.	ENS.
ASHER, J.M.	F1c
BARAN, S.	S1c
BEAUDETTE, L.W.	CQM
BRITT, H.N.	F2c
BROOKS, R.A.	StM2c
BUSBY, M.S.	QM2c
BUSCH, W.R.	FC3c
CHEWNING, W.M.	LT.
CLARK, J.G.Jr	SC2c
CURTISS, G.R.	F1c
DALTON, E.A.	SC1c
DAUGHTERTY, G.W.Jr	S2c
EK, J.R.	S2c
EMERICK, J.W.	EM1c
ENNIS, R.E.Jr	MM1c
FAHEY, J.M.	F2c
FIOROT, E.B.	TM3c
FINSKE, R.W.	RM3c
FLOYD, R.L.	S1c
FOSTER, E.L.	CMoMM
FOSTER, N.B.	S2c
GABEL, G.F.	EM3c
GHENT, C.C.Jr	MoMM1c
GREEN, D.L.Jr	CRM
GRISHAM, S.E.	CTM
HALE, B.D.	CMoMM
HALL, D.K.	MoMM2c
HALPIN, J.E.	EM3c
HASTY, A.W.	S1c
HAVRILECZ, M.	MoMM1c
HAZEL, L.P.	S1c
HEMPHILL, W.P.Jr	RM2c
HOTZ, F.D.	SM2c
JACKSON, E.	CK2c
JONES, E.E.	F1c
JORDAN, V.F.Jr	F2c
LENSE, L.N.	ENS.
LLOYD, R.D.	TM2c
LOKEN, W.E.	MoMM2c
MAIER, M.L.	F2c
MADISON, G.O.	MoMM2c
MALONEY, T.J.	TM3c
MANNING, J.R.	S1c
MAUTNER, M.	PhM1c
MC HOLLAND, F.O.	MoMM2c
MEIZLIK, J.H.	GM3c
MICHA, M.F.	MoMM1c
MILLER, V.A.	EM1c
MURPHY, D.F.Jr	S2c
NESBITT, H.L.	EM1c
OCUMPAUGH, E.IV	LT.
OLIVER, P.C.	S1c
OSBURN, R.W.	EM3c
PITARYS, S.J.	Cox
REARDON, F.J.	F3c
REDMAN, J.L.	F1c
ROAK, J.B.	LT.
ROBB, A.F.	TM1c
ROBERTS, M.H.	Y1c
ROONEY, R.S.	CDR.C.O.
ROSTA, J.	TM3c
RYDER, E.M.	RM2c
SCHLADENSKY, P.	EM3c
SCHLESS, L.I.	EM2c
SCHULDT, G.P.	S2c
SCHULZ, W.K.	TM2c
SIMUNACI, F.W.	MoMM1c
SLAGLE, W.R.	S2c
SLOAN, D.K.Jr	LT.Exec.
SMITH, B.F.	CEM
SMITH, J.D.	LT.(JG)
ST. AUBIN, R.J.	GM2c
SUMMERS, R.E.	TM1c
THOBEN, F.A.	SC3c
THOMAS, J.L.	RM3c
TOMS, T.	MoMM1c
TROJAN, C.A.	TM2c
WADE, L.R.Jr	F1c
WILLIAMS, B.E.	MoMM2c
WOOD, E.E.	CEM

SCULPIN (SS191)

Enroute to Johnston Island, SCULPIN, under Cdr. Fred Connaway, left Pearl Harbor on 5 November 1943. After topping off with fuel, she left Johnston on 7 November to conduct her ninth patrol in an area in the Caroline Islands. Her mission was to support the action of our surface forces in the Gilbert Islands by intercepting and attacking any enemy forces which might be proceeding from Truk toward the Marshall Islands to oppose our surface forces. She was to leave her area on 14 December, and return to Pearl Harbor, stopping at Johnston for fuel if necessary. SCULPIN was not heard from following her departure from Johnston Island on 7 November.

During the patrol, Commander John P. Cromwell (promoted to Captain during the patrol) was aboard SCULPIN. He was to take charge of a coordinated attack group consisting of SCULPIN, SEARAVEN, and either APOGON or SPEARFISH, if formation of the group were directed by despatch. Should the group be ordered formed, Captain Cromwell would transmit his orders to them by low frequency radio from SCULPIN. On the night of 29 November, the vessels were directed to form and APOGON was named as the third member of the group. When no rendezvous orders were given by Captain Cromwell after 40 hours, new orders were sent by ComSubPac. SCULPIN was to proceed immediately to Eniwetok, make a close observation, and report any enemy shipping. This was done in order to avoid confusion among the other submarines, and to determine whether SCULPIN was all right. Although the new orders to SCULPIN were sent repeatedly on 1 December and other orders a few days later, no answer came from her. On 30 December SCULPIN was reported as presumed lost.

Meanwhile, long before tension mounted at the bases concerning her, SCULPIN was meeting her test. The story presented here is reconstructed from statements made by members of her crew recovered from enemy prison camps since the close of the war.

CAPT. JOHN P. CROMWELL
WOLF PACK COMMANDER

On the night of 18 November, SCULPIN made a radar contact on a fast convoy, and made an end around at full power. Submerging on the enemy track for a dawn attack, SCULPIN began what promised to be a successful approach. However, she was detected in the attack phase, and the convoy zigged toward, forcing her deep. There was no depth charge attack at this time. About an hour later, the ship surfaced to begin another end around, but immediately dove again, having surfaced 6,000 yards from a destroyer which was lagging the convoy. Depth charging started as soon as she dove again.

Early in the ensuing attack a string of depth charges did the ship minor damage. Lt. G. E. Brown, the only officer survivor, was relieved as diving officer to make an inspection and found her fundamentally sound. At this time the submarine had succeeded in shaking the enemy, but before Brown returned to the control room the ship had broached when the diving officer had tried to bring her to periscope depth and the depth gauge had stuck at 125 feet. The depth charge attack was renewed at once.

About noon on 19 November, a close string of 18 depth charges threw SCULPIN, already at deep depth, badly out of control. The pressure hull was distorted, she was leaking, steering and diving plane gear were damaged and she was badly out of trim. Commander Connaway decided to surface and to fight clear. The ship was surfaced and went to gun action. During the battle Commander Connaway and the Gunnery Officer were on the bridge, and the Executive Officer was in the conning tower. When the destroyer placed a shell through the main induction, and one or more through the conning tower, these officers and several men were killed. Lt. Brown succeeded to command. He decided to scuttle the ship ,and gave the order "all hands abandon ship". After giving the order the last time the ship was dived at emergency speed by opening all vents. About 12 men rode the ship down, including Captain Cromwell and one other officer, both of whom refused to leave it. Captain Cromwell, being familiar with plans for our operations in the Gilberts and other areas, stayed with the ship to insure that the enemy could not gain any of the information he possessed. For this action, ComSubPac recommended that he be given the Congressional Medal of Honor. In all, 42 men were taken prisoner by the Japanese destroyer, but one was thrown over the side almost immediately because he was severely wounded. Another man escaped being thrown overboard only by wrenching free of his captors and joining the other men.

The group of 38 enlisted men and 3 officers were taken to Truk where they were questioned for ten days. Then they were loaded on two carriers (21 on one, 20 on the other) and started for Japan. Enroute to its destination, the carrier CHUYO, carrying 21 SCULPIN survivors, was torpedoed and sunk by SAILFISH on 31 December 1943, and only one American escaped. This was a particularly coincidental and tradjic event since SCULPIN stood by SQUALUS (later recommissioned SAILFISH) when she sank off Portsmouth, New Hampshire in 1939. At Ofuna, the 21 survivors were repeatedly questioned, and they learned they were in an unofficial Navy prison camp. They were released from the camp a few at a time when the enemy became convinced that they could get no informattion from them, and were sent to work in the copper mines of Ashio. There they were allowed to register as prisoners of war, and received at least enough food to live on, although not enough to maintain health properly. They remained at Ashio until released by American forces on 4 September 1945.

This submarine, on her first eight patrols sank nine ships for 42,200 tons and damaged ten, totaling 63,000 tons. Her first patrol off the east coast of the Philippines group resulted in one sinking, the 3,124 ton transport KANKYO MARU on 10 January, 1942. During her second patrol in the region east of Celebes, she sank a destroyer type vessel and did damage to a light cruiser. Her third patrol was conducted in the Molukka Sea, and SCULPIN damaged a freighter. On her fourth patrol, conducted in the South China Sea, she is credited with having sunk a freighter, damaged a freighter and damaged three tankers.

SCULPIN went to the Solomons area for her fifth patrol, and is credited with sinking two large tankers and a transport. She damaged a freighter on this patrol. Going back to the Solomons for her sixth patrol, SCULPIN damaged a tanker. SCULPIN made her seventh patrol in May and June 1943 in the Aleutians. Here she sank two small patrol craft and damaged two freighters. On her eighth patrol in the East China Sea, SCULPIN sank a freighter-transport.

U.S.S. SCULPIN

ALLEN, N.J. .... LT. Exec.	LAMAN, H.D. MoMM2c
* ANDERSON, E.N. SC2c	LAWTON, C.J. F1c
APOSTOL, E. CK1c	MAGUIRE, S.W. EM2c
ARNATH, E. S2c	MARCUS, G.W. RM3c
BAGLIEN, J.W. RM3c	MARTIN, M.G. FC3c
* BAKER, C.E. F2c	McCARTNEY, J.W. EM3c
* BAKER, J.N.Jr. F2c	McTAVISH, J.F. S1c
BARRERA, M. CK1c	MILBOURN, H.S.Jr. .... F1c *
BEIDLEMAN, E.M.Jr. RT2c	MILLER, C.E. TM3c
BENTSEN, F.G. S2c	MOORE, W.E. .... CSM(PA)
BERRY, W.R. TM1c	MORETON, A.F. EM1c
BLUM, A.G. EM3c	MORRILLY, R.M. EM3c
BRANNUM, B.C. F1c	MURPHY, P.L. .... F1c *
* BROWN, G.E.Jr. .... LT.	MURRAY, E.T. SM3c
BROWN, T.V. S2c	MURRAY, L.J. .... MoMM1c *
CARTER, R.W. S2c	PARR, J. RDM3c
CLEMENTS, K.B. MoMM2c	PARTIN, W.H. S1c
COLEMAN, C.S. MoMM1c	PETERSON, J.G. .... RM2c *
CONNAWAY, F. .... CDR.C.O.	PITSER, C.E. TM2c
* COOPER, B.M. QM2c	RICKETTS, E.F. .... MoMM2c *
CROMWELL, J.P. .... CAPT.	ROCEK, G. .... MoMM1c *
DAYLONG, J.E. MoMM2c	ROURKE, J.P. .... GM3c *
DEFREES, J.R.Jr. .... LT.	SALVA, F. .... FC3c(M)
DeLISLE, M.S. F1c	SCHNELL, E.V. TM3c
DIEDERICH, D.L. EM3c	SCHROEDER, D.E. Y2c
ELLIOTT, H.L. F1c	SHIRLEY, D.B. SM3c
EMBURY, G.R. .... LT.(JG)	SMITH, C.G.Jr. .... ENS.
* ESKELDSEN, L.A. F1c	SMITH, L.H. EM2c
FIELDER, W.M. .... ENS.	SUEL, J.T. S1c
GABRUNAS, P.J. ..... CMoMM(AA)	SWIFT, J.B. EM1c
GAMEL, J.W. .... ENS.	TAYLOR, C.G. RM3c
GOORABIAN, G. S1c	TAYLOR, R.H. S1c
* GORMAN, M.T. S2c	THOMAS, H.J. .... TM1c *
GUILLOT, A.B. F1c	TODD, P.A. .... PhM1c *
HARPER, J.Q. TM3c	TONEY, H.F. .... TM3c *
* HAVERLAND, W.H. .... CMoMM(AA)	VAN BEEST, H. S1c
HEMPHILL, R.E. .... CMM(AA)	WARREN, E.E. EM2c
HOLLAND, E.R. MoMM1c	WEADE, C.H. .... CTM(AA)
JOHNSON, G.E. MoMM2c	WELSH, W.H. S1c
KANOCZ, S. EM3c	WHITE, D.J. MoMM2c
* KELLER, E.K.F. S2c	WRIGHT, E. .... EM3c *
KENNON, J.B.Jr. SC3c	WYATT, R.O. .... GM2c *

** - Men recovered from Japanese prison camps.*

U.S.S. SCULPIN (SS191)

CAPELIN (SS289)

Returning from her first war patrol after only 17 days out, CAPELIN (Cdr. E. E. Marshall) came into Darwin on 16 November 1943 with a defective conning tower hatch mechanism, excessively noisy bow planes, and a defective radar tube. These flaws were corrected to the satisfaction of the Commanding Officer, and the ship then departed for her second patrol on 17 November. Her area was in the Molukka and Celebes Seas, and she was to pay particular attention to Kaoe Bay, Moratai Strait, Davao Gulf and trade routes in the vicinity of Siaoe, Sangi, Talaud and Sarangani Islands. She was to leave her area at dark 6 December.

Nothing has been positively heard from CAPELIN since she departed. However BONEFISH reported having seen a U. S. submarine at 1°-14'N, 123°-50'E on 2 December 1943. This position is in the area assigned to CAPELIN at this time. An attempt to reach CAPELIN by radio, on 9 December 1943, elicited no response.

E. E. Marshall

On 23 November an American submarine was attacked off Kaoe Bay, Halmahera, 1°-34'N, 123°-07'E. However the Japanese state that this attack was broken off, and the evidence of contact was rather thin. The only positive statement which can be made is that CAPELIN was lost in Celebes Sea, or in Molukka Passage or the Molukka Sea, probably in December 1943. Enemy minefields are now know to have been placed in various positions along the north coast of Celebes in CAPELIN's area, and she may have been lost because of a mine explosion. In her 17 day first patrol, CAPELIN sank two Japanese medium freighters for 7,400 tons of merchant shipping. This first patrol was conducted among the islands immediately west of New Guinea.

U.S.S. CAPELIN

ARNEY, B.J.............S2c
BALL, C.M.............BM2c
BECK, C.I.Jr...........CTM
BLAIR, G.R............EM3c
BRAGG, O.C............QM3c
BRITTON, R.L..........ENS.
BROWN, E.S.Jr..........S1c
BUTLER, M.H............CRM
CALLAHAN, F.T.......... CY
CALLAHAN, J.J.Jr...MoMM2c
CAVANAUGH, J.P.........S1c
CHEATHAM, E..........StM1c
CLIFFORD, E.R.........TM2c
COLYER, C.W...........TM1c
CROSS, J.L............MM1c
CROWLEY, J.D...........F2c
DE FREYTAS, C.F.......EM3c
DEVINE, W.F...........RM3c
DEVINE, W.J...........TM2c
DILL, P.L.............TM3c
EKLUND, L.T...........FC3c
EVERHART, C.L........PhM1c
GANLEY, J.F.Jr.......CMoMM
GILLEN, P.J.........MoMM2c
GRABNICKAS, P.........SC2c
GREENLEAF, D.T.......CMoMM
HICKS, M.J............EM2c
HOLT, J.W.Jr...........CEM
JACOBS, D..............F1c
KEATON, L.O...........TM3c
KENNEDY, D.G.Jr.......EM1c
KLEIN, I.I............EM2c
KRAIL, E.J............EM1c
KOZIOL, J.W............F3c
LAFFERTY, W.A..........S1c
LANGE, D.W.............S1c
LANDRES, L.A.........CMoMM
LESTER, E.J.........MoMM1c
LEWITT, W.M...........EM2c

LUTLEY, J.L............F2c
MADDOX, J.W............S1c
MADEY, A..............EM1c
MARSHALL, E.E..LT.CDR.C.O.
MASON, W.F.Jr......LT.CDR.
MELBIN, G.R............S1c
MOELLER, O.F..........TM2c
MORGAN, H.F...........RM1c
NORRIS, E.A............F1c
NOVOTNY, C.R..........EM1c
O'DONNELL, M.B........RM3c
OLSEN, S.R..........MoMM1c
O'NEAL, T.E...........TM2c
O'NEIL, C.F........LT.(JG)
PETTIGREW, H.E.Jr...MoMM1c
PERRY, F.............StM2c
PERRY, L.A............TM3c
PILKINTON, W.N........RT2c
POTEAT, E.L.........MoMM2c
POWELL, R...........MoMM1c
RAMINSKI, W.E.......MoMM2c
RHIMANN, R.C.......LT.(JG)
RHODES, J.E.Jr......MoMM2c
ROBERTS, C.W........MoMM1c
ROBERTSON, E.D.LT.CDR.Exec.
SHARER, W.A.............LT.
SIMON, H..............GM1c
SMITH, D.T..........MoMM2c
SMITH, R.L............RM2c
SMITH, L.C..........MoMM2c
SMOLENSKI, E.J.........S1c
SNYDER, N.W............F3c
STASIK, W.W.........MoMM2c
STEEGE, E.H...........TM1c
STICKLE, R.G..........EM3c
TERRELL, R.W........MoMM2c
THIBEAULT, J.L........TM3c
VASSAR, C.L.Jr........SC1c
VAUGHAN, C.W...........S1c
WINKLER, H.H.Jr.......QM3c

CAPELIN Surfaces After A Dive

SCORPION (SS278)

Departing Pearl Harbor on 29 December 1943, SCORPION (Cdr. M. G. Schmidt) stopped at Midway to top off with fuel, and left that place on 3 January 1944 to conduct her fourth war patrol. Her assigned area was in the northern East China and Yellow Seas.

On the morning of 5 January, SCORPION reported that one of her crew had sustained a fracture of the upper arm and requested a rendezvous with HERRING (SS233) which was returning from patrol and was near her. The rendezvous was accomplished on the afternoon of 5 January in 30°-07'N, 167°-30'E but heavy seas prevented transfer of the injured man to HERRING. The latter reported this fact on 6 January, and stated "SCORPION reports case under control." SCORPION was never seen or heard from again after her departure from the rendezvous. On 16 February 1944, STEELHEAD and SCORPION were warned that they were close together, and that an enemy submarine was in the vicinity.

M. G. Schmidt

When no report was received from her by 24 February 1944, Midway was directed to keep a careful watch for her, and SCORPION was directed to make a transmission. Neither of these measures proved fruitful, and SCORPION was reported on 6 March 1944 as presumed lost.

No information has been received from the Japanese which indicates that SCORPION's loss was the result of enemy anti-submarine tactics. There were, however, several mine lines across the entrance to the Yellow Sea. The presence of these mine lines and the "restricted area" bounding them was discovered from captured Japanese Notices to Mariners at a much later date. In the meantime several submarines had made patrols in this area, crossing and recrossing the mine lines without incident, and coming safely home. It is probable that these mine lines were very thin, offering only about a 10 percent threat to submarines at maximum, and steadily decreasing in effectiveness with the passage of time. SCORPION was lost soon after these mines were laid, or at a time when they presumably offered the greatest threat. She could have been an operational casualty, but her area consists of water shallow enough so that it might be expected that some men would have survived. Since we know of no survivors, the most reasonable assumption is that she hit a mine.

In her first three patrols, SCORPION sank ten ships, for a total of 24,100 tons, and damaged two more, for 16,000 tons. Her first war patrol was in the approaches to Tokyo in April 1943. Here she sank two freighters, four sampans and two patrol craft. In addition, she damaged a freighter. On her second patrol, conducted in the Yellow Sea, she sank two freighters. Her third patrol was made in the Marianas Islands, and resulted in damage to a tanker.

U.S.S. SCORPION

Name	Rating
ALEXANDER, J.S.	EM2c
APPLETON, C.W.	SC3c
BAUSMAN, L.L.	SC1c
BELL, H.F.	S1c
BROWN, R.T.	LT.(JG)
BYNUM, R.H.	QM1c
CHAMBERLAIN, F.J.	EM2c
CHRISTMAN, H.F.	S1c
CLOUGH, J.E.	TM2c
CORNELIUS, T.T.	CMoMM
CUNNINGHAM, J.W.	CRM
DEANE, L.W.	TM3c
DEWS, R.P.	StM1c
DRAKE, V.R.	ENS.
DRANE, R.B.	LT.(JG)
ECHORST, E.L.	TM2c
ELLIS, R.H.	LT.(JG)
ENGLISH, E.J.	MoMM1c
FABER, L.M.	S1c
FASNACHT, J.A.	QM2c
FAUSTMAN, L.D.	MoMM1c
FERGUSON, N.	St3c
FLAHERTY, W.A.Jr.	CQM
GLAZIER, J.F.	GM2c
HARVEY, P.L.	EM2c
HARVEY, R.D.Jr.	F3c
HEIDENRICH, J.T.	TM1c
HEINZ, C.P.	MoMM1c
HOOD, F.E.	S2c
HUND, C.M.	CGM
HUTCHINSON, R.E.	TM3c
INGRAM, G.E.	MoMM2c
JACOBS, R.L.	S2c
KOSTER, N.L.	CMoMM
KRAWCZYKOWICZ, E.	F1c
LABARTHE, W.C.	MoMM2c
LARIMORE, B.E.	TM2c
LLOYD, R.W.	MoMM1c
MANGSNELLO, L.A.	CCS
MATTHEWS, S.E.	RM1c
MC MILLAN, F.K.	MoMM1c
MC NALLY, F.A.Jr.	RT2c
MILLER, P.J.Jr.	EM2c
MORGAN, H.W.	QM2c
MOSBEY, L.E.	EM2c
PIERCE, C.B.	LT.Exec.
RAIRDEN, R.M.	Y3c
RANDOLPH W L.	EM1c
RAWLINGS, J.P.	CEM
ROBILARD, F.J.	S1c
ROCHE, T.E.	TM2c
ROWE, A.V.	S2c
SAUNDERS, B.	S1c
SCHEU, D.S.	LT.
SCHMIDT, M.G.	CDR.C.O.
SEAMAN, D.A.	MoMM1c
SEARS, W.I.	EM1c
SETVATE, M.W.	TM3c
SHAKE, J.	F2c
SHAPIRO, I.S.	PhM1c
SHEA, P.D.	F1c
SINK, R.O.	F1c
SKELTON, S.R.	TM3c
SMITH, D.E.	RM3c
SMITH, J.F.	TM3c
SPEARS, C.R.	CMoMM
STURGES, E.A.	MoMM1c
TARBELL, W.E.	EM1c
TOWSEND, J.	RM3c
WISE, R.J.Jr.	LT.
UDICK, R.V.	TM1c
VOORHEES, J.L.	TM2c
WEIDENBACK, R.F.	FC3c
WILLIFORD, R.R.	F1c
WOMACK, R.L.	MoMM2c
ZIMMERMAN, K.	RM2c

HOMEWARD BOUND - Painting By Vandis

GRAYBACK (SS 208)

GRAYBACK, under Cdr. J. A. Moore, left Pearl Harbor on 28 January 1944, to begin her tenth war patrol in the East China Sea east of the coast of Chekiang Province, China. She topped off with fuel at Midway, and departed from there on 3 February. On 12 February, she was sent orders to patrol the area running east and west between Luzon and Formosa from that date until sunset 20 February 1944, and then to proceed to her original area.

Cdr. J.A. Moore

GRAYBACK made her first report on 24 February in latitude 25°-14'N, longitude 122°-58'E, stating that she had sunk or damaged 44,000 tons of shipping thus far on her patrol. She had sunk a TARAYASU MARU class ship on 19 February and sunk a TATUTA MARU class on 24 February, also damaging a freighter and tanker of unknown classes during the latter attack. She had five torpedoes left aft and one left forward.

The following day she reported from a position about 22 miles northeast of her former position, telling of new successes. She had fired four torpedoes aft, and had made three hits on two enemy freighters. When this message was received, she was ordered to return to Midway, and she was expected about 7 March 1944. Had she failed to receive this message and remained her full time on station she would have reached Midway about 23 March.

On 10 March, in an effort to establish her position, GRAYBACK was requested to furnish information as to where she had found the best hunting. No answer was received, and on 30 March 1944, GRAYBACK was reported as presumed lost. Commander Moore had been known for his conservative estimates of damage inflicted on the enemy, and at the time of the report concerning her

loss, it was recommended that GRAYBACK be credited with the claims made by him in his despatches.

Japanese information made available since the cessation of hostilities records an anti-submarine attack which probably explains GRAYBACK's fate. It came on 26 February 1944, and in about the expected position of GRAYBACK at that time. The enemy tells of finding a surfaced sub at 25°-47'N, 128°-45'E. A carrier plane "gave a direct hit at the sub, which exploded and sank immediately". The attack was continued by surface craft at the point where bubbles rose, and an oil slick appeared covering an area of 100 by 250 meters.

GRAYBACK was credited with an estimated 25,000 tons sunk and 25,000 tons damaged on her final patrol. In the first nine patrols of this vessel, she is credited with 22 ships sunk, for 83,900 tons, and 9 damaged for 49,300 tons. She began her career as a patroller in February 1942, in the Bonin Islands. On her first patrol GRAYBACK sank two freighters and a patrol craft. This vessel made the passage from Pearl Harbor to Fremantle, Western Australia on her second patrol, and encountered no enemy vessels in the mandates enroute. GRAYBACK covered the South China Sea approaches to Saigon, French Indo-China, in her third patrol, but made no successful attacks. She went to the Solomons for her fourth patrol, and sank two large transports, while damaging a large freighter. Her fifth patrol was in the same area, and she sank four landing craft and damaged an enemy submarine. In addition she acted as a reference vessel for a bombardment of Munda on 4-5 January 1943, and rescued six U. S. Army aviators stranded ashore the following evening.

In the Solomons area, GRAYBACK's sixth patrol resulted in the sinking of one freighter. She made the passage from Australia to Pearl Harbor for overhaul on her seventh patrol. Enroute she damaged five freighters and a destroyer...Her eighth patrol, in the South China Sea, resulted in GRAYBACK's being credited with a freighter sunk, an unidentified vessel sunk, a transport sunk in cooperation with CERO, and a freighter damaged. In her ninth patrol, GRAYBACK went to the East China Sea area. She sank four freighters, a sampan, a patrol vessel, and damaged another freighter. In addition, during this patrol on 18 December 1943, GRAYBACK sank the Japanese destroyer NUMAKAZE near Okinawa. GRAYBACK has been awarded the Navy Unit Commendation for the period of her last four patrols.

U.S.S. GRAYBACK

BANGERT, G.H.........MoMM1c
BARBOUR, H.K.........MoMM2c
BARNETT, J.E...........SC1c
BELL, F.R..............TM2c
BENNETT, J.W...........EM3c
BLANAN, R.P..........MoMM1c
BLOODSWORTH, R.........QM3c
BOYER, F.L...........MoMM1c
BRANDT, J.L............EM3c
BRASCH, W.J............RM1c
BUKOWSKI, T.............CRM
CAMPBELL, W.E........MoMM2c
CAPSHAW, R.L..........PhM1c
CAREY, R.E..............S2c
CASE, H.L............MoMM2c
CHOTAS, J.N............RM3c
COBURN, F.M..........MoMM2c
COX, L.R...............SC3c
DAVIDSON, M.R..........TM3c
DAVIS, V.E..............Y2c
DODSON, J.R.............Cox
FERRY, G.R.Jr...........S1c
FIEBER, G.E............EM3c
FIELDING, C.F...........F2c
FORSYTHE, J.R.Jr.......SM1c
FOX, K.W.Jr..........MoMM2c
FRANCIS, M.L.........MoMM3c
GAVLAK, C.B............FC2c
GEORGE, M.L..........MoMM3c
GILDO, B,..............St1c
GRAY, J.H............MoMM3c
HALPERT, A.S...........RM1c
HALL, F.A..............TM2c
HALVORSON, E.E..........S1c
HANDLOWICH, L.I.........S1c
HANSEN, R.V............RT1c
HEFLER, T..............EM1c
HITCH, R.B.............EM1c
HOLZMANN, F.C.Jr.......TM2c
HOOKS, W.C..............F1c
HRUDKA, A..............QM2c
IRIZARRY, F.A..........SM3c
JACKSON, A.N...........TM2c
JACOBS, L.F.............S1c
JAMES, F.R..............F1c
JONES, J.A.............TM1c
KING, J.P..............EM3c
KNOPS H.T...............CEM
KOLLER, W.A..........MoMM2c
LaRIVIERE, R.E..........S1c
LEAF, L.H............MoMM3c
LITTLEJOHN, R.O.........ENS.
LOCKYER, D.H.N.........TM3c
MAYO, R.L.......CDR.P.C.O.
McKELVEY, F.H...........ENS.
MEYER, F.W.H...........TM3c
MEYERS, L.J..........MoMM2c
MOORE, J.A..........CDR.C.O
NICHOLSON, W.G........CMoMM
NORTHAM, J.T...........EM3c
O'MEARA, T.F...........TM2c
PARKS, R.A.............EM1c
PHILLIPS, M.C.......LT.(JG)
PINHO, A.Jr............EM3c
RALSTON, W.L...........EM3c
RAUBER, V.M.............ENS.
RIVERA, V.U............St2c
ROY, W.C.Jr..............LT.
SCHELLINGER, G.K........S2c
SESSLER, E.F...........TM1c
SHAW, R.T...............CTM
SILVERA, I.V...........RM3c
SMITH, C.H...............LT.
SOLOMON, S.............EM3c
SOUTHERN, A.H..........TM3c
STANFORD, L.C.........CMoMM
STEWART, J.H.........LT.Exec.
STOCKMAN, R.E...........S2c
WALISZEWSKI, S.J.......SC1c
YATT, J.C..............GM1c

GRAYBACK - August 1943 - Note Decreased Silhouette to Aid Invisibility and Extra Limber Holes to Decrease Diving Time

TROUT (SS202)

The veteran patroller TROUT (Lt. Cdr. A. H. Clark) left Pearl Harbor on 8 February 1944, enroute to area for her eleventh patrol. She topped off with fuel at Midway, and left there on 16 February, never to be heard from again. She was to patrol between 20°-00′ N and 23°-00′ N from the China coast to 130°-00′ E.

TROUT was scheduled to leave her patrol area not later than sunset on 27 March 1944, and was expected at Midway about 7 April 1944. -When she did not arrive, she was reported as presumed to be lost on 17 April 1944.

From information received from the Japanese since the close of the war the following facts have been gleaned. On 29 February 1944 SAKITO MARU was sunk and another ship badly damaged in position 22°-40′ N, 131°-45′ E. TROUT is the only U. S. submarine which could have made an attack at this time in this position. Since TROUT did not report this action it is assumed that she was lost during or shortly after this attack.

In her first ten patrols, TROUT sank 23 enemy ships, giving her 87,800 tons sunk, and damaged 6 ships, for 75,000 tons. TROUT's first patrol resulted in no enemy damage, but her second patrol was a most unusual one. She delivered ammunition from Pearl Harbor to Corregidor in January 1942. To compensate for the weight of ammunition delivered, she brought back as ballast 20 tons of gold. silver and securities which was delivered to Pearl Harbor, from where it was taken to Washington for safekeeping. Also during the patrol TROUT sank a medium freighter and a patrol craft. In the period from mid-March to mid-May 1942 TROUT conducted her third patrol in the Empire. Here she sank a large tanker, three freighters and a gunboat, and damaged a large freighter. TROUT's forth patrol covered the period during which she was part of the forces defending Midway. She made no successful attacks here. The area south of Truk was the scene of TROUT's fifth patrol; here she sank a trasport and damaged an aircraft carrier.

During her sixth patrol, in the Southern Solomons, TROUT had but one attack opportunity. She made no hits on a battleship sighted on 13 November 1942. In the South China Sea on her seventh patrol, she sank a freighter, a tanker and two sampans, and damaged two other large tankers. The same general area was the scene of her eighth patrol; TROUT sank two sampans and damaged an auxiliary vessel. In May and June 1943 TROUT patrolled the lesser Philippines and sank two tankers, a freighter and wo small schooners, also damaging a freighter. TROUT's tenth patrol was a passage from Fremantle to Pearl, with a patrol of the Davao area enroute. She sank a freighter, a transport, a sampan and a submarine. The latter was I-182, sunk by TROUT in Surigao Strait on 9 September 1943. This vessel was awarded the Presidential Unit Citation for the period of her second, third and fifth patrols.

A. H. Clark

U.S.S. TROUT

ABBOTT, R.E..............F2c
ADAMS, A.W..............Bkr3c
BARKER, J.B.Jr..........GM3c
BECKLEY, C.V............ENS.
BENNETT, T.W.Jr.........RM3c
BOLAND, J.J.............CPhM
BOND, R.V...............S1c
BRANDT, N.A.............FC1c
BROCKMAN, R.J...........CTM
BROWNLOW, E.............CCS
CALLAN, K.T.............EM1c
CARRICO, R.E......LT.(JG)
CLARK, A.H....LT.CDR.C.O.
CLARKE, J.B.............EM1c
COAKLEY, J.E............GM2c
COPT, L.J...............EM1c
COREY, F.J..............EM2c
CRAIN, E.F.Jr...........ENS.
CROWLEY, J.R............Y3c
CUNNINGHAM, E.H. III.MoMM1c
DECESARE, F.P.Jr........CRM
DECKER, F.J.............CMoMM
DORTCH, W.H.............S2c
EHLERDING, J.G..........RM1c
EWELL, J.E..............StM2c
EYE, O.R................TM3c
FESTIN, B...............TM3c
FINNEY, W.O.............MoMM2c
FROGNER, G.I............RM1c
FRONTINO, J.N...........TM2c
FROST, C.F..............MoMM1c
GARRISON, R.L...........TM2c
GAYLORD, W.H............LT.
GIONET, R.C.............MoMM2c
GUNYER, A.L.............SM1c
GURNEY, H.R.............CY
GWYNN, R.P..............S1c
HALL, O.................EM1c
HALTERMAN, A.M..........TM1c
HANFORD, S.J............MoMM3c
HARRISON, D.W...........CEM

HOY, J.E................MoMM1c
HUGHES, R.L.............CEM
HUGHES, P.W.............S1c
JOHNSON, A.W............TM2c
KAISER, R.W.............MoMM2c
KELTNER, M.H............ENS.
KERR, R.................QM2c
KING, E.................BM2c
KNUTSON, G.J............MoMM1c
KUNSTMAN, R.............EM3c
LEWIS, A.S..............StM2c
MAGNER, J.F.............MoMM1c
MASSETT, P.J............MoMM2c
MAUER, L.L..............MoMM2c
MC DUFFIE, W.B..........SC3c
MILLION, F.A............EM3c
MILLNER, C.C............StM1c
MOLLOHAN, G.D...........TM2c
MURPHY, T.J.............TM3c
MYERS, L.E.Jr...........LT.
NEARMAN, K.E............RM2c
PERRY, R.R..............ENS.
RICHARDSON, J.W.........CTM
ROWAN, L.R..............GM3c
RUBER, J.E..............MoMM2c
SCOTT, K.I..............MoMM1c
SEERING, S.R............TM3c
SMITH, A.L..............CMoMM
STANFORD, W.W...........CMoMM
SWENTZEL, L.M...........F2c
TAYLOR, H.F.............EM3c
TEISEN, A.T.............MoMM1c
THOITS, E.E.............TM3c
THURMAN, A.J............S1c
TIERNEY, H.T............RT3c
TRACY, J.T..............EM3c
WALKER, E.I.............SM3c
WILKOWSKI, J.B..........SM2c
WINTER, W.A.............QM1c
WOODWORTH, H.E....LT.Exec.

TULLIBEE (SS284)

On 5 March 1944, TULLIBEE, commanded by Cdr. C. F. Brindupke, departed Pearl Harbor to start her fourth war Patrol. She stopped at Midway to top off with fuel, and having left that place on 14 March, she was not heard from again. The area assigned to TULLIBEE was an open sea area north of Palau, and she was to cooperate with surface forces in the first carrier strike on Palau.

TULLIBEE was to leave her area not later than 24 April 1944, and on that date a despatch was sent directing her to proceed to Majuro for refit. She was expected at Majuro about 4 May, but instructions stated that a submarine unable to transmit would not go to Majuro, but to Midway. On 6 May 1944, Midway was alerted for a submarine returning without transmission facilities, but the lookout was not rewarded and TULLIBEE was presumed lost on 15 May 1944.

C. F. Brindupke

The following story of TULLIBEE's loss is taken from a statement made by the lone survivor, C. W. Kuykendall, GM2c. He reports that the boat arrived on station, 25 March, and on the night of 26 March a radar contact was made. The contact was found to be on a convoy consisting of a large troop and cargo ship, two medium sized freighters, two escort vessels and a large destroyer.

Having solved the convoy's speed and course, TULLIBEE made several surface runs on the large transport. but held fire, being unable to see her due to squally weather. The escorts had detected the submarine's presence, and dropped 15 to 20 depth charges. The submarine came in to 3,000 yards, still unable to see the target, and fired two bow tubes. A minute or two later a terrific concussion shook the boat, and Kuykendall, who had been on the bridge, soon found himself struggling in the water. Since range and bearing of escorts was known, the survivor states that he is sure the explosion was the result of a circular run of one of TULLIBEE's torpedoes.

There were shouting men in the water when Kuykendall first regained consciousness after the blast, but after about ten minutes everything was silent, and he never again saw or heard any of the other TULLIBEE men. At 1000 on 27 March, an escort vessel located the swimming man, and after firing on him with machine guns, came in and picked him up. He learned here that the transport they had fired at had sunk.

The story of his captivity is much the same as the stories of survivors of GRENADIER, SCULPIN, TANG, PERCH, and other U.S. submarines. He was questioned assiduously by English speaking officers, and beaten when he refused to give any more information than international law required. In April 1944, he was taken to Ofuna Naval Interrogation Camp, where he stayed until 30 September. From that date

until rescue on 4 September 1945, he was forced to work in the copper mines of Ashio.

This submarine began her career in the Submarine Force in July 1943, with a patrol in the western Caroline Islands. In this patrol she sank one freighter and damaged another. Her second patrol was in the area south of Formosa off the China coast; here she sank a transport ship and damaged a large tanker and another transport. On her third patrol, in the Marianas area, TULLIBEE sank a small freighter. This gave TULLIBEE a total of three ships sunk, totaling 15,500 tons, and three damaged, for 22,000 tons.

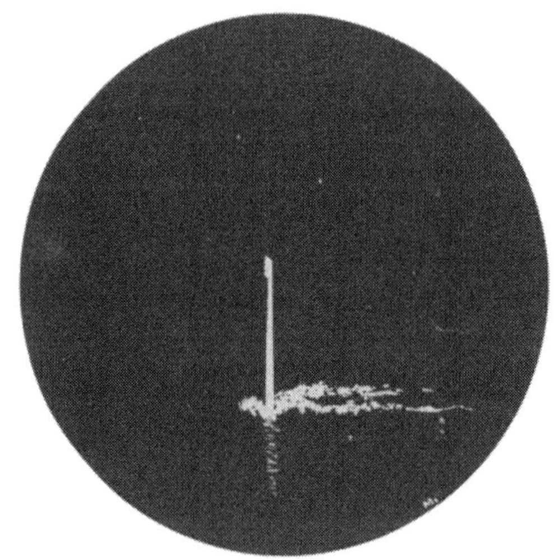

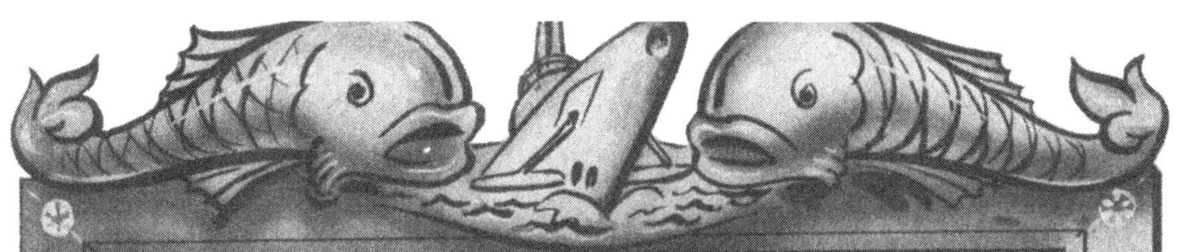

U.S.S. TULLIBEE

ABNET, P.R............S1c
ANDERSON, W.R........TM3c
ARNOLD, D.T...........QM1c
BARCOOZY, J.Jr........QM2c
BEEHLER, R.E........MoMM2c
BETSILL, J.E........MoMM2c
BLANCHARD, L.P....SC2c(B)
BRINDUPKE, C.F...CDR.C.O.
BRITT, M.L............TM3c
BROCKLESBY, A.F.......SM1c
BROWN, J.C..........MoMM2c
BURASCO, N.A...........S2c
BUTLER, D.............ENS
CIRALDO, F..........MoMM3c
CLAY, J.P.............TM2c
CLIFFORD, G.K..........F1c
CRANE, L.B............TM3c
CROSSMAN, R.H.Jr......EM2c
DEETZ, H.W..........MoMM2c
DEGENHARDT, C.H.......RM1c
DELANEY, T.M......CGM(AA)
DOUGLAS, C.............S2c
DUCANS, G.A.Jr.LT.CDRExec.
DZIK, E.H.............SC1c
ELLIS, L..............St1c
EVANS, W.A.........LT.(JG)
FARLEY, E.M.Jr.........S1c
FRANK, W.J............TM2c
GAGE, C.S...........MoMM1c
GRAHAM, D.A............S1c
GRENIER, R.A..........RT1c
GROSZ, J.N............FC2c
HALL, M.J...........MoMM3c
HEATH, C.N.Jr..........F1c
HENKEL, F.M............F1c
HICKS, C.J............TM2c
HIERONIMUS, L.J.......EM1c
HOEFLER, W.E...........S1c
IRWIN, H.T.Jr...........LT.
JODER, W.B.....CMoMM(AA)
KEATING, H.F........MoMM1c
KEENER, T.M.Jr........TM3c
KISMAN, F.H...........RM2c
*KUYKENDALL, C.W.......GM2c
LANDON, C.L.........MoMM1c
LINDSAY, F.............F1c
LOVETT, C.M...........EM3c
MANN, D.R...........MoMM2c
MC CONNELL R.F........EM3c
MC DONALD, W.G........EM3c
MC FADDEN, M.L......MoMM1c
MOFFITT, J.J..........RM2c
MUOIO, C.J.............F1c
NICHOLAS, E.R..........F1c
NOPPER, A.W...........RT1c
PATTEE, C.E...........EM1c
PAWLIK M.S............EM2c
PETERSON, R.H......LT.(JG)
REHN, C...............EM2c
REGER, F.B............EM3c
ROBY, R.H...........MoMM1c
SATERFIELD, P.T........ENS.
SCHOENROCK, W.L....CSS(PA)
SEIBERT, H.D...........F1c
STEARNS, K.C..........EM1c
STRACHAN, H.L..........S2c
SMITH, A.F.............F1c
SULLIVAN, E.E...CMoMM(PA)
SYMKIEWICZ, A.A.......TM1c
THACKER, H.L........PhM1c
TICKNOR, G.O.......CEM(PA)
TRYTKO, S.............RM3c
VIGEANT, P.R..........TM3c
WALLIS, G.C...........SM3c
WASHINGTON, R.Jr....StM1c
WAGNER, J.J.............Y2c
WENDT, R.J............TM3c
WILSON, D.S.............LT.
WISER, H.J............FC3c
WOOD, J.K..............ENS.

* - Survivors

AIR-SEA RESCUE - Painting By Vandis

GUDGEON (SS211)

Armed with the pride borne of her successes on eleven previous war patrols, GUDGEON, under Lt. Cdr. R. A. Bonin, sailed from Pearl Harbor on 4 April 1944 to conduct her twelfth patrol in an open sea area in the northern Marianas. She left Johnston Island on 7 April 1944, after having topped off with fuel, and was never heard from again.

R. A. Bonin

Originally scheduled to leave her area on 16 May, she was ordered on 11 May to depart her area in time to take station for a special assignment. An acknowledgement for this message was required and when none was received, it was asked for again on 12 May. On 14 May, her special assignment was given to another submarine, and GUDGEON was told to return to Midway. She should have arrived at Midway about 23 May but failed to do so and on 7 June she was reported as presumed lost.

GUDGEON's area was the space from 17°N to 21°N, and 143°E to 147°E but if she arrived earlier than 22 April 1944, she was to patrol the rectangle from 21°N to 24°N, 143°E to 147°E until that time. Using normal cruising speed, she would have arrived in the area assigned about 16 April. Assuming that nothing irregular happened enroute, she might be expected to have been in the northern area from 16-22 April. On 18 April, enemy planes claimed that they dropped bombs on a submarine. "The first bomb hit a bow, the second bomb direct on bridge. The center of the submarine burst open and oil pillars rose." The position given for this attack is 166 miles bearing 13°T from "Yuoh" Island. No island approaching the spelling or sound of this word can be found in the Pacific, and it is assumed that a mistake has been made either by the Japanese or in translation of the position. If the island referred to could be Maug, the position given would be in the middle of the area in which GUDGEON should have been at the time specified. The attack described cannot be correlated with any known attack on a U. S. submarine near this time, but it is felt that the possible errors in assuming that this attack sank GUDGEON are too great to list as anything but a possibility.

On 12 May 1944, a number of submarines patroling the Marianas reported that the enemy engaged in intensive anti-submarine tactics in about 15°-15'N, 145°-30'E. Early in the afternoon, SANDLANCE states, "while patrolling off Saipan looking for convoy, we heard about forty depth charges eight to ten miles away." Later SANDLANCE received three bombs and twenty-one depth charges herself. SILVERSIDES heard both the first attack and the attack made on SANDLANCE. TUNNY heard depth charging during the afternoon. No submarine returning from the area reported having been attacked on 12 May except SANDLANCE. Japanese data for the attack gives little information save that it was made by planes in cooperation with ships. With so many submarines in the vicinity, and the enemy conscious of their presence, as they undoubtedly were, the attack which was not on SANDLANCE might easily have been on a false contact.

The probability as to the cause for GUDGEON's loss is that she was depth-charged, bombed, or both. The attack of 12 May occurred slightly south of GUDGEON's area, but it was not unusual for submarines to leave their areas temporarily for tactical reasons. Since the anti-submarine measures in the Marianas were so intense, it is not unlikely that GUDGEON would be unable to transmit a receipt for the message of 10 May for several days. All of these conclusions are presumptive, and there is a great likelihood that GUDGEON was lost during an unrecorded enemy attack.

During her first eleven patrols, GUDGEON was a most active submarine. She sank 25 ships, for 166,400 tons, and damaged 8 more, for 41,900 tons. She started for the Empire but four days after the attack at Pearl Harbor, and there sank a freighter and a submarine. By sinking the Japanese submarine I-173 on 27 January 1942, GUDGEON became the first United States submarine in history to sink an enemy combatant ship. She patrolled the South China Sea in her second war run and sank a large freighter-transport and a medium freighter. Her third patrol was as member of the forces fighting the Battle of Midway. She inflicted no damage in the Battle. Passing from Pearl Harbor to Fremantle, Western Australia for her fourth patrol, GUDGEON patrolled the Truk area enroute. Here she sank three freighters and a freighter-transport, all of fairly large size. Her fifth patrol was in the Bismarck Archipelago, and resulted in the sinking of three freighters and damage to another.

GUDGEON patrolled Davao Gulf, Ambon Island and Timor Island on her sixth patrol. She made no attacks on this patrol, but did reconnoiter the latter two islands. In the Java Sea and Strait of Makassar on her seventh patrol, GUDGEON sank two tankers and two freighters and damaged a third freghter. Her eighth patrol covered a passage from Fremantle to Pearl with principal patrol in the Philippine areas. She sank the largest (17,500 ton) transport ship the Japanese had, a small freighter-transport, a trawler, and damaged a freighter. GUDGEON patrolled Saipan and Rota on her ninth run, and sank a freighter and damaged another freighter and patrol craft. The East China Sea north of Formosa was GUDGEON's area during her tenth war patrol. She sank a large transport, a small freighter, and the coastal defense vessel WAKAMIYA on 23 November 1943. She also damaged a large tanker. In the same area for her eleventh patrol, this vessel sank a large transport and a sampan, and damaged a second sampan. GUDGEON was awarded the Presidential Unit Citation for the period covering her first eight patrols.

U.S.S. GUDGEON

ABBOTT, O.A. TM3c
ANKENY, W. QM3c
BALL, J.R. S1c
BARRETT, M.P. GM3c
BIRCHFIELD, P.H. MoMM3c
BLESSING, J.H. TM1c
BONIN, R.A. ..... LT.CDR.C.O.
BOSSONG, J.G. FM2c
CARNEY, J.R. SM3c
CHRISTIAN, R.O. TM3c
COGHLAN, J.W.S. ..... LT.(JG)
COLLINS, R.C. .... LT.
COPELAND, C.B.Jr. EM2c
CRANDALL, G.E. EM2c
DICKENSON, B.W. .... ENS.
DODSON, E.H. EM3c
DONOVAN, J.P. TM3c
EVANS, J.W. MoMM1c
EVERHART, A.R. Y3c
FEIKERT, W.E. MoMM1c
FERNANDEZ, A. StM2c
FOURNIER, J.A. EM3c
GARRETT, H.O. EM2c
GAUGHAN, E.C. MoMM2c
HAMMOND, K.L. MoMM3c
HEGERFELD, L.G. TM2c
HENRY, W.R. F1c
HENSLEY, E.C. MoMM2c
HEYES, B.L. .... LT.(JG)
HITT, R.M. GM3c
HUGHART, R.E. TM2c
KELLER, D.W. RM3c
KELLER, N.C. S2c
KOHUT, S. .... CMoMM
KRUEGER, K.P. RM2c
LANGDALE, L.A. SC2c
LEFFERTS, G.W.Jr. ... MoMM3c
LEWIS, R.J. S1c
McCORQUADALE, D.B. .. LT.(JG)
MC KENNA, J.R. TM3c

MC LALLEN, J.W. TM3c
MC NICOL, W.R. RM3c
METZGER, L.L. TM1c
MIDGLEY, D.R. ..... LT.Exec.
MORRIS, E. MoMM3c
MURPHY, W.J. EM3c
NICKEL, H.C. MoMM1c
NORRIS, M.P. EM3c
ORFILA, H.F. QM3c
OSTLUND, W.C. ...... LT.(JG)
PATRIQUIN, H.F. SC2c
PATTERSON, T.E. .... CEM
PIENIADZ, F.J. RT2c
PILLER, J.A. S1c
PINKLEY, A.B. ...... LT.(JG)
POWLES, J.M. .... CPhM
REMALEY, W.D. RM1c
RICE, J.R. TM3c
SENNEWALD, W.J. MoMM3c
SEWELL, M.A. S2c
SHULTS, L. MoMM2c
SIMON, R.P. TM2c
SPONHEIMER, W.H. S1c
SULLIVAN, O.J. MoMM1c
SWINSON, P.W. StM2c
TAYLOR, R.H. F2c
TAYLOR, S.H. S1c
THOMAS, C.F. MoMM3c
UPDIKE, H.E. TM3c
VANCE, N. S1c
VAN NORDEN, F.E. EM2c
WALKER, J.M.Jr. RM2c
WATERS, H.A. MoMM2c
WATSON, G.J. EM3c
WEBSTER, E.A.Jr. F1c
WHITE, T.J. FC3c
WHITELOW, J. MoMM2c
WORTHINGTON, W.W.Jr. ... EM2c
ZIMMERMAN, C.A. GM3c

GUDGEON
FIND 'EM
CHASE 'EM
SINK 'EM
Gudgeon

HERRING (SS233)

HERRING, under Lt. Cdr. D. Zabriskie, Jr., left Pearl Harbor on 16 May 1944 to conduct her eighth patrol in the Kurile Islands. On 21 May she topped off with fuel at Midway and departed for the Kurile region. No word was received from HERRING direct after her departure from Midway, but she did accomplish a rendezvous with BARB on 31 May 1944.

These two boats were to patrol the Kurile Islands area cooperatively, and at the rendezvous, as recorded in BARB's report of her eighth war patrol, the areas which each were to be responsible for were delineated. A few hours after leaving HERRING early on the afternoon of 31 May, BARB made contact with two Japanese merchantmen. While developing the contacts BARB heard distant depth charging, which she took as an indication that HERRING was making an attack.

Later that evening BARB picked up a prisoner who revealed that HERRING had sunk the escort vessel of the convoy BARB had been attacking. The ship sunk was ISHIGAKI, a new type DE built in 1942, and it was sunk with one torpedo hit. The sinking resulted in the scattering of the three ship convoy and two ships, which subsequently passed near BARB, were sunk by her. Post-war information reveals that HERRING sank the third merchantman of the convoy.

On 3 June 1944 orders were sent to BARB and HERRING directing them to stay outside of a restricted area in which friendly surface ships would be operating during the Marianas Campaign. A receipt was required for this message, but none was heard from HERRING. BARB was unable to contact her after 31 May. Consequently on 27 June, Midway was directed to post a sharp lookout for HERRING, which might be returning without ability to transmit by radio, and was expected by 3 or 4 July. When she had not appeared by 13 July 1944, HERRING was reported as presumed lost.

D. Zabriskie, Jr.

Japanese information indicates that HERRING was sunk on 1 June 1944, two kilometers south of Point Tagan on Matsuwa Island in the Kuriles. The report states that two merchant ships, HIBURI MARU and IWAKI MARU, were sunk by American torpedoes while at anchor at Matsuwa. In a counter-attack, a shore battery scored two direct hits on the conning tower, and "bubbles covered an area about 5 meters wide, and heavy oil covered an area of approximately 15 miles". The position of this attack was around 150 miles from the position where HERRING met BARB; the attack occured on the day after the BARB picked up her prisoner. BARB and HERRING were the only U. S. submarines in the area at the time and BARB did not make the attack on the anchored ships referred to above. As a result of the attacks reported by BARB and by the Japanese, HERRING has been credited with

four ships and 13,202 tons sunk for her last patrol.

For her first seven patrols, HERRING sank nine ships, totaling 45,200 tons, and damaged two, totaling an additional 8,400 tons. Her first four patrols were in the Atlantic, the first three off the coast of Spain, and the fourth near Iceland. The first netted an Axis freighter, while on the second HERRING saw no enemy ships. Her third patrol saw her sink a Nazi U-boat, and her fourth was again unproductive of enemy targets. Her fifth patrol was the passage from the United Kingdom, where she had been based for her Atlantic patrols, to New London, Conn., thence to Pearl Harbor. She patrolled the East China Sea on her sixth war run, and sank two large transports, a freighter, and a small escort type vessel. HERRING's seventh patrol was in the area just south of the Japanese home islands; here she damaged a destroyer type vessel.

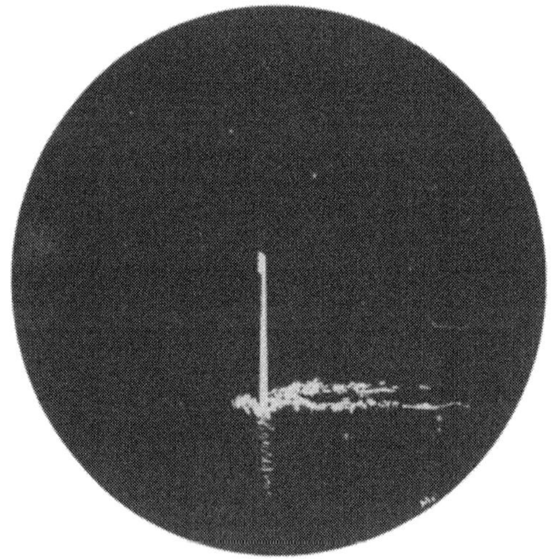

U.S.S. HERRING

ANDERSON, F.H.........RT2c
ANDERSCN, J.L.Jr...MoMM2c
ARMSTRONG, J.E.......RM1c
BALESTRIERI, S.......ENS.
BLEVINS, J.T.. ....S1c
BOUCHER, L.J..........S1c
BRENNAN, J.J..........TM2c
BLAIR, J.L.............F1c
BRONDER, J.J..........SC2c
BROWN, W.J.............S2c
BURKETT, T............CK1c
BURTON, C.E........MoMM2c
CAMPBELL, N.........StM2c
CARROLL, M.D........CMoMM
CARTER, R.A............S1c
CHOUINARD, R.J.......TM1c
CHRISTOPHERSON, R.W..TM1c
COMPTON, J.N......LT.(JG)
COOK, A.J...........MoMM2c
CUNNINGHAM, E.P......ENS.
CUSHION, H.L..........EM1c
DAWKINS, J.R.......MoMM1c
DEVENPORT, R.E.......TM3c
EDGINTON, F.K..........F1c
EITELBACK, W.J.Jr..MoMM1c
FLEMING, C.D...........S2c
FRENCH, G.W.........MoMM3c
GAGNON, D.R............F2c
GREGORY, J.L..........TM3c
GROSHENS, G.C.........EM2c
GROTE, C.H............RM3c
GUERRA, A.A...........CPHM
HARPER, P.............TM3c
HASKELL, R.G.... ..MoMM2c
HILL, B.G..............S2c
HOFMAN, W.A.......LT.(JG)
ISBELL, L.H...........SC3c
JOHNSON, J.M.......MoMM2c
JOHNSCN, L.K...........S2c
JOHNSON, S.L.Jr.......RM3c
KELLEY, E.A...........EM2c
KOSTAL, M.F.Jr....LT.(JG)

LEAHY, F.L.Jr...........LT.
LEWIS, W.E.............TM3c
LOFTIS, R.H.........MoMM1c
MACK, R.L..............RM3c
MASON, W.J.........LT.Exec.
MAYES, J.B.............SM3c
MC CREARY, J.W.Jr......CQM
MC LENDON, W.R........TM3c
MERRIMAN, J.A.Jr....SoM2c
MILLIS, R.S.............CEM
MITCHELL, G.R.........EM3c
MUCH, H.B...............F1c
ODOM, L.................F2c
O'HOWELL, H.J.......CMoMM
PAYNE, R.E.............GM2c
PEPERA, G.J...........FCS2c
PERKINS, J.G............S2c
POLAND, C.E...........SM3c
POTVIN, O.P...........QM3c
PRESSNAL, W.B..........ENS.
PRICE, S.H.............EM2c
RILEY, C.E........ MoMM2c
ROBBINS, D.L........MoMM3c
ROCKWELL, E.E.........EM1c
RYAN, D.E...........MoMM3c
SAARM, A.H..........MoMM3c
SCHMIDT, C.A............F1c
SMILEY, W.K...........GM3c
STERN, W................S1c
STONEKING, R.R.........SC3c
SUTHERLAND, J.A.........F1c
SWANSON, F.A............Y2c
TWIGG, A.W.............EM1c
VAN MATRE, V.H........EM3c
VREELAND, L.M...........Cox
WAGONER, G.E..........FC3c
WALKER, C.D.........MoMM2c
WALSH, J.R.............EM3c
WAY, K.K................S1c
WILSON, H.R............TM2c
WUERTELE, E.C..........S1c
ZABRISKIE, D.Jr.LT.CDR.C.O.

U.S.S. HERRING (SS233) Diving Trim

GOLET (SS 361)

Enroute to her second patrol, GOLET (Lt. Cdr. J. S. Clark) left Midway on 28 May 1944, for the entire area off the northeast coast of Honshu. No word was heard from her after she departed Midway.

GOLET was scheduled to depart her area on 5 July 1944, and was expected at Midway about 12 or 13 July. On 9 July 1944, she was sent a message which required an acknowledgement, but none came. On 11 July, a sharp lookout was posted at Midway for a submarine coming in without being able to transmit. By 26 July 1944, the ship had not returned, and it was reported as presumed lost.

In the reports covering Japanese anti-submarine attacks, made since war's end, one is recorded as having been made on 14 June 1944, at 41°04'N, 141-30°E. This attack is considered to explain GOLET's loss, since the enemy, in his report, states, "On the spot of fighting we later discovered corks, raft, etc., and a heavy oil pool of 50 by 5,200 meters". GOLET was credited with no sinkings or damage to enemy ships on her first patrol, conducted in the Kuriles, and the area south of Hokkaido and east of Honshu.

U.S.S. GOLET

BARLOW, G.R. ... Ens.
BARNES, E.C. ... EM2c
BARTA, R.A. ... MoMM1c
BARTZ, E.L. ... MoMM1c
BEAULIEU, D.W. ... GM3c
BELCHER, DL. ... McMM3c
BICKHAM, C.P. ... SM2c
BLACKBURN, E.R. ... RT1c
BREUNIG, J.W. ... MoMM3c
BROWN, J.W. ... LT.(JG)
BUTOR, J.A. ... CTM.
CARR, A.H. ... TM3c
CLARK, J.S. ... LT.CDR.CO
CORAM, W.M. ... EM3c
DANKO, R.K. ... QM1c
DAVIDSON, W.D. ... SM2c
DOWEY, C. ... MoMM2c
EARLE, V.J. ... S1c
EDWARDS, W.A. ... GM1c
GERMANN, L.L. ... MoMM3c
GREENHALGH, J.F. ... TM3c
GRUMET, S.E. ... MoMM3c
GUEST, O.C.Jr. ... MoMM1c
GOETZ, H.C. ... S2c
GORMLEY, G.L. ... F1c
HARDY, R.F. ... TM3c
HANLEY, RE. ... RM3c
HARVILLE, R.L. ... CEM
HENDLEY, G.D. ... EM1c
HOFFMAN, R.E. ... MoMM2c
HUGHES, E.J. ... FC2c
HUMBLE, J.J. ... RM3c
INFALT, R.W. ... TM2c
JOHNSON, C.H. ... LT.(JG)
KANE, W.M. ... LT.CDR
KOLBUCAR, J. ... QM3c
KOUTSOS, J.M. ... S1c
LEINWAND, L.R. ... EM3c
LEONARD, C.B. ... MoMM2c
LEWIS, G.J. ... S1c
LOCKWOOD, G.G. ... MoMM2c
LYTLE, H.P. ... TM3c
MARTIN, C.L. ... EM2c
MC CULOUGH, W.E. ... StM1c
MC LAUGHLIN, H.B. ... LT.
MILLER, E.W. ... CPhM
MILLHOUSE, L.G. ... EM2c
MILUS, P.P. ... CPC
NUMAIR, S.J. ... F1c
PARRY, M. ... TM2c
PETERSON, M.L. ... RM1c
PINTER, G.A. ... EM3c
POGRAIS, F.R. ... EM1c
REICHELT, R.C. ... MoMM1c
ROCKWOOD, A.J. ... SC1c
ROBE, J. ... GM2c
RYMAL, J.G. ... S2c
SADLER, W.R. ... LT.
SCHLEMMER, A.E. ... MoMM1c
SCHRAMM, E.F. ... MoMM3c
SEDERSTRAND, C.E. ... CEM
SIERACKI, E.F. ... TM3c
SIMANDL, R.A. ... TM3c
SMITH, D.B. ... RM2c
STERLING, G.Jr. ... St3c
STONE, A.R. ... CMoMM
STROUT, J.C. ... EM2c
STULL, W.G. ... MoMM1c
STURDIVAN, J.E. ... TM1c
SUTHERLAND, E.H. ... MoMM1c
SWARTZBACK, W.W. ... Y1c
TARR, A.H. ... S1c
TINKER, R.B. ... SC2c
THOMPSON, R.N. ... TM2c
WADSWORTH, A.B.III. ... LT.CDR.
WALZ, R.R. ... MoMM2c
WESLEY, J.H. ... BM2c
WHITE, J.S. ... ENS.
WHITNEY, E.E.Jr. ... LT.
WILLIAMS, R.E. ... EM1c
WINKLE, W.J. ... TM2c
WRIGHT, H.D. ... SC1c

S-28 (SS132)

On 20 June 1944 Lt. Cdr. J. G. Campbell assumed command of S-28, his first command. The ship had finished a normal upkeep period on 12 June, and continued on her assigned duty of training enlisted personnel and engaging in sonar exercises with ships under control of ComDesPac.

On 3 July S-28, in accordance with orders from ComDesPac, got underway from the Submarine Base, Pearl Harbor, to conduct a week's normal operations. During the day on 3 July, S-28 acted as a target for anti-submarine warfare vessels until about 1700 local time. At that time she made two practice torpedo approaches on the U. S. Coast Guard Cutter RELIANCE. On 4 July S-28 again carried out sonar exercises as on the previous day, and at 1730 again undertook a practice approach on RELIANCE

At 1730 S-28 dived about 4 miles distant from RELIANCE. At about 1805 RELIANCE made sound contact with S-28 at a range of 1700 yards. The range decreased to about 1500 yards and then steadily increased, as the bearing drifted aft. Although sound contact was temporarily lost by RELIANCE at 3,000 yards, she picked up the submarine again at 3,300 yards. At 1820, with range 4,700 yards, RELIANCE permanently lost sound contact on S-28. At no time during the approach or the ensuing sound search were distress signals from S-28 seen or heard, nor was any sound heard which indicated an explosion in S-28.

When by 1830, S-28 had not surfaced or sent any signals, RELIANCE retraced her course and tried to establish communication with her. Although previous tests had showed that no difficulty would be experienced in exchanging messages by sound gear at ranges up to 2,000 yards, RELIANCE was unable to contact S-28. The Coast Guard vessel called in other vessels from Pearl Harbor at 2000, and a thorough search of the area was instituted, lasting until the afternoon of 6 July 1944. A slick, which was unmistakably made by diesel oil, was the only sign of S-28.

The Court of Inquiry which investigated the sinking determined that S-28 sank shortly after 1820 on 4 July 1944 in 21°-20'N, 158°-23'W, in 1400 fathoms of water. Because of the depth of the water, salvage operations were impossible. The Court recorded its opinion that S-28 lost depth control "from either a material casualty or an operating error of personnel, or both, and that depth control was never regained. The exact cause of the loss of S-28 cannot be determined." The Court found, further, that, "the material condition of S-28 was as good or better than that of other ships of her class performing similar duty.", and that, "the officers and crew on board S-28 at the time of her loss were competent to operate the ship submerged in the performance of her assigned duties". It was opined that the loss of S-28 was not caused by negligence or inefficiency of any person or persons.

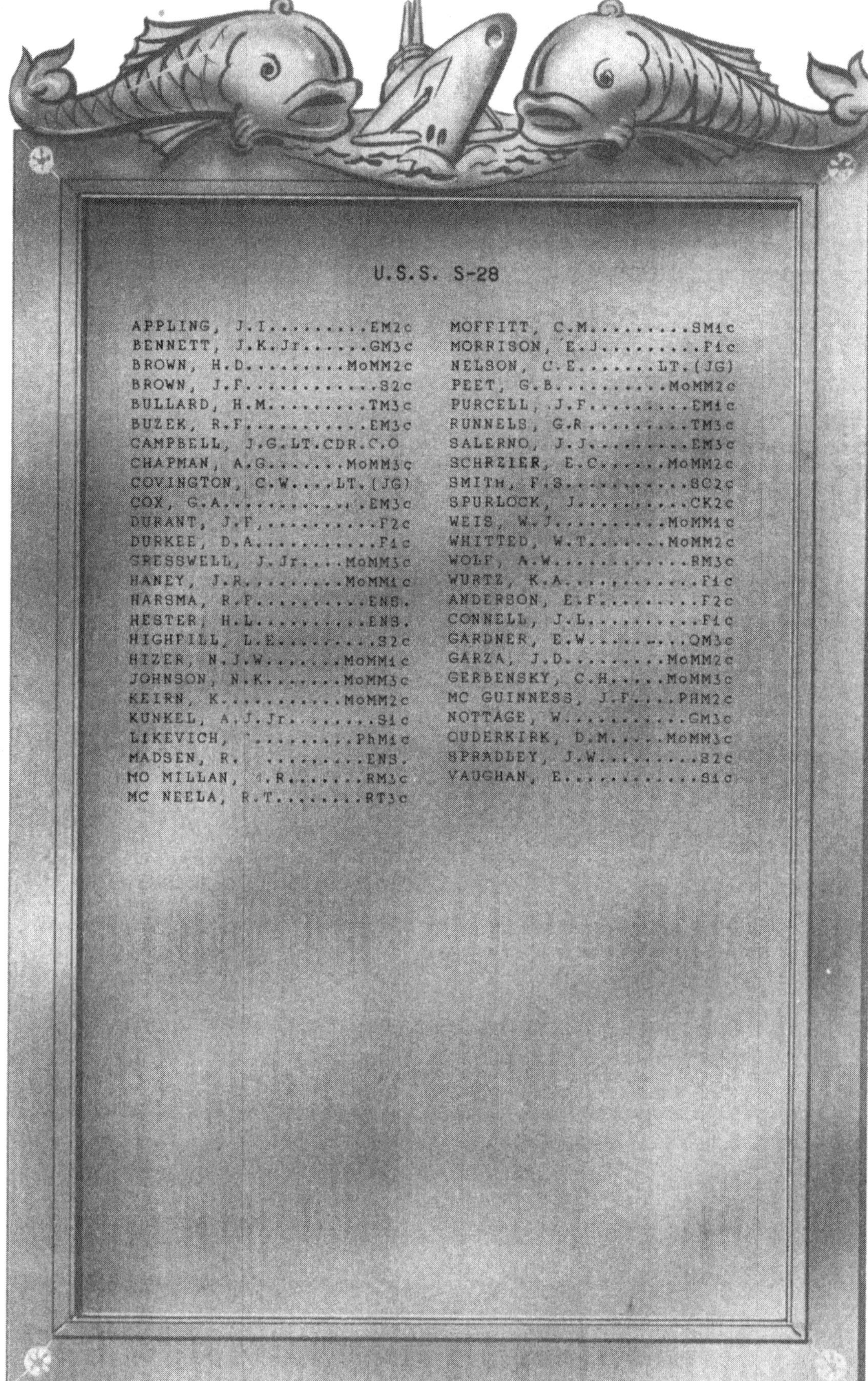
U.S.S. S-28
APPLING, J.I..........EM2c
BENNETT, J.K.Jr.......GM3c
BROWN, H.D..........MoMM2c
BROWN, J.F.............S2c
BULLARD, H.M..........TM3c
BUZEK, R.F............EM3c
CAMPBELL, J.G.LT.CDR.C.O
CHAPMAN, A.G........MoMM3c
COVINGTON, C.W....LT.(JG)
COX, G.A..............EM3c
DURANT, J.F,...........F2c
DURKEE, D.A............F1c
GRESSWELL, J.Jr....MoMM3c
HANEY, J.R..........MoMM1c
HARSMA, R.F...........ENS.
HESTER, H.L...........ENS.
HIGHFILL, L.E..........S2c
HIZER, N.J.W........MoMM1c
JOHNSON, N.K........MoMM3c
KEIRN, K............MoMM2c
KUNKEL, A.J.Jr.........S1c
LIKEVICH, ...PhM1c
MADSEN, R. ....ENS.
MC MILLAN, .R.........RM3c
MC NEELA, R.T.........RT3c
MOFFITT, C.M..........SM1c
MORRISON, E.J..........F1c
NELSON, C.E.......LT.(JG)
PEET, G.B...........MoMM2c
PURCELL, J.F..........EM1c
RUNNELS, G.R..........TM3c
SALERNO, J.J..........EM3c
SCHRZIER, E.C.......MoMM2c
SMITH, F.S............SC2c
SPURLOCK, J...........CK2c
WEIS, W.J...........MoMM1c
WHITTED, W.T........MoMM2c
WOLF, A.W.............RM3c
WURTZ, K.A.............F1c
ANDERSON, E.F..........F2c
CONNELL, J.L...........F1c
GARDNER, E.W..........QM3c
GARZA, J.D..........MoMM2c
GERBENSKY, C.H......MoMM3c
MC GUINNESS, J.F.....PHM2c
NOTTAGE, W............GM3c
OUDERKIRK, D.M......MoMM3c
SPRADLEY, J.W..........S2c
VAUGHAN, E.............S1c

ROBALO (SS 273)

ROBALO under Cdr. M. M. Kimmel, departed Fremantle on 22 June 1944 to conduct her third war patrol in the South China Sea in the vicinity of the Natuna Islands. After traversing Makassar and Balabac Straits, she was to arrive on station about 6 July, and stay there until dark on 2 August 1944.

On 2 July a contact report stated ROBALO had sighted a Fuso class battleship with air cover and two destroyers for escort in 3°-29'N, 119°-26'E, just east of Borneo. No other messages were received from ROBALO and when she did not return from patrol, she was reported as presumed lost.

The following information was received via the Philippine guerrillas and a U. S. Navy enlisted man who was a prisoner of war at Puerto Princessa Prison Camp, Palawan, P. I. On 2 August 1944, a note dropped from the window of the prison cell in which survivors from ROBALO were held was picked up by an American soldier who was in a work detail and given to H. D. Hough, Y2c, USN, another prisoner. On 4 August 1944, Hough contacted Mrs.Trinidad Mendosa, wife of guerrilla leader Dr. Mendosa, who furnished further information on the survivors. From these sourees, he put together the following facts.

ROBALO was sunk 26 July 1944, two miles off the western coast of Palawan Island as a result of an explosion of her after battery. Four men swam ashore, an officer and three enlisted men: Samuel L. Tucker, Ens.; Floyd G. Laughlin, QM1c; Wallace K. Martin, SM3c, and Mason C. Poston, EM2c. They made their way through the jungles to a small barrio northwest of the Puerto Princessa camp. They were captured there by Japanese Military Police, and confined in the jail. They were held for guerrilla activities rather than as prisoners of war, it is said. On 15 August 1944, they were evacuated by a Jap destroyer, and no other information is known regarding their destination or whereabouts. It is possible that they may have been executed by the Japanese or that the destroyer in which they were embarked was sunk. At any rate they were never recovered, and their note stated that there were no other survivors

M. M. Kimmel

It is doubted that a battery explosion could be sufficiently violent to cause the sinking of the ship and it is expected that the loss of ROBALO was caused by striking an enemy mine.

In her first patrol, in the area west of the Philippines, ROBALO damaged a large enemy freighter. Her second patrol was in the South China Sea near Indo-China; here she sank a 7500 ton tanker.

Photograph of U.S.S. ROBALO - Off Starboard Bow

U.S.S. ROBALO

ACKLEY, J.W. S1c
BAILEY, J.B. TM2c
BELL, P.S. SM1c
BOEHLES, J.P. TM1c
BREEDEN, C.E. EM3c
BRERETON, W.A. MoMM1c
BROCKMAN, G. S1c
CAGLE, C.L. MoMM1c
CARTER, H.E. .... LT.CDR.
CHANGARY, S.J. MoMM3c
CLARK, E.O. S1c
CLIFFORD, M.D.R. S1c
COOPERMAN, H.M. RT2c
COTTERMAN, S.N. PhM1c
GRESS, D.C. RM3c
DICKERSON, D.E. .... CMoMM
DITTMAN, C.L. TM2c
DOWNEY, S.L. MoMM2c
DVORACEK, J.L. Jr. F1c
ERVIN, L.F. MoMM1c
FELL, C.W. ..... LT.CDR.Exec.
FINK, D.E. RM3c
FLANAGAN, A.J. GM2c
FONDON, G.M. F1c
FRICKER, J.J. SC2c
GERDES, H.G. .... ENS.
GLEATON, E. Jr. CK2c
GRAHAM, K.E. EM1c
HAMILTON, H.L. Jr. TM3c
HART, J.J. Jr. TM3c
HOOD, H.T. TM3c
HURST, J.A. MoMM2c
IVEY, H.B. RT1c
JACKSON, N.M. TM2c
JAMBOR, W.E. GM1c
JOHNSON, E.H. MoMM1c
JOHNSON, N.Y. SC1c
KESTERSON, W.G. MoMM2c
KIMMEL, M.M. .... LT.CDR.C.O.
KONEN, A.C. S2c
*LAUGHLIN, F.G. QM1c
LEAHEY, R.J. SC3c
LEFEBVRE, J.W. .... CEM
LEVY, D.J. MoMM3c
LOVELL, D.W. EM1c
LUTMAN, J.A. .... ENS
MARTIN, R.E. EM2c
MARTIN, W.K. .... SM3c *
MARX, M.T. EM2c
MATTHEWS, W.G. Y1c
MILLER, E.D. MoMM1c
MC KNIGHT, H.F. Jr. .. LT.(JG)
NICHOLS, H.E. F1c
NICLAS, J.R. MoMM2c
O'BRIEN, J.J. MoMM2c
O'ROURKE, E.P. F1c
PAW, E.J. FC2c
PHELPS, B.B. TM1c
POSTON, M.C. .... EM2c *
PRIDDIS, J.F. .... CEM
PROSEUS, R.J. .... LT.
RAMSIER, H.L. MoMM1c
ROOT, C.A. MoMM1c
RUSSELL, S.J. F2c
SMITH, S.W. GM3c
SONEMANN, W.F. RM3c
SPEENER, R.W. S1c
SPENCER, S.E. .... CTM
TAYLOR, H.P. MoMM1c
TUCKER, S.L. .... ENS. *
USEALMAN, H.E. S2c
VAN DEURZEN, J.R. ... MoMM3c
VARNEY, E.G. S1c
VIRGA, C.R. F1c
VOGEL, F.P. TM3c
WAREHEIM, J.C. S1c
WILKERSON, D.F. MoMM2c
WILLIAMS, D.L. StM1c
WILSON, F. .... CMoMM
WINNAN, F.O. EM3c
WLODARCZYK, S.J. F1c
WOOD, C.E. Jr. QM3c
ZEA, C.K. TM3c

*– Denotes men who survived sinking, but have not been recovered following the end of the war.

FLIER (SS250)

FLIER, commanded by Cdr. J. D. Crowley, left Fremantle, Western Australia on 2 August, 1944 to conduct her second war patrol. Her area was east of Saigon, French Indo-China, and she was to pass through Lombok Strait, Makassar Strait, the Celebes Sea, Sibutu Passage and the Sulu Sea in proceeding to her station. By evening of 13 August she had come through the Sulu Sea and was transiting Balabac Strait, south of Palawan, P.I. when, at 2200, disaster struck. Suddenly a terrific explosion, estimated to have been forward on the starboard side, shook the ship.

Several of the men on the bridge were injured, and the Commanding Officer was thrown to the after part of the bridge, where he regained his senses a moment later. Oil, water and debris deluged the bridge. There was a strong smell of fuel, a terrific venting of air through the conning tower hatch, and the sounds of flooding and of screaming men below. Lt. Liddell, the Executive Officer, had stepped below the hatch to speak to Cdr. Crowley; he was blown through it, and men poured out behind him. Within 20 or 30 seconds FLIER sank while still making 15 knots through the water. The Commanding Officer's opinion is that the explosion was caused by contact with a mine.

Those men who survived have stated that the following men were seen in the water after the ship went down: Crowley, J. D., Cdr; Liddell, J. W., Jr., Lt.; Jacobson, A. E., Ens.; Howell, A. G., CRT.; Tremaine, D. P., FCR3c; Miller, W. B., MoMM3c; Russo, J. D., QM3c; Baumgart, E. R., MoMM3c; Knapp, P., Lt.; Casey J. E., Lt.; Reynolds, W. L., Lt. (jg); Mayer, P. S., Ens.; Pope, C. D., CGM; Madeo, G. F., F2c. Lt. (jg) Reynolds was wounded, as was Hudson, and when the word was passed for all survivors to gather together, they and Pope did not reappear. Ens. Mayer was being assisted by Howell, but after about 20 minutes he was unconscious and had to be abandoned.

J. D. Crowley

The first impulse was to swim to Comeran Island, but when the question was weighed, and the possibility of falling into Japanese hands was considered, Crowley decided to strike out for the coral reefs to the northwestward. Meanwhile Lt. Knapp became separated from the group and was not seen or heard again. The sky was overcast, and it was difficult to swim toward the objective at all times; an occasional flash of lightning helped to keep the swimmers oriented. After moonrise, at 0300 on 14 August, maintaining proper direction was easier.

All this time Lt. Casey had been unable to see, having been partially blinded by oil. At about 0400 he became exhausted and the others were forced to leave him. Commander Crowley realized that the only hope for anyone laying in swimming at best speed, and all hands were told to do the best they could toward land, which was now in sight. Madeo now began to fall behind, and was not seen after 0500.

At 1330 five of the group, Cdr. Crowley, Lt. Liddell,, Ens. Jacobson, Howell and Baumgart reached a floating palm tree and used this to aid themselves in remaining afloat and pushing toward land. This group came ashore on Mantangule Island at 1530 and were met there by Russo, who had swum the entire distance. At 1700 Tremaine was found on the eastern end of the island by Lt. Liddell. A lean-to was constructed and the night was spent on the beach.

In the days following plans were laid to obtain food and water and to make contact with friendly natives. A raft was made of drifted bamboo lashed together, and the party began working from island to island, with Palawan the ultimate objective. On 19 August they contacted natives who led them to a U. S. Army Coast Watcher Unit on Palawan. This unit made its communication facilities available to the group, and arrangements were made for evacuation by submarine. On the night of 30 August the survivors from FLIER embarked in two small boats, and, having made their way safely around a Japanese merchant ship anchored near the rendezvous point, were picked up by REDFIN early in the morning of 31 August.

FLIER's first patrol was conducted west of Luzon in June 1944. She sank four freighters, and damaged a fifth freighter and a tanker for 19,500 tons sunk and 13,500 tons damaged.

U.S.S. FLIER

ABRAHAMSON, A.J......MoMM2c
ANDERSON, V.I.........TM2c
BANCHERO, G.J.......MoMM2c
BANKS, C..............CK3c
BAEHR, H.A............ENS.
BARRON, P.F...........RM2c
*BAUMGART, E.R.......MoMM3c
BIVENS, W.O...........S1c
BOHN, T.L.............EM3c
BORLICK, E.A........MoMM1c
BROOKS, W.J..........CMoMM
BRUBAKER, E.S..........F1c
CANADY, E...........MoMM1c
CASEY, J.E.............LT.
CHRISTENSEN, C.J.......S1c
CLAWSON, C.W..........S1c
COSGROVE, R.J.........TM2c
COURTRIGHT, C.L........S1c
COWHEY, W.F...........EM1c
COWIE, J.B............EM3c
CUSHMAN, R.A........MoMM2c
*CROWLEY, J.D.......CDR.C.O.
DAGGY, W.H..........MoMM3c
DAROS, P.A..........MoMM1c
DONOVAN, T.A..........TM2c
DORRICOTT, W.E. Jr.......Y2c
DRESSELL, E.W..........QM2c
ELDER, J.E..............Y2c
ERICSON, H.G...........EM3c
FALOWSKI, F.W..........EM3c
FENDER, T.E.........MoMM1c
FITE, B.V..............RM3c
FREEMAN, W.D...........S1c
GAIDECZK, P.A.........PhM1c
GALINAC, J.J...........GM3c
GERBER, C.A............TM1c
GETCHELL, M.G.........Bkr3c
GRIMSHAW, J.W.......MoMM2c
GWINN, K.L.............CTM
HARDY, G.W.............BM2c
HELLER, E.W............S2c
HOLTYN, H.S.........MoMM2c
*HOWELL, A.G.........CRT(AA)

HUDSON, E.W..........CMoMM
JACOBSON, A.E.Jr.......ENS.*
KANTOR, S.............TM3c
KISAMORE, O.W.......MoMM3c
KNAPP, P...............LT.
KLOCK, W.J............RM1c
KUCINSKI, J.W.........EM1c
LADERBUSH, G.R........TM2c
LAMBERT, R.A..........TM3c
LEROY, J............MoMM1c
LIDDELL, J.W.Jr..LT.Exec.*
LINDEMAN, B.O.........TM1c
MAYER, P.S............ENS.
MC COY, E.H...........S1c
MC LANE, V.C.......MoMM3c
MADEO, G.F............F2c
MILLER, W.B........MoMM3c*
MINER, H.A............ENS.
MOENCH, V.L...........S1c
MURAWSKI, V.J.........F1c
MYERS, H.L............EM1c
NICHOLSON, J.G........TM3c
NORDHOF, H.D..........RM2c
PARKER, C.W...........EM1c
PAYNE, C.W............S1c
PHILLIPS, G.W.Jr...MoMM3c
POOLE, M..............CEM
POPE, C.D.............CGM
POURCIAU, K.J.........S1c
REYNOLDS, W.L......LT.(JG)
RICCIARDELLI, M.N..MoMM1c
ROSE, R.C..........MoMM1c
RUSSO, I.D...........GM3c*
SEE, D.N..............F1c
SKOW, A.L............SC3c
SNYDER, I.E.........CMoMM
TAYLOR, J.C...........EM1c
TREMAINE, D.P.......FCR2c*
TURNER, J.C..........StM1c
VEST, P.A..........MoMM2c
VOGT, J.F.............RT2c
WALL, L.P.............TM1c
WESTMORELAND, J.E.....S1c

* - Denotes survivors.

HARDER (SS257)

Commander S. D. Dealey guided his eminently successful fighting ship, HARDER, out of the harbor at Fremantle, Australia on 5 August 1944 to begin the sixth war patrol of that vessel. In company with HAKE, HARDER conducted training exercises enroute to Darwin. These two submarines topped off with fuel at Darwin, and on 13 August, together with HADDO, left for their assigned area west of Luzon, P. I. They were to patrol as a coordinated attack or wolfpack group, with Cdr. Dealey in charge.

On the afternoon of 20 August 1944, RAY, patrolling the same area, tracked a large convoy into Paluan Bay on the northwestern coast of Mindoro. An hour after surfacing, she contacted HARDER just outside the bay and held a megaphone conversation with Sam Dealey. Dealey formulated a plan for a concentrated dawn wolfpack attack on the convoy. HARDER came alongside HADDO at 0130 on the morning of 21 August and told Lt. Cdr. C. W. Nimitz, Jr., that at least 16 enemy ships were holed up in the bay. When the convoy made its exit at dawn (as convoys were wont to do) RAY was to approach from the northwest, HADDO from the west, and HARDER from the southwest. GUITARRO also had been drafted by Dealey, and was to attack from the northwest near Cape Calavite Lighthouse.

During the attacks which ensued, four ships, totaling 22,000 tons, were sunk, by Japanese admission. It is thought likely that HARDER sank one of them.

On the following day, HADDO and HARDER conducted a combined attack on three small vessels off Bataan. All three were sunk; these were the coast defense vessels MATSUWA, SADO and HIBURI. HADDO and HARDER each received credit for sinking one vessel, and shared credit for the third sinking.

S.D. Dealey

The morning of 23 August HADDO contacted a tanker escorted by a destroyer, and blew the bow off the destroyer in a down the throat shot. She fired her last torpedo in this attack, and in response to urgent calls for assistance, HAKE and HARDER rendezvous with her. HADDO, being out of torpedoes, "received Sam's blessing" and left his wolfpack, heading south. HAKE and HARDER discussed plans for finishing off the damaged destroyer and then departed for their common objective off Caiman Point.

At 0453 on the morning of 24 August HAKE dove not far from Caiman Point and about four miles off Hermana Major Island, west coast of Luzon, with HARDER in sight 4500 yards south of her. HAKE heard echo ranging to the south and soon sighted two ships. At first they appeared to be a three stack light cruiser and a destroyer, but upon later inspection were dentified as a three stack Thailand destroyer (the PHRA RUANG, of 1,035 tons) and a minesweeper of less than 1,000 tons. HAKE broke off the attack and headed north when the target zigged away apparently to enter Dasol Bay, while the minesweeper stayed outside..

At 0647 upon coming to a northerly course, HARDER's periscope was seen dead ahead at about 600-700 yards.. Sound also reported faint screws on this bearing, so HAKE turned away toward the south. At this point the minesweeper gave three strong pings, whereupon HAKE saw her 2,000 yards away swinging toward the two submarines. HAKE figured he had sound contact and went deep. The enemy kept pinging, but seemed to have the two targets located and to be undecided what to do about it. At 0728, HAKE heard 15 rapid depth charges, none close. Two sets of screws were heard and each continued pinging on either quarter of HAKE as she evaded to the westward. By 0955 all was quiet.

HARDER never was heard from again. Her periscope was last sighted at 15°-43'N, 119°-43'E. Japanese records reveal that an anti-submarine attack was made on the same day at 15°-50'N, 119°-43'E with 440 pound depth charges. The enemy said, "much oil, wood chips and cork floated in the neighborhood". Presumably HARDER perished in this depth charge attack.

HARDER was officially credited with having sunk 20.5 enemy ships, (The half credit was given for a ship sunk cooperatively with HADDO). This gave HARDER a total of 82,500 tons sunk and she damaged seven ships for 29,000 tons.

Her first patrol was conducted in Empire waters, starting in June 1943. She sank three freighters, and damaged seriously a freighter-transport and another freighter, a transport and a tanker. She went to the Empire again for her second patrol, and sank three freighters and a tanker, while she damaged a trawler.

HARDER was part of a wolfpack, of which PARGO and SNOOK were the other members, on her third patrol. In the open sea north of the Marianas, she sank a freighter, three freighter-transports and an armed trawler. HARDER's fourth patrol was in the Carolines. On 13 April 1944 she sank the Japanese destroyer IKAZUCHI. She also sank a freighter and damaged a second destroyer. HARDER departed for her fifth patrol in the Celebes Sea on 26 May 1944. She picked up coast watchers from northeastern Borneo, and gave a very valuable contact report on a major task force leaving Tawi Tawi anchorage, Sulu Archipelago, in preparation to engaging in the first Battle of the Philippine Sea. She sank the destroyer MINATSUKI on 6 June 1944. On the next day the destroyer HAYANAMI fell victim to HARDER's torpedoes, and sank tail first. The destroyer TANIKAZE was HARDER's next victim, sunk on 9 June. On 10 June she damaged another destroyer. By the time HARDER returned from this patrol, she had earned the reputation of being the Submarine Force's most terrible opponent of destroyers.

HARDER received the Presidential Unit Citation for her first five patrols, and Commander Dealey was posthumously awarded the Congressional Medal of Honor for his outstanding contribution to the war effort on HARDER's fifth patrol.

U.S.S. HARDER

ALTHERR, C.R........MoMM2c
BABER, R.O..........MoMM2c
BEUTELSPACHER, W.F....SC3c
BLUM, R.A...........MoMM3c
BOURG, S..............GM3c
BROSTROM, W.A.........SM1c
BUCKNER, T.W.......LT.(JG)
BULL, C.A.............RM2c
CASH, V.J...........MoMM1c
CHENARD, R.R...........F1c
CLARK, W.L............RT2c
CONLEY, J.C.........MoMM1c
CRASK, H.F.............S1c
CROMWELL, J.E.........Stm2c
DAHLHEIMER, D.B.....MoMM2c
DALLESSANDRO, V.L.....TM1c
DEALEY, S.D.........Cdr.CO
DE VOE, E.W............F1c
DIAMOND, W.V..........RM1c
EDGAR, J.M............FC2c
FINNEY, C.E...........Mach.
FISHER, G.R.Jr......MoMM3c
GIFFORD, R.L..........TM3c
GLUECKERT, J.L......MoMM2c
GULLY, D.J.............Y1c
HALOUPEK, W.O..........Ens.
HATFIELD, H.D....Rad.Elec.
HOOD, E.V.............TM1c
HUTCHERSON, V.W......CMoMM
JAMES, D.R.........LT.(JG)
JONES, R.E..........MoMM3c
KECKLER, R.W.......CEM(AA)
KELLOGG, J.H..........EM2c
LAKEY, G.W.............S1c
LANE, J.M.............EM3c
LAWSON, H.W.........MoMM3c
LEVIN, G.B............RT2c
LILLEY, S.B............S1c
LO CASCIO, A..........PhM1c
LONAS, I.P...........CMoMM
LYNN, H.A.Jr..........TM3C
LOGAN, S.M..........LT.Exec
MAJURI, F.P.jr........EM1c
MANNING, R.E..........EM2c
MC GREVY, F.B.........EM2c
MC WILLIAMS, G.K.....Bkr3c
MEDLEY, B.R...........RM2c
MILLER, C..............CTM
MILLS. R.R............EM3c
MOFFETT, C.A.Jr.....MoMM2c
MOORE, O.J............SM2c
MOORE, R..............CK2c
MORGAN, A.B...........EM2c
MOSS, R.B..............S1c
MURRAY, M.H...........TM2c
OGILBIE, T.D...........S1c
OPISSO, L.A.........MoMM2c
PAQUET, F.Jr..........GM1c
PECK, E.R..............S1c
PICK, R.S..............S1c
PRATT, R.E.............S1c
PRZYBILLA, R.P........EM2c
ROGERS, M.M...........TM3c
ROGERS, M.M............S1c
ROOSEVELT, R.B.........ENS.
SAMPSON, P.T...........ENS.
SCHEIBELHUT, F.S....MoMM2c
SCHWARTZ, M.........MoMM3c
SIMON, D.J............RM3c
SLOGGETT, V.L......LT.(JG)
SMITH, A..............TM2c
SNIPERS, J.W.Jr.....MoMM1c
SNYDER, W.L...........TM3c
SOMMERSCHIEFLD, L.H....Cox
SPICE, N............MoMM3c
SWAGERTY, J.T.......MoMM3c
WHITE, L.M............TM3c
YOUNG, B.J............SC2c
ZANDER, W.G.........MoMM2c

Submarines Pacific Fleet

Be it known that

Commander S. D. Dealey

UNITED STATES NAVY

While Commanding Officer of the

U. S. S. Harder

has so Distinguished himself by his Conspicuous Gallantry and Extraordinary Heroism above and beyond the Call of Duty and has been awarded the

Congressional Medal of Honor

for sinking five enemy combatant vessels on his outstandingly successful fifth war patrol.

SEAWOLF (SS 197)

SEAWOLF (Lt. Cdr. A. L. Bontier) left Brisbane on 21 September 1944 beginning her 15th patrol, and arrived at Manus on 29 September. Leaving Manus on the same day, SEAWOLF was directed to carry certain stores and Army personnel to the east coast of Samar.

Lt. Cdr. A.L. Bontier

On 3 October SEAWOLF and NARWHAL exchanged SJ radar recognition signals at 0756. Later the same day an enemy submarine attack was made at 2°-32'N, 129°-18'E, which resulted in the sinking of U. S. S. SHELTON (DE407). Since there were four friendly submarines in the vicinity of this attack, they were directed to give their positions, and the other three did, but SEAWOLF was not heard from. On 4 October, SEAWOLF again was directed to report her position, and again she failed to.

U. S. S. ROWELL (DE403) and an aircraft attacked a submarine in the vicinity of the attack on SHELTON, having at that time no knowledge of any friendly submarines in the area, and it was thought that SEAWOLF must be held down by these anti-submarine activities. It is possible that SEAWOLF was the submarine attacked.

SEAWOLF Sinks Patrol Boat #39

The report from ROWELL indicates that an apparently lethal attack was conducted in conjunction with a plane which marked the spot with dye. ROWELL established sound contact on the submarine, which then sent long dashes and dots which ROWELL stated bore no resemblence to the existing recognition signals. After one of the several hedgehog attacks a small amount of debris and a large air bubble were seen. It has been established that the Japanese submarine RO-41 sank SHELTON on 3 October, and was able to return to Japan.

In view of the above facts, and the fact that there is no attack listed in the Japanese report of anti-submarine attacks which could account for the loss of SEAWOLF, it is possible that SEAWOLF was sunk by friendly forces in an anti-submarine attack on 3 October 1944, in the vicinity of 02°-32'N, 129°-18'E. It is also possible that she was lost due to an operational casualty or as a result of an unrecorded enemy attack.

During her first fourteen patrols, SEAWOLF sank 27 enemy ships, and damaged 13. This gave her total tonnage for ships sunk and damaged of 108,600 and 69,600, respectively. On the day the war began she started patrolling in the vicinity of northern Luzon, but returned with no damage to her credit. Her second patrol was the passage from Manila to Port Darwin and SEAWOLF did not meet any enemy ships. On her third patrol SEAWOLF transported a cargo of .50 caliber anti-aircraft ammunition to Corregidor in January 1942 and then took passengers from there to Surabaya. Patrolling the vicinity of Lombok Straits for her fourth run, SEAWOLF sank a transport and damaged three light cruisers, two transports and a freighter. She received the Navy Unit Commendation for this patrol. Returning to the Philippine area for her fifth patrol, SEAWOLF sank a freighter. In the Makassar Strait for her sixth patrol, SEAWOLF sank a tanker and a freighter-transport, while she damaged another tanker.

On her seventh patrol, SEAWOLF made the passage from Fremantle to Pearl Harbor, patrolling at Davao Gulf, Palau and Yap enroute. She sank the Japanese freighter-transport SAGAMI-MARU 40 miles inside the mouth of Davao Gulf on 3 November 1942. In addition, SEAWOLF sank two other freighter-transports and damaged a freighter on this patrol. On her eighth patrol, in the Bonins-Formosa Area, SEAWOLF sank a large freighter, a tanker, two sampans, and, on 23 April 1943, Patrol

Boat number 39, a converted Japanese destroyer. Going to an area off the China coast north of Formosa for her ninth patrol, SEAWOLF sank a freighter-transport and a sampan, and damaged a destroyer escort.

SEAWOLF's tenth patrol was in the East China Sea in August and September 1943; here she sank three large freighters and two sampans, while she damaged a third sampan. She conducted her eleventh patrol in the South China Sea and sank a large freighter-transport and an unidentified ship, and damaged a freighter. In the East China Sea north of Formosa SEAWOLF sank a freighter-transport, three freighters and damaged three more freighters on her twelfth war patrol. SEAWOLF's mission on her thirteenth patrol was a photographic reconnaissance of Palau. She also rescued two downed aviators during a U. S. carrier air raid there. On her fourteenth patrol, SEAWOLF delivered cargo to guerrilla activities in the Philippines.

U.S.S. SEAWOLF

ASA, M.L...........LT.(JG)
ASTARITA, H.M..........S1c
BALCH, L.R............EM1c
BALLARD, R.A..........GM2c
BANNISTER, J.........Bkr3c
BARGENQUAST, A.F...MoMM1c
BECK, W.B.......F1c(MoMM
BEKKE, G.E.........CRM(SS)
BENNETT, R.J...........S1c
BERGEVIN, P.K..........S1c
BOLON, D.V.........F1c(EM)
BONTIER, A.M..LT.CDR.C.O.
CALL, J.B........RM1c(SS)
CARITHERS, J.P..F1c(MoMM)
CARNEGIE, R.J.....F1c(EM)
CASH, W.L...(MoMM3c(T)(SS)
CHAPMAN, E..CMoMM(AA)(SS)
COON, N.D.........RT2c(SS)
COPAS, C.M.............Y1c
COTTON, W.J...........SC3c
COX, R.L...............LT.
CUNNALLY, J.P..MoMM1c(SS)
DOANE, P...............LT.
DEVITT, R.F.....MoMM2c(SS)
EWING, J.L............QM3c
FIXLER, R.N............S1c
FLYNN, K.J.......EM1c(SS)
FRANCO, P......MoMM2c(SS)
GEORGE, L.........EM3c(SS)
GRIMES, J.........QM2c(SS)
HADLEY, W.T.CPhM(AA)(T)(SS)
HARRIS, J.G.....F1c(MoMM)
HOWARD, A.H.......TM2c(SS)
HUFF, R.E.....(MoMM2c(SS)
JOHNSON, J.E.....RM2c(SS)
JURINIC, M........SC1c(SS)
KENNEY, J.E........S1c(SS)
KREMPA, C.S....MoMM1c(SS)
KUEHN, A.E........QM1c(SS)
LAWSON, V.G......TM2c(SS)
LEEMAN, M.H.Jr.........S1c
LIKERT, G.R,.....BM1c(SS)
LYNCH, C.D........EM2c(SS)
MALONE, D.L.......TM2c(SS)
MARSTON, G.F.Jr..TM3c(SS)
MAUS, C.R..........SM2c(SS)
McCOY, W.G...........CMoMM
MICHAEL, F.S..........RM3c
MILLER, R.V.D.....LT.(JG)
MILLER, R.L.............S2c
MILLER, R.T.......TM2c(SS)
MILLS, L.T.Jr...........F1c
MITCHELL, H.E.....S2c(FC)
MORRIS, E.L.......FC2c(SS)
MORRIS, J.A........S1c(SS)
NAZAY, G.G.....MoMM3c(SS)
NAZE, D.J.....CTM(AA)(SS)
NEEDHAM, G.M.....EM1c(SS)
NIVISON, C.L.....EM1c(SS)
O'BRIEN, E.F.Jr........LT.
PAGE, A.F.........EM2c(SS)
PAGE, L.A......MoMM1c(SS)
PETERSON, E.N..MoMM1c(SS)
POLITYLO, W......EM3c(SS)
REILAND, W.F.Jr... ..ENS.
RHOADS, G.B....MoMM1c(AA)
RIGGLE, M.R......TM2c(SS)
ROCAYA, S.........St2c(SS)
ROGERS, B.F...CRT(AA)(SS)
SADLER, J.C......TM2c(SS)
SAINT, J.W.....MoMM1c(AA)
STEINECKER, G.A........F1c
STRAUSSER, C.E.........F1c
SZENDREY, E.J.....LT.(JG)
UNDERHILL, W.H.MoMM2c(SS)
VAN ANDEL, J..........ENS
WALL, V.P......MoMM1c(SS)
WARREN, T.W.......TM2c(SS)
WIEGENSTEIN, M.P.CMoMM(SS)
WYATT, D.B.........S1c(TM)
YOUNG, R.P............EM3c
ZUEL, E.A..........EM2c(SS)

PASSENGERS

KOPP, H.S..........Captain
MILLER, G.F........1st LT.
WISE, B.L.............C.W.O
PERALTA, G.E.......1st Sgt
ALMERO, E.A.........Ts/Sgt
IBEA, A.I.............S/Sgt
BUENO, G.B...............Sgt
PUGOSE, E.L..............Sgt
FRIA, A.B.................Cpl
CENDONIA, O.C...........T/5
RUIZ, R.R.................T/5
RAMOS, O.B...............Pfc
RIMANDO, J.F.............Pfc
HAMMILL, C.H..........S/Sgt
FRAMISCO, A.C.........S/Sgt
RODRIGUEZ, I.R............Sgt
HERBIG, R.P...............Sgt

All passengers U.S. Army Personnel.

DARTER (SS227)

On 1 September 1944, DARTER, commanded by Cdr. D.H. McClintock, left Brisbane for a period of training enroute to her fourth war patrol. She topped off with fuel at Darwin on 10 September and left that place on the same day to perform routine reconnaissance duty in the Celebes Sea from 14 September to 24 September.

Proceeding thence to the South China Sea with DACE commanded by Cdr. B. D. Claggett, DARTER formed a coordinated attack team with that vessel. The period from 12 October to 24 October was productive of many targets and attacks for DARTER, and she sank 9,900 tons of enemy shipping and damaged 19,900 tons in this time.

In the early morning of 23 October 1944 both DARTER and DACE contacted and tracked a large enemy force heading north through Palawan Passage enroute to engage our forces in the Battles for Leyte Gulf. They attacked while the enemy were unable to alter course appreciably, and in brilliant pre-dawn submerged attacks, sank the heavy cruisers ATAGO and MAYA, and so severely damaged the heavy cruiser TAKAO that she was useless for the rest of the war. During daylight, DARTER tried a submerged attack on TAKAO, which had been stopped, but was driven off by screening destroyers. Thus a night coordinated attack plan was drawn up by the two boats.

Since she could not surface to take sights, DARTER was forced to navigate on a 24-hour-old Dead Reckoning plot. At 2200 TAKAO got underway, and DARTER began a surface attack. Detecting two radars sweeping, she decided to do an end around, and then make an attack at radar depth. At 0005 on 24 October 1944, DARTER grounded on Bombay Shoal, and, making 17 knots at the time, rode up to a draft of nine feet forward. Efforts to get off the reef were unsuccessful, and a message was sent to

D. H. McClintock

DACE requesting assistance.

DACE closed DARTER and, after confidential gear had been smashed and classified matter burned, the men of DARTER were transferred to DACE. This was all done before dawn, and there were no losses of DARTER personnel.

DARTER's demolition charges failed to go off properly, and DACE used her remaining torpedoes in trying to destroy her without success, the torpedoes hitting the reef and exploding before they could reach their target. She did, however, score 21 four inch hits on DARTER. ROCK was called in and fired ten torpedoes at DARTER, with similar lack of success due to their hitting the reef.

NAUTILUS, on her 13th patrol, arrived on 31 October 1944, and scored 55 six inch hits on DARTER. Her report states, "It is doubtful that any equipment in DAR-

TER at 1131 this date would be of any value to Japan - except as scrap. Estimated draft of DARTER - 4 Feet".

It must be realized that Commander McClintock understood fully the dangers involved in the end around maneuver in which DARTER grounded—indeed, the incident is a classic example of calculated risk, and he was not held in any way at fault in the incident. It was simply one of the unfortunate tactical losses which must be expected in wartime, but which, in this case, was minimized by the fact that DARTER's full complement of personnel was saved. In order to keep this fighting and successful crew together the entire DARTER crew was ordered to take over the submarine MENHADEN, then building at Manitowoc, Wisconsin.

DARTER's four patrols (including her last) resulted in 23,700 tons of enemy ships being sent to the botom, and 30,000 tons being damaged. She began her patrolling career south and west of Truk in January and February 1944. She damaged a freighter on this first patrol. In the second patrol of this vessel, she covered the area in and around the Celebes Sea; she sank a freighter here. DARTER's third patrol was again in the eastern Celebes Sea, and she sank the large mine layer TUGARU on 29 June 1944. She was credited with sinking the heavy cruiser ATAGO and damaging the heavy cruiser TAKAO on the night of 23 October 1944, shortly before she stranded. DARTER was awarded the Navy Unit Commendation for the last patrol.

DARTER Aground on Bombay Shoal

SHARK 2 (SS314)

Joining SEADRAGON and BLACKFISH at Pearl Harbor, the second SHARK (Cdr. E. N. Blakely) left that place on 23 September 1944, and proceeded to Saipan to begin her third war patrol. The three vessels left the latter island on 3 October to conduct a coordinated patrol in the vicinity of Luzon Strait. Commander Blakely had command of this coordinated attack group, called Blakely's Behemoths.

On 22 October, SHARK reported having contacted four large enemy vessels in Latitude 20°-28'N, Longitude 117°-50'E. She still had her full load of torpedoes aboard, so had not made an attack. SHARK addressed no further messages to bases, but on 24 October, SEADRAGON received a message from her stating that she had made radar contact with a single freighter, and that she was going in to attack. This was the last message received from SHARK.

However, on 13 November 1944, a despatch originated by Commander Naval Unit, Fourteenth Air Force, stated that a Japanese ship enroute from Manila to Japan with 1800 American prisoners of war had been sunk on 24 October by an American submarine in a torpedo attack. No other submarine reported the attack, and since SHARK had given SEADRAGON a contact report only a few hours before the sinking, and could not be raised by radio after it, it can only be assumed that SHARK made the attack described, and perished during or after it. Five prisoners who survived and subsequently reached China stated that conditions on the prison ship were so intolerable that the prisoners prayed for deliverance from their misery by a torpedo or bomb. Because many prisoners of war had been rescued from the water by submarines after sinking vessels in which they were being transported, U. S. submarines had been instructed to search for Allied survivors in the vicinity of all sinkings of Empire bound Japanese ships. SHARK may well have been sunk trying to rescue American prisoners of war. All attempts to contact SHARK by radio failed and on 27 November she was reported as presumed lost.

E. N. Blakely

A report from the Japanese received after the close of the war on anti-submarine attacks records the attack made by SHARK on 24 October 1944, in Latitude 20°-41'N, Longitude 118°-27'E. Depth charges were dropped 17 times, and the enemy reports having seen "bubbles, and heavy oil, clothes, cork, etc." Several American submarines report having been attacked on this date near the position given, but in view of the fact that none reported the attack on the convoy cited above, this attack is considered the most probable cause of SHARK's loss.

SHARK sank five ships, totaling 32,200 tons and damaged two, for 9,900 tons prior to her last patrol. Her first patrol was in the area west of the Marianas. SHARK sank two freighters, a transport and a large tanker, and damaged a freighter. In her second patrol in the Bonins, SHARK sank a medium freighter.

U.S.S. SHARK DOWN THE WAYS

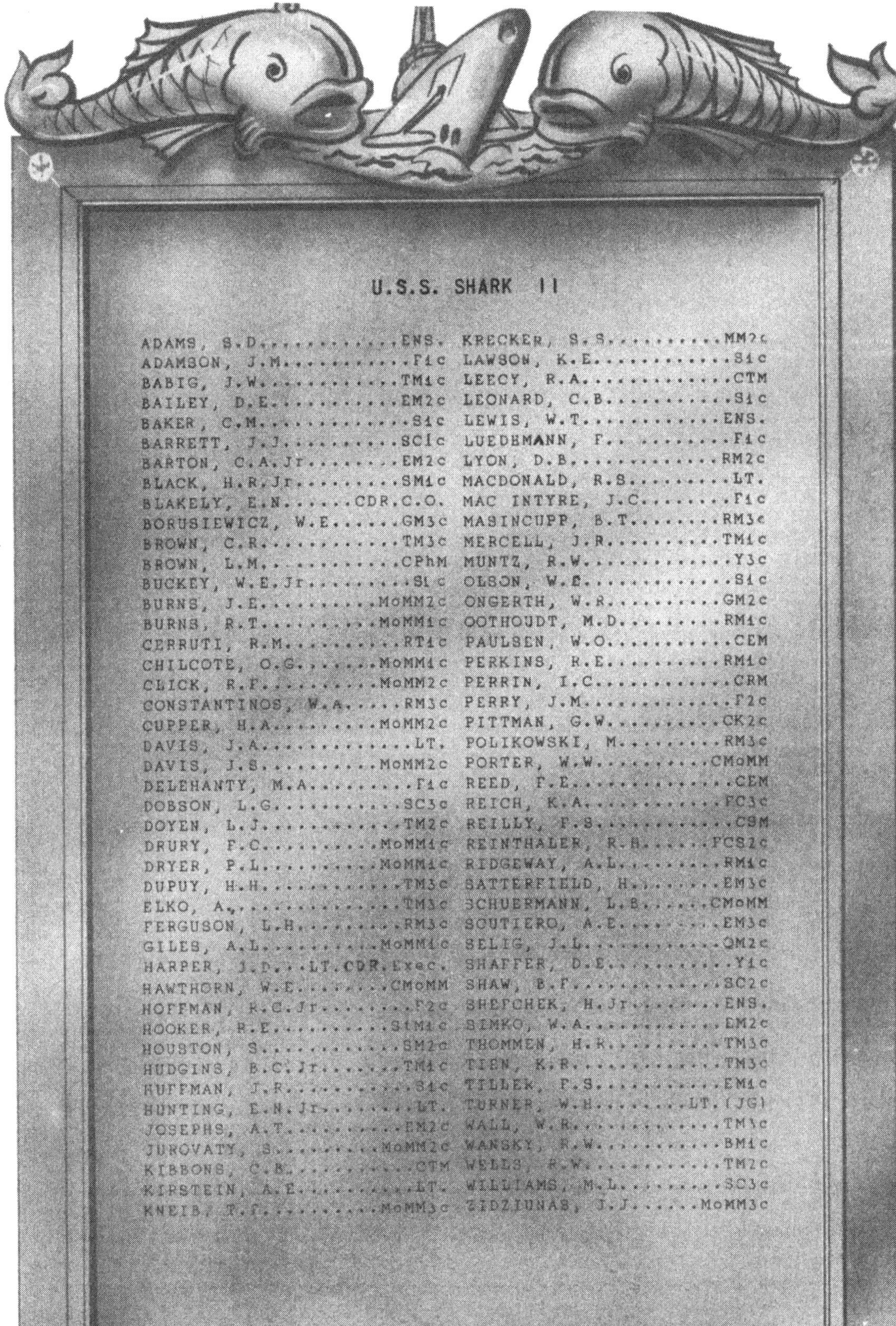

U.S.S. SHARK II

ADAMS, S.D............ENS.
ADAMSON, J.M...........F1c
BABIG, J.W............TM1c
BAILEY, D.E...........EM2c
BAKER, C.M.............S1c
BARRETT, J.J..........SC1c
BARTON, C.A.Jr........EM2c
BLACK, H.R.Jr.........SM1c
BLAKELY, E.N.......CDR.C.O.
BORUSIEWICZ, W.E......GM3c
BROWN, C.R............TM3c
BROWN, L.M............CPhM
BUCKEY, W.E.Jr.........S1c
BURNS, J.E..........MoMM2c
BURNS, R.T..........MoMM1c
CERRUTI, R.M..........RT1c
CHILCOTE, O.G.......MoMM1c
CLICK, R.F..........MoMM2c
CONSTANTINOS, W.A.....RM3c
CUPPER, H.A.........MoMM2c
DAVIS, J.A.............LT.
DAVIS, J.S..........MoMM2c
DELEHANTY, M.A.........F1c
DOBSON, L.G...........SC3c
DOYEN, L.J............TM2c
DRURY, F.C..........MoMM1c
DRYER, P.L..........MoMM1c
DUPUY, H.H............TM3c
ELKO, A...............TM3c
FERGUSON, L.H.........RM3c
GILES, A.L..........MoMM1c
HARPER, J.D...LT.CDR.Exec.
HAWTHORN, W.E.........CMoMM
HOFFMAN, R.C.Jr........F2c
HOOKER, R.E..........StM1c
HOUSTON, S............SM2c
HUDGINS, B.C.Jr.......TM1c
HUFFMAN, J.R...........S1c
HUNTING, E.N.Jr........LT.
JOSEPHS, A.T..........EM2c
JUROVATY, S.........MoMM2c
KIBBONS, C.B...........CTM
KIRSTEIN, A.E..........LT.
KNEIB, T.F..........MoMM3c
KRECKER, S.S..........MM2c
LAWSON, K.E............S1c
LEECY, R.A.............CTM
LEONARD, C.B...........S1c
LEWIS, W.T............ENS.
LUEDEMANN, F...........F1c
LYON, D.B.............RM2c
MACDONALD, R.S.........LT.
MAC INTYRE, J.C........F1c
MASINCUPP, B.T........RM3c
MERCELL, J.R..........TM1c
MUNTZ, R.W.............Y3c
OLSON, W.E.............S1c
ONGERTH, W.R..........GM2c
OOTHOUDT, M.D.........RM1c
PAULSEN, W.O...........CEM
PERKINS, R.E..........RM1c
PERRIN, I.C............CRM
PERRY, J.M.............F2c
PITTMAN, G.W..........CK2c
POLIKOWSKI, M.........RM3c
PORTER, W.W..........CMoMM
REED, F.E..............CEM
REICH, K.A............FC3c
REILLY, F.S............CSM
REINTHALER, R.H......FCS2c
RIDGEWAY, A.L.........RM1c
SATTERFIELD, H........EM3c
SCHUERMANN, L.B......CMoMM
SOUTIERO, A.E.........EM3c
SELIG, J.L............QM2c
SHAFFER, D.E...........Y1c
SHAW, B.F.............SC2c
SHEFCHEK, H.Jr........ENS.
SIMKO, W.A............EM2c
THOMMEN, H.R..........TM3c
TIEN, K.R.............TM3c
TILLER, P.S...........EM1c
TURNER, W.H.........LT.(JG)
WALL, W.R.............TM3c
WANSKY, R.W...........BM1c
WELLS, R.W............TM2c
WILLIAMS, M.L.........SC3c
ZIDZIUNAS, J.J......MoMM3c

TORPEDOMEN AT PLAY

TANG (SS 306)

TANG, under Cdr. R. H. O'Kane, set out from Pearl Harbor on 24 September 1944, to begin her fifth war patrol. On 27 September she topped off with fuel at Midway and left there the same day, heading for an area between the northwest coast of Formosa, and the China Coast.

In order to reach her area, TANG had to pass through narrow waters known to be heavily patrolled by the enemy. A large area streching northeast from Formosa was known to be mined by the enemy, and O'Kane was given the choice of making the passage north of Formosa alone, or joining a coordinated attack group (SILVERSIDES, TRIGGER, SALMON. under Commander Coye in SILVERSIDES) which was to patrol off northeast Formosa, and making the passage with them. TANG chose to make the passage alone and these vessels never heard from TANG, nor did any base, after she left Midway.

The story of TANG's sinking comes fron the report of her surviving Commanding Officer. A night surface attack was launched on 24 October 1944 against a transport which had previously been stopped in an earlier attack. The first torpedo was fired, and when it was observed to be running true, the second and last was loosed. It curved sharply to the left, broached, porpoised and circled. Emergency speed was called for and the rudder was thrown over. These measures resulted only in the torpedo striking the stern of TANG, rather than amidships.

The explosion was violent, and people as far forward as the control room received broken limbs. The ship went down by the stern with the after three compartments flooded. Of the nine officers and men on the bridge, three were able to swim through the night until picked up eight hours later. One officer escaped from the flooded conning tower, and was rescued with the others.

Cdr. R.H. O'Kane

The submarine came to rest on the bottom at 180 feet, and the men in her crowded forward as the after compartments flooded. Publications were burned, and all assembled to the forward room to escape. The escape was delayed by a Japanese patrol, which dropped charges, and started an electrical fire in the forward battery. Thirteen men escaped from the forward room, and by the time the last made his exit, the heat from the fire was so intense that the paint on the bulkhead was scorching, melting, and running down. Of the 13 men who escaped, only eight reached the surface, and of these but five were able to swim until rescued.

When the nine survivors were picked up by a destroyer escort, there were victims of TANG's previous sinkings on board, and they inflicted tortures on the men from TANG. With great humanity, O'Kane states, "When we realized that our clubbings and kickings were being administered by the burned, mutilated survivors of our own handiwork, we found we could take it with less prejudice."

The nine captives were retained by the Japanese in prison camps until the end of the war, and were treated by them in typical fashion. The loss of TANG by her own torpedo, the last one fired on the most successful patrol ever made by a U. S. submarine, was a stroke of singular misfortune. She is credited with having sunk 13 vessels for 107,324 tons of enemy shipping on this patrol, and her Commanding Officer has been awarded the Congressional Medal of Honor.

On her last patrol TANG fired twenty four torpedoes in four attacks. Twenty two torpedoes found their mark in enemy ships, sinking 13 of them; one missed, and the last torpedo, fired after a careful checkover, sank TANG. This vessel was awarded the Presidential Unit Citation twice during her career. Commander O'Kane has been called the Submarine Force's most outstanding officer; he served as Executive Officer of the very successful WAHOO before taking command of TANG.

In her five patrols, TANG is credited with sinking 31 ships, totalling 227,800 tons and damaging two for 4,100 tons. This record is unexcelled among American submarines. In her first patrol, spending February 1944 west of Truk and Saipan, she sank three freighters, a large tanker and a submarine tender. TANG's second patrol was in the area west of Palau, east of Davao and at Truk. She made no ship contacts worthy of attack, but at the latter island she rescued twenty two Navy airmen during a carrier based strike at Truk on 30 April-1 May 1944. This vessel's third patrol was in the East China and Yellow Seas. Here she sank six freighters, a tanker, and a large aircraft transport. She covered the waters along the southern coast of Honshu in August 1944. She sank a freighter, a large transport, a tanker and two patrol craft, while she damaged another freighter and small craft.

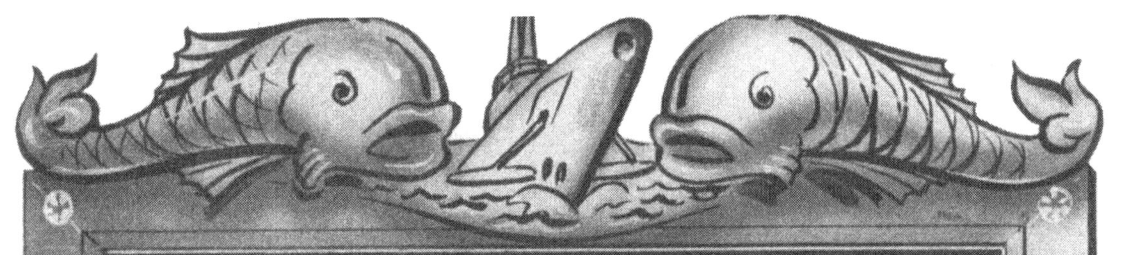

U.S.S. TANG

ACCARDY, J.G.........SM3c
ADAMS, R.F...........StM2c
ALLEN, D.D...........MoMM2c
ANDERSON, P.E.........TM3c
ANDRIOLO, C.L.........RM2c
ANTHONY, H............F1c
BALLINGER, W.F........CTM
BAUER, E.C............S1c
BEAUMONT, E.H.........LT.
BERGMAN, E.F..........RM1c
BISOGNO, F.N..........TM3c
BOUCHER, W.J..........TM3c
BRESETTE, B.V.........S1c
BUSH, J...............EM2c
*CAVERLY, F.M.........RT1c
CHIAVETTA, B..........S1c
CLARK, W.J............S1c
COFFIN, R.J...........EM3c
CULP, J.B.............CEM
DARIENZO, A.J.........EM2c
*DISILVA, J.B.........MoMM3c
*DECKER, C.O..........MoMM3c
DE LAPP, M.V..........CMoMM
DORSEY, W.E...........MoMM1c
ENOS, F.M.Jr..........LT.(JG)
ERICKSEN, L.H.........F1c
FELLICETTY, D.C.......Y3c
FINCKBONE, D.H........EM2c
*FLANAGAN, H.J........LT.(JG)
FLUKER, J.W...........TM1c
FOSTER, J.M...........TM1c
GALLOWAY, W.C.........TM2c
GORAB, G.J.Jr.........EM3c
GENTLE, T.E...........F1c
GREGG, O.D............S1c
HAINLINE, H.W.........S1c
HAWS, G.O.............MoMM2c
HARMS, F.G............MoMM2c
HENRY, J.P............F1c
HEUBECK, J.H..........LT.(JG)
HUDSON, A.L...........CMoMM
IJAMES, H.W...........S2c
IMWOLD, S.B...........MoMM2c
JENKINS, D.M..........S1c

JONES, S.W............CQM
KAISER, L.C...........MoMM3c
KANAGY, J.T...........EM1c
KASSUBE, J.T..........S1c
KEY, J.S..............SC3c
KNAPP, R.B............FCS3c
KROTH, R.J............LT.(JG)
LANE, L.R.............EM1c
LARSON, P.L...........CPhM
LEE, R.P..............RM3c
LEIBOLD, W.R..........CBM *
LLEWELLYN, L.H........RM3c
LONDON, C.W...........F1c
LOVELESS, C...........EM1c
LYTTON, E.............MoMM1c
MCMORROW, R.V.........MoMM2c
MCNABB, J.J...........F1c
NAROWANSKI, P.........TM3c
O'KANE, R.H...........CDR.C.O. *
PARKER, J.J...........CCS
PEARCE, B.C.Jr........ENS.
RAIFORD, R.M..........CK3c
REABUCK, F.J..........F1c
RECTOR, D.D...........GM3c
REINHARDT, E..........F1c
ROBERTS, J.L..........SC3c
ROBERTSON, G.L........MoMM2c
SAVADKIN, L...........LT. *
SMITH, S.G.Jr.........QM3c
SPRINGER, F.H.........LT.Exec.
STEPIEN, E.F..........F1c
SUNDAY, F.L...........EM3c
TRUKKE, H.O...........TM2c *
VAUGHN, P.B.Jr........Cox
WADSWORTH, C.W........TM3c
WALKER, H.M...........St3c
WEEKLEY, L.S..........CTM
WELCH, R.E............QM3c
WHITE, J.M............GM1c
WILLIAMS, W.H.........Y2c
WINES, P.T............LT.(JG)
WUKOVICH, G...........MoMM1c
ZOFCIN, G.............MoMM1c

* - Survivors

"Cdr. R.H.O'Kane, USN and 22 aviators rescued by USS TANG"

ESCOLAR (SS294)

ESCOLAR (Cdr. W. J. Millican) departed Pearl Harbor on 18 September 1944, to proceed to Midway to top off with fuel. There she joined CROAKER and PERCH and left on 23 September to conduct a coordinated patrol (ESCOLAR's first patrol) in the Yellow Sea north of 30°-00'N. Commander Millican was in command of this coordinated attack group, which was designated "Millican's Maurauders."

On 30 September, when ESCOLAR was estimated to be about north of the Bonin Islands, the following partial message was received from her "This from ESCOLAR X attacked with deck gun boat similar to ex Italian Peter George five OTYI- - - -". Although no further transmissions have ever been received by bases from ESCOLAR, who was forced to break off the transmission and the engagement with the gunboat at this time, the Commanding Officer of CROAKER has stated that she suffered no damage and was in frequent communication with PERCH and CROAKER until 17 October 1944.

PERCH reported that on 17 October she had received a message from ESCOLAR stating that she was in position 33°-44'N 127°-33'E, and was heading for Latitude 33°-44'N, Longitude 129°-06'E. Neither PERCH nor CROAKER could raise ESCOLAR by radio after this transmission was received.

Had ESCOLAR left her area on the scheduled date, she would have arrived at Midway about 13 November 1944. All attempts to contact ESCOLAR failed and she was reported on 27 November 1944 as presumed lost. It is assumed that she was lost about 17 October. Information supplied by the Japanese on anti-submarine attacks gives no clue as to the cause of her loss, but the Yellow Sea area is thought to have been mined. A course line plotted between the two positions given above does not cross any known Japanese mine lies, but positions of mines laid before April 1945 are not definitely located. The known minefields in Tsushima Strait were laid in April 1945. However, there were mines in the general area of ESCOLAR's predicted position, and the most likely explanation for her end at present is that she detonated a mine.

U.S.S. ESCOLAR

ABRAM, L.L..........MoMM2c
ANDERS, D.W...........RM3c
BABB, T................LT.
BAILEY, L.L............CEM
BALFE, D.L............TM2c
BECKER, F.E...........EM3c
BENDER, J.J.........PhM1c
BLAHA, F......LT.CDR.Exec.
BONES, R.E.............F1c
BONK, B.W..............S1c
BRABHAM, C.E...........CRM
BROECKER, G.J.........RT2c
BROUSKIE, F...........EM1c
BROWN, E.E.............F1c
CAHILL, J.M.........MoMM3c
CALABRESE, R.L........TM3c
CALDWELL, W.T.Jr......TM1c
CAMPBELL, K.S.........RM1c
CHEOSKY, M.J..........EM3c
CIFRODELLA, J.J.......TM2c
CLARY, J.W...........CMoMM
COLEMAN, D.E..........QM3c
CUMMINGS, J.M.......MoMM1c
DANIELS, L.C.Jr.......QM2c
ENNIS, J.F.............S1c
EVANS, B.............StM1c
FARRAR, R.L............LT.
FARWELL, J.C............CY
FINE, F.J.............TM2c
FOSTAIR, J.E..........QM2c
FOSTER, A.B...........GM2c
FOX, L.B..............RT1c
FULTON, D.A. MoMM1c
GANCARZ, W............EM1c
GLADING, D.H........MoMM3c
GORECKI, A.E...........CCS
HAHN, F.L.............TM3c
HAMPTON, C.L..........QM1c
HILL, C.J..............LT.
HORODYNSKI, E.S.......FC2c
JEFFREY, L.V..........ENS.
JOHNSON, J.G........MoMM3c
KELLAM, J.H...........EM2c
KILLOUGH, D.C.......MoMM1c
KOMES, H.B............SC2c
KRAUSE, F.B.Jr........SM1c
LARUE, V.J.............S1c
LATHAM, H.C.........LT.(JG)
LIEDER, A...........MoMM1c
LYONS, W.C.Jr.......MoMM2c
MASLOSKI, J............F1c
MC SLOSKEY, T.D.......RM2c
MILLER, S.D............CEM
MILLICAN, W.J.....CDR.C.O.
MORRIS, J.J............S1c
MUNSEL, J.M.........MoMM3c
NEWTON, R.B.Jr.........CTM
NORFORD, R.N...........F1c
O'CONNELL, J.A.Jr...MoMM1c
PENNINGTON, B.L......CMoMM
PHILLIPS, D.W..........F1c
RALEY, J.A...........StM2c
ROMOND, J.L.........MoMM3c
SEARIS, R.W.........LT.(JG)
SHIRAH, R.A...........EM3c
SLAVIK, J.A............F2c
SMITH, A.R.............S1c
SMITH, B.T.............F1c
SPOUST, D............Bkr3c
TOLARCHEK, A..........GM1c
TRENSCH, H............EM3c
TUCKER, J.B............S1c
TUCKER, T.R............F1c
TURNER, R.C...........EM2c
VALENTINO, R........MoMM2c
VELTEN, W.............TM3c
WALLACE, G.M..........TM1c
WELLS, N.P.............S1c
WHITEHOUSE, J.H.......ENS.
WYBROW, R.W...........SC3c
YAWORSKY, W...........TM3c
ZUMAR, A...............S1c

ALBACORE (SS 218)

ALBACORE with Lt. Cdr. H. R. Rimmer in command, left Pearl Harbor on 24 October 1944, topped off with fuel at Midway on 28 October, and departed there for her eleventh patrol the same day, never to be heard from again. Her area was northeast of Honshu and south of Hokkaido, and because of the danger of mineable waters, she was ordered to stay outside of waters less than 100 fathoms deep.

She was to depart her area at sunset on 5 December 1944, and was expected at Midway about 12 December. When she had not been seen nor heard from by 21 December despite the sharpest of lookouts for her, she was reported as presumed lost.

Enemy information available now indicates that ALBACORE perished by hitting a mine. The explosion occurred on 7 November 1944, in latitude 41°-49'N, longitude 141°-11'E while ALBACORE was submerged, and was witnessed by an enemy patrol craft. The craft reports having seen much heavy oil and bubbles, cork, bedding and various provisions after the explosion.

Prior to her loss, ALBACORE had been a very successful submarine, especially in her engagements with Japanese combat vessels. Her record of enemy combatant ships sunk is the best of any United States submarine. She sank a total of 13 ships, totaling 74,100 tons, and damaged five, for 29,400 tons, during her first ten patrols. She began her series of patrols with one at Truk in September 1942, damaging two freighters and a tanker. On her second patrol, near New Britain, ALBACORE sank a transport, and, on 18 December 1942, the Japanese light cruiser TENRYU. Her third patrol was in the Bismarck Archipelago; ALBACORE sank an escort vessel and a destroyer. The latter was OSHIO sunk near the New Guinea coast on 20 February 1943. During her fourth patrol again in the Bismarck-Solomons-area, ALBACORE was able to inflict no damage on the enemy herself, but she sent contact reports which

Lt.Cdr. H.R. Rimmer

enabled GRAYBACK to sink several enemy ships. In her fifth patrol, ALBACORE covered the same area and damaged a transport. She patrolled the Truk area on her sixth war run, sinking one freighter and damaging another.

ALBACORE's seventh and eighth war patrols were both in the area north of the Bismarck Archipelago during the period from mid-October 1943 to the end of February 1944. In her seventh patrol she sank a freighter and in her eighth a transport. In addition, during her eighth patrol on 14 January, ALBACORE sank the Japanese destroyer SAYANAMI. ALBACORE was ordered to patrol west of the Marianas and in the Palau area during the Allied invasion of these places in June 1944. On 19 June she intercepted a Japanese task force proceeding from Tawi Tawi anchorage, in the Sulu Archipelago, toward Saipan to engage our surface forces in the first Battle of the Philippine Sea. ALBACORE torpedoed and sank the aircraft carrier

TAIHO. In addition, she sank a small freighter on this ninth patrol. ALBACORE conducted her tenth patrol near the southern coast of Shikoku, Japan. Here she sank a medium freighter, a medium tanker and a large patrol craft. ALBACORE has been awarded the Presidential Unit Citation for her second, third, eighth and ninth patrols, the ones in which she sank enemy combatant vessels.

Lt. Cdr. H.R. Rimmer Receives Silver Star
From Adm. Lockwood 25 October 1944

U.S.S. ALBACORE

Name	Rate
BARBER, W.H.Jr.	S1c
BAUMER, K.R.	GM2c
BIGELOW, H.F.	ENS.
BLACKMON, E.B.	CPhM
BOWER, W.W.	LT.(JG)
BRANNAM, A.R.	MoMM2c
BURCH, H.H.	RT2c
CADO, N.J.	S1c
CARANO, J.J.	F1c
CARPENTER, C.L.	MoMM1c
CARPENTER, J.L.	StM2c
CARRACINO, P.C.	F1c
CHAPMAN, D.S.	S2c
CHILDRESS, D.	FCS3c
CHILDS, F.H.Jr.	TM1c
COLLOM, P.A.	TM2c
CRAYTON, A.C.	MoMM2c
CUGNIN, J.E.	TM3c
CULBERTSON, J.W.	EM3c
DAVIS, P.H.	EM2c
DAVIS, R.E.	GM3c
DAY, F.W.	MM3c
DELFONSO, J.	TM3c
DE WITT, J.L.	TM2c
DUNLAP, J.T.	MoMM1c
ESKEW, C.H.	RT3c
FORTIER, J.P.Jr.	ENS.
FULLILOVE, G.H.Jr.	S1c
GANT, J.W.	MoMM3c
GENNETT, J.P.	CEM
GIBSON, W.H.	SC1c
GILKESON, J.F.	LT.(JG)
HALL, C.C.	F1c
HARRELL, J.K.	QM3c
HILL, R.D.	SC1c
HUDGINS, A.D.	F2c
HUGHES, D.P.	TM3c
JOHNSON, B.P.	EM2c
JONES, S.P.	QM2c
KAPLAFKA, G.	S1c
KELLEY, N.Jr.	S2c
KINCAID, M.K.	SM1c
KINON, V.[illegible]	F1c
KRIZANEK, J.M.	MoMM2c
KRUGER, A.S.	S2c
LANG, W.E.Jr.	LT.
LITTLE, J.A.	EM3c
MANFUL, K.W.	S1c
mC KENNA, P.K.	S1c
MERCER, J.N.	CEM
MOSS, L.D.	GM2c
NAUDACK, R.J.	TM3c
NEVAREZ, E.	S1c
NORTHAM, J.H.	S1c
NYSTROM, F.R.	S2c
O'BRIEN, R.J.	F1c
PETERSON, E.H.	CTM
PIERINGER, C.F.Jr.	TM2c
PORTER, J.T.	MoMM1c
REED, J.W.Jr.	S1c
RILEY, F.A.	LT.
RIMMER, H.R.	LT.CDR.C.O.
ROBERTS, A.B.	CQM
ROWE, J.E.	S1c
SHOENTHAL, P.	CRM
SISK, G.M.	SC2c
SPARATT, J.L.	MoMM2c
STANTON, A.L.	CMoMM
STARACE, R.J.	EM2c
ST CLAIR, H.W.	MoMM3c
STEPHENSON, J.H.	EM2c
STRATTAN, M.C.	Y2c
TANNER, E.R.	MoMM1c
TESSER, W.G.	EM3c
TOMICH, P.R.	RM3c
TRAYNOR, C.E.Jr.	LT.(JG)
WALKER, T.T.	LT.Exec.
WEISENFLUH, E.	EM3c
WELCH, J.D.	EM3c
WEST, R.A.	MoMM2c
WILLIANS, W.J.	MoMM2c
WILMOTT, L.A.	F1c
WOOD, D.R.	RM2c
WRIGHT, S.M.	StM2c

Albacore (SS-218) at Mare Island, Calif.

GROWLER (SS215)

Early in November 1944, GROWLER, HAKE and HARDHEAD were operating together west of the Philippine group as a coordinated search and attack group under command of Commander T. B. Oakley, Jr., Commanding Officer, GROWLER. The patrol was GROWLER's eleventh. On 7 November, GROWLER reported having made temporary repairs to her SJ radar which made it usable, but that she urgently needed spare parts for it. A future rendezvous was arranged with BREAM for the purpose of delivering the parts.

In the early morning hours of 8 November, GROWLER, then in 13°-21'N, 119°-32'E, made SJ radar contact on an enemy target group, and reported it to HARDHEAD. Commander Oakley directed HARDHEAD to track and attack from the convoy's port bow. Shortly thereafter, HARDHEAD made contact with both the target group and GROWLER. After about an hour had passed HAKE heard two distant explosions of undetermined character, and HARDHEAD heard an explosion which sounded like a torpedo. At the same time, the targets zigged away from GROWLER. Shortly after, HARDHEAD heard three distant depth charges explode.

A little over an hour after these explosions, HARDHEAD attacked the target from the port bow, obtained three or four hits, and HAKE saw a tanker sink. HARDHEAD was subjected to a severe counter attack from which it emerged undamaged, while HAKE was worked over thoroughly later in the morning. All attempts to contact GROWLER after this attack were unsuccessful, and she has never been seen or heard from since. The rendezvous with BREAM for the delivery of SJ spare parts was not accomplished. Since GROWLER had tracked targets by radar for at least an hour, it appears that her temporary SJ repairs must have been satisfactory.

Although Japanese records mention no

T. B. Oakley, Jr.

anti-submarine attacks at this time and place, it is evident that depth charges were dropped in the vicinity of GROWLER, but in the absence of more conclusive evidence the cause of her loss must be described as unknown. The Japanese admit that a tanker was sunk that night which checks with HARDHEAD's sinking. HARDHEAD was heavily depth charged following her own attack and later that morning HAKE was expertly worked over presumably by the same escorts. This leads to the belief that if GROWLER were sunk by depth charging it was at hands of a skillful anti-submarine group.

The explosion described by HARDHEAD as "possibly a torpedo" may have been a depth charge or a torpedo explosion. It is unlikely that a torpedo hit was made on the convoy at this time because if the tanker had been hit she probably would either have burst into flame, as she subsequently did when hit by HARDHEAD, or slowed down if hit in the engine room. She did neither, nor was there any evidence that any of the three escorts were hit. However, since only three subsequent explosions were heard by HAKE, and a number of depth charges generally are dropped in an accurate or persistent anti-submarine attack, a number of possibilities exist as to GROWLER's end.

She could have been sunk as the result of a premature or circular run of her own torpedo, and the three depth charges heard by HAKE may have been only a token attack by the escort. Although there was a quarter moon, the night was somewhat misty, and she might have made the approach at radar depth. If so, she could have been rammed, thus making it unnecessary for the escort to drop many depth charges. She could have been caught at either radar or periscope depth and the anti-submarine group, evidently a good one, might have verified the results of their attack immediately. An escort could have hit her with a torpedo and only dropped a few depth charges to insure a kill. In any event, sinking by her own torpedoes is only a slight possibility. It is doubtful whether a report by the escorts of this convoy would help to decide this question. In the cases of TULLIBEE and TANG, where surviviors' statements leave little doubt that destruction was by their own torpedoes, the Japanese ships which picked up survivors claimed to have sunk the submarines themselves.

GROWLER was the ship commanded by Cdr. Howard W. Gilmore on her fourth patrol when, mortally wounded by machine gun fire after GROWLER had rammed a patrol vessel, he ordered the ship submerged while he lay on the bridge. The Commanding Officer, the assistant officer of the deck and a lookout were lost, and Cdr. Gilmore was posthumously awarded the Congressional Medal of Honor.

During her first ten patrols GROWLER sank 17 ships, for a total tonnage of 74,900 and damaged 7 ships, for 34,100 tons. Her first patrol began in June 1942, and was in Aleutian waters. She began her career by sinking a destroyer and severely damaging two. The one sunk was ARARE, sunk while at anchor on 5 July 1942. GROWLER's second patrol was off Formosa; here she sank a large tanker, two medium freighters, a transport and sampan. In her third patrol, this ship sighted eight vessels, but none could be closed for an attack. The area was near Truk. GROWLER's fourth patrol was on the traffic lanes from Truk to Rabaul. She sank a freighter and a large gunboat, also damaging a second freighter. The fight with the gunboat was the incident which cost the Commanding Officer and two other men their lives.

GROWLER's fifth patrol, in the Bismarck Archipelago, was productive of but two attack opportunities; she sank a medium freighter and damaged a large freighter. From mid-July to mid-September 1943 GROWLER made her sixth patrol in the same area as her fifth, but was unable to do any damage to the enemy, having only one opportunity to attack. She returned to this area for her seventh patrol, but this run was cut short by battery and generator difficulties, and no attacks were made. In March and part of April of 1944, GROWLER made her eighth patrol in the East China Sea area. In this patrol she sank a small patrol craft and damaged a medium freighter. GROWLER covered the Marianas, the Eastern Philippines and the Luzon Strait areas on her ninth patrol, and was credited with sinking a large tanker and damaging a destroyer escort. She patrolled the Luzon and Formosa Straits in her tenth war patrol. She sank a large tanker, a freighter, a destroyer, a coast defense vessel, and an unidentified escort type vessel. She also damaged two more freighters. The destroyer she sank was SHIKINAMI, sent to the bottom on 12 September, while the coast defense vessel was HIRATO, sunk in the same day.

S.D. Miller, GM1/c being presented Letter of Commendation with Ribbon

U.S.S. GROWLER

ABEL, J.H............TM1c
ARCHER, H.W..........EM2c
BAKER, H.C...........S1c
BEATTY, T.M..........GM3c
BERGFELD, W.V........EM1c
BLACKSTON, H.H.......S2c
BOOKER, W.D..........TM2c
BOONE, C.R..........CMoMM
BRIDGE, R.S.........RM2c
CARR, W.K...........ENS.
CHAMBLIN, R.L.Jr.....QM2c
CLARK, L.C........MoMM3c
CLEVELAND, B........St3c
DALLMAN, G.B.........F1c
DARBY, J.A........MoMM1c
DAUGHTREY, G.P......FCS2c
DAWSON, F.E.........EM1c
DURAND, A.L.Jr.......F1c
ERIKSON, R.D.........F1c
FERRARIO, A........CMoMM
FLIPPENS, W........StM2c
FREDMAN, C.E......MoMM1c
FRYER, A.J..........EM2c
GEORGE, H.A..........F1c
GREGORY, W.M.....LT.(JG)
HAKANSON, R.E.......TM2c
HARRIS, R...........TM3c
HEALD, H.F...........S1c
HEDRICK, W.E........SC2c
HICKEY, W.C.......MoMM2c
HOPE, R.E...........TM3c
JACOBS, A.M.........EM3c
JEWETT, G.W......LT.(JG)
JOHNSON, L.S.....LT.(JG)
KACZMAREK, H.A.......Y3c
KUBA, D.J.........MoMM1c
LADERMAN, R.S.......RT2c
LANE, R.E...........RM1c
LEVEILLE, M.P.....MoMM1c
LORIO, E.P...........F1c
LYNCH, G.............S1c
MADDUX, J.H.........TM1c
MANESS L.B...........CEM
MANNING, W.S......MoMM2c
MASON, R.K.Jr....LT.Exec.
MCLAUGHLIN, J.J.....QM3c
MCMULLEN, L.R.......TM2c
MELANCON, C.M.....MoMM2c
METZLER, A.........FCS3c
MILLER, D.C.........GM3c
MINKLE, A.J..........F1c
MORRISON, W.........EM2c
NAYLOR, N.W..........LT.
NATOV, B............RT2c
NIXON, C.F...........F1c
OAKLEY, T.B.Jr...CDR.C.O.
ORTH, L.R...........SC1c
OWEN, A.D...........RM2c
PADILLA, J...........S2c
PARUS, H.R.Jr........S2c
PICARD, R.J.......MoMM2c
POST, E.W...........TM3c
RATNECHT, C.H.....MoMM3c
READ, E.P..........CMoMM
RHODES, H.E..........S1c
ROTHENBERGER, E.W....RM3c
SCHULZ, K.G..........Y2c
SEBESTYN, P.Jr......TM3c
SHAY, C.O............S1c
SIMMONS, D.G........RT2c
SMITH, W.D.......LT.(JG)
SMITH, W.L...........CTM
STEVANOVICH, N.L....QM3c
STOINER, S.J.........S1c
STUBBLEFIELD, J.W...CMoMM
SUBA, C.F............S1c
TANNER, J.A.......MoMM2c
THIGPEN, D.T.........F1c
THOMAS, F.P..........LT.
TULLIER, R.B.........F1c
VAIL, P.F...........EM2c
VECERE, R...........EM3c
WELCH, R.D..........EM2c
WETERINGS, R.L.......S1c
WORKMAN, C.A......MoMM3c

Damage to GROWLER on Fourth Patrol, and A New Bow
Being Hoisted Into Place at Brisbane, Australia

SCAMP (SS277)

Leaving Pearl Harbor on 16 October 1944, SCAMP (Cdr. J. C. Hollingsworth) headed for Midway, topped off with fuel there, and departed that place for her eighth patrol on 21 October 1944. SCAMP was to patrol in the vicinity of the Bonin Islands. On 8 November, her area was changed to the vicinity of 29°-00'N, 141°-00'E.

On 9 November, SCAMP was told to stay clear of the Bonins area south of 28°N during B-29 raids and she acknowledged, saying she was in 28°-44'N, 141°-44'E, and had made no torpedo attacks. This was the last communication received from SCAMP. In order to provide rescue services for downed aviators during Saipan-based B-29 assaults on Tokyo, SCAMP was ordered to lifeguard duty on 14 November. She was told to proceed to a point just east of the peninsula which forms the eastern boundary of Toyko Bay, on Honshu. Between that date and 26 November 1944, numerous messages were sent to SCAMP which required no acknowledgement, thus rendering it impossible to tell whether she received any or all of them.

On 29 November 1944, information was received of an enemy minefield in the vicinity of Inubo Saki, a point on the previously mentioned peninsula, and all submarines in that area were warned. Since all transmissions to SCAMP after 9 November 1944 remained unacknowledged, and she had not appeared by 21 December 1944, she was reported as presumed lost on war patrol in enemy waters.

Since the end of the war, the following facts have been learned from Japanese sources. On 11 November 1944, a Japanese patrol plane bombed what appeared to be oil trails left by a submarine, in 33°-38'N, 141°-00'E. A coast defense vessel was led to the scene by the plane and dropped some seventy depth charges in three runs on the target whereupon a large oil pool appeared.

J. C. Hollingsworth

The position of the attack is one in which SCAMP might be expected to be on 11 November, in proceeding toward her lifeguard station. On 13 November GREENLING, herself on a lifeguard station, contacted a ship at 29°-41'N, 140°-10'E. Due to the nature of radar interference, GREENLING thought that her contact was on SCAMP, although she was unable to sight anything.

On 16 November two attacks were made by the Japanese, one in 32°-10'N, 139°-30'E, the other in 29°-21'N, 141°-30'E. Amplifying data on these attacks reveal that on the latter attack, "Great explosive sounds came as a result of this attack". It would seem then, that SCAMP was attacked several times during her period of lifeguard duty. Whether she was badly damaged and withdrawing from the Japanese coast at the time of the last two attacks, is impossible to say. No attack cited here ties in with any anti-submarine attacks reported by submarines returning from patrol. It is probable that damage to SCAMP became progressively more serious as she absorbed each successive attack, and she may have been withdrawing from the Empire without transmission facilities when the end came.

SCAMP, in the seven patrols completed before her loss, sank six ships, totaling 49,000 tons, and damaged eight, for 40,400 tons. Her first patrol was in the southern approaches of the Japanese Empire in March 1943. Plagued by poor torpedo performance, she could only damage a tanker and two freighters. In the Bismarcks-Solomons area on her second patrol, SCAMP sank a large freighter. The same area was the scene of her third patrol, which netted SCAMP a submarine and a large tanker, both damaged. SCAMP's fourth patrol was in the same area as the previous two; this time she sank a freighter and a freighter-transport, and damaged a destroyer escort.

On her fifth patrol this ship covered the Truk-Kavieng traffic lanes. She sank a freighter-transport , and damaged a heavy cruiser and a transport. Her sixth patrol, in the same area from mid-December 1943 to February 1944 resulted in the sinking of a single large tanker. In her seventh patrol, conducted in the New Guinea - Palau - Mindanao area, SCAMP sank a small trawler by gunfire. During this patrol, SCAMP was severely damaged by a close enemy aircraft bomb, and was saved only by the heroic work of her Commanding Officer and crew.

U.S.S. SCAMP

ABAD, R.M..............RM2c
ADAMS, J.D..............S1c
ANDERSON, H.E.........TM2c
BARLOW, A.W.............F1c
BARRIOS, I.F........MoMM2c
BASS, O...............StM2c
BATH, C.E...............LT.
BAYSA, P.F.............CS2c
BLANKENSHIP, A.L......ENS.
BOWAN, H.A.............EM1c
BRANDT, A.F.............CRM
BRAZEE, H.E............EM2c
BURNS, W.D.Jr.......MoMM2c
CAPPEL, R.L............EM3c
CARTEE, M.A.............Y1c
CARY, R.L...........MoMM1c
CERVENY, V.............TM2c
CHAPMAN, W.W...........GM1c
CLAGUE, G.C.........MoMM2c
COGAN, A.B..............S2c
COLLINS, W.W...........ENS.
COTT, G.F...............F1c
CRAWFORD, R.S.......MoMM3c
CUSTER, B.C.............S2c
DIENNO, B.S.............S1c
DI NICOLA, O.J..........S2c
DUCKWORTH, D.F......MoMM1c
DZIAMBA, A.............SC1c
ECKHARDT, G.H.......LT.(JG)
FELBER, D.E.............F1c
FERGUSON, J.R...........F1c
FOJTIK, J.P.........MoMM2c
GLODOWSKI, C.F..........S1c
GRAHAM, R.N............TM3c
GRAPHIA, A.J...........SC3c
HAGEN, T.A..............S1c
HAIGLER, G.W...........EM1c
HEGMANN, R.C............F2c
HILL, R.J...........MoMM2c
HITTSON, J.F...........EM1c
HOLLINGSWORTH, J.C.CDR.C.O
HOUCHEN, N.P..........FCS3c
HOWELL, J.W............EM3c
IVEY, W................EM2c
JANISH, F.M............RT1c
JOHNSON, A.H............CQM
JONES, C.A..............S1c
JONES, E.R.Jr.......MoMM3c
KUSHNER, S..........MoMM1c
LANDES, C.O............EM3c
LANGDON, C.N...........TM1c
LYNN, C.W..............RM3c
MARK, D.A..............RM3c
MARKHAM, J.T............F1c
MC CLUNNY, R.L..........S1c
MC KEE, E.O.........MoMM3c
MK KINNEY, E.W.........RT3c
MC LAUGHLIN, W.A.......SM1c
MC NEILL, J.R...........CEM
MILLS, H.F..............CTM
MOORE, E.S.............ENS.
PAPPAS, J.M............QM2c
PENROSE, R.W...........SC1c
PRILLER, C.M...........CPhM
RASMUSSEN, R.C.Jr.......F1c
RIDDLE, E.D............TM3c
RODRIGUEZ, F.W..........S1c
SAVAGE, J.H............TM3c
SHAFFER, W.L............LT.
SIMPSON, J.............TM2c
SMITH, E.W..........MoMM3c
SPROUSE, J.M.Jr.........S1c
STEINBRINK, E.Z.........F1c
STEINMANN, J.W.........TM1c
SUTHERLAND, T.S.LT.CDR.Exec.
SWICK, C.O.............RT2c
THOMPSON, P.R.........CMoMM
TINSLEY, E.L........MoMM3c
VRANCICH, W............GM3c
WARD, A.L...........MoMM2c
WAYTASZIK, E.J.........EM1c
WICKHAM, M.F..........CMoMM
WILKINSIN, T.H..........LT.

SCAMP Comming Into Pearl Harbor

SWORDFISH (SS193)

SWORDFISH, under Cdr. K. E. Montross, left Pearl Harbor on 22 December 1944, to carry on her thirteenth patrol in the vicinity of Nansei Shoto. She topped off with fuel at Midway on 26 December and left that day for her area. In addition to her regular patrol, SWORDFISH was to conduct photographic reconnaissance of Okinawa, for preparation of the Okinawa Campaign.

On 2 January, SWORDFISH was ordered to delay carrying out her assigned tasks in order to keep her clear of the Nansei Shoto area until completion of carrier based air strikes which were scheduled. She was directed to patrol the general vicinity of 30°-00'N, 132°-00'E until further orders were received. In the last communication received from SWORDFISH, she acknowledged receipt of these orders on 3 January.

On 9 January 1945, SWORDFISH was directed to proceed to the vicinity of Okinawa to carry out her special mission. It was estimated that the task would not take more than seven days after arrival on station, which she should have reached on 11 January. Upon completion of her mission, SWORDFISH was to proceed to Saipan, or to Midway if she was unable to transmit by radio. Since neither place had seen her by 15 February, and repeated attempts to raise her by radio had failed, she was reported as presumed lost on that date.

In the report of her loss, mention was made that KETE, which at the time was patrolling the vicinity of Okinawa, reported that on the morning of 12 January she contacted a submarine by radar. It was believed that contact was with SWORDFISH since it was in 27°-00'N, 128°-40'E. Four hours later KETE heard heavy depth charging from this area, and it was believed that this attack might have been the cause of SWORDFISH's loss.

Japanese information on anti-submarine

K. E. Montross

attacks does not mention the attack heard by KETE on 12 January, and records no attacks in which SWORDFISH is likely to have been the victim. However, it is now known that there were many mines planted around Okinawa, since the Japanese were expecting an Allied invasion of that Island. The majority of the mines were planted close in. It is considered about equally likely that SWORDFISH was sunk by depth charge attack before she reached Okinawa for her special mission or that she was lost to a mine at that place.

SWORDFISH, in the twelve patrols before her fatal thirteenth, sank twenty-one ships, amounting to 113,100 tons, and damaged an additional eight, totaling 45,800 tons. Her first patrol began the day after the attack on Pearl Harbor, and was conducted west of the Philippines. SWORDFISH sank four freighters, varying from 3,900 tons to 9,400 tons, and damaged a fifth. At the time, this was the most successful patrol in the war. She conducted her second patrol in the lesser Philippine group and among the small islands between Celebes and New Guinea. Here she sank three medium freighters and a tanker. She also evacuated President Quezon, his family, Vice President Osmena, Chief Justice Santos, and three officers in the Philippine Army from Corregidor and took them to Panay, where they boarded a motor tender. SWORDFISH returned to Manila Bay and evacuated eleven more Philippine officials. SWORDFISH's primary mission on her third patrol was to deliver 40 tons of supplies to the beleaguered Corregidor. However, on 10 April 1942 ComSubsAF told SWORDFISH to neglect her special mission and patrol offensively. SWORDFISH made no attacks on this patrol, but did perform reconnaissance of several islands.

The South China Sea area was the scene of this ship's fourth patrol, and she sank a freighter and a tanker, while she damaged two freighters. She returned to the South China Sea for her fifth patrol, but did no damage to the enemy. SWORDFISH went to the area west of Bougainville for her sixth patrol, and sank a medium freighter and damaged a second freighter. She went again to the Solomons for her seventh patrol and sank a freighter. On her eighth patrol, SWORDFISH covered the Palau-Truk-Rabaul areas during August and September 1943. Here she sank a freighter and a transport, while damaging a freighter-transport. Her ninth patrol was made south of Japan, but she made no attacks, and the patrol was cut short by material defects in SWORDFISH. On her tenth patrol, in the same area as her ninth, SWORDFISH sank a freighter-transport, and two medium freighters.

This ship covered the Marianas on her eleventh patrol; she damaged two freighters. On her twelfth patrol, conducted in the Bonins, SWORDFISH sank a freighter and two small trawlers, while she damaged a third trawler. In addition, during this patrol, on 9 June 1944, SWORDFISH sank the Japanese destroyer MATSUKAZE in a night submerged attack as the enemy ship was bearing down for an attack. SWORDFISH was awarded the Navy Unit Commendation for the period of her first, second and fourth patrols.

Ship's Co. U.S.S. SWORDFISH at the End of Their Tenth War Patrol

U.S.S. SWORDFISH

ABRAHAMSON, A..........CCS
AROLD, R.G..........MoMM2c
BAKER, G.S..........MoMM1c
BASTA, J.J............RM1c
BATES, M...............F1c
BAUGHMAN, D.S. JR...LT.CDR.
BENBENNICK, C.J........S1c
BILLY, M............MoMM2c
BLANCHARD, J.R.L......RM3c
BAECKLER, D.........PhOM3c
BLEASDELL, L.J......MoMM2c
BOGDAN, W.C.........MoMM2c
BRALEY, A.E.........MoMM3c
BROWN, R.J............SC1c
CAULEY, R.M.Jr..........CRT
CLARK, A.D............EM2c
CONNORS, T.J..........TM3c
COX, M.E.Jr...........RM3c
DALY, R.F...............LT.
DAVIS, H.W EM2c
DELLADONNA, J.V.........LT.
DILLON, W.............TM2c
DRAGA, G.K.............S1c
DUNCAN, L.H...........EM2c
DUNTON, E.W.Sr......MoMM1c
ECHOLS, L.O..........Bkr3c
EDWARDS, G.V..........TM2c
EMMINGHAM, R.L........EM3c
FAUSSET, E.R..........GM3c
FEISS, K.F.............F1c
FORSYTHE, E.J.........TM1c
FOWLER, J.G............S1c
FUNK, N...............EM1c
GALLEY, E.A.Jr........SM2c
GAMBRELL, D.E.Jr......QM2c
GARZA, E............MoMM3c
GERAGHTY, B.J.Jr.......S1c
GILFILLIAN, H.M.....MoMM2c
GRAF, J.V...........MoMM1c
GRAHAM, G.P...........RM3c
GRANDY, W.P..........StM1c
HAFTER, R.L...........EM1c
HALL, C.E..............CEM
HASERODT, R.W.......MoMM1c
HASKINS, W.C..........EM3c
HAYNES, J.E...........TM3c
HOLLAND, R..........MoMM2c
HOOPES, R.D.Jr..........LT.
HRYNKO, F.A.........MoMM3c
JANES, R.L.........LT.(JG)
JOHNSON, R.E........MoMM3c
JOHNSON, S.J........PHOM3c
KELLEY, J.R............F1c
KIRK, V................St3c
KOHLER, W.E.........MoMM3c
KREMER, R.B...........MM2c
KROLL, R.E............TM3c
LAUDERDALE, H.O........F1c
LINDSAY, D.C........MoMM3c
LOONEY, G.A..............CY
LO PRESTI, R...........S1c
MADDEN, J.J.Hr........TM3c
MC CAFFREY, M.F.......RT3c
MAYFIELD, J.M.........EM2c
MARVIN, P..............ENS.
MEACHAM, W.T.Jr......FCS2c
MONTROSS, K E......CDR.C O.
PENCE, K.E............GM2c
PETTY, F..............BM2c
PLOURD, G.R...........PhM1c
POLLARD, C.L...........ENS.
PRESTON, E.W.Jr........S1c
PYE, J.B......LT.CDR. Exec.
ROBINSON, H.N.Jr....MoMM3c
RUSSELL, W.E...........CQM
SISKANINETZ, W..........Cox
SKELDON, J.A..........QM3c
SLATER, C.F..........CMoMM
SOFFES, M...........MoMM2c
SPENCER, F.H.Jr.......EM3c
STATTON, W.G........MoMM1c
STONE, H.A............TM2c
SCHWENDENER, K.D........LT.
TARBOK, F.A...........EM3c
TAYLOR, J.F............S1c
VAN HORN, E.K.........TM3c
WAGNER, A.J...........TM2c
WILLIAMS, T.A.........TM1c
WREN, J.E.............EM3c

BARBEL (SS316)

BARBEL, commanded by Lt. Cdr. C. L. Raguet, departed Fremantle for her fourth war patrol on 5 January 1945. She proceeded to Exmouth Gulf, conducting training exercises enroute. Having topped off with fuel, she left Exmouth Gulf on 8 January, and proceeded via Lombok Strait, Java Sea and Karimata Strait to patrol an area in the South China Sea. At dark on 16 February she was to leave her area and commence her return to Fremantle.

On 13 January, BARBEL was directed to join BLUEGILL and BREAM in covering the western approaches to Balabac Strait. On 27 January she was ordered to form a wolfpack with PERCH and GABILAN and cover the western approaches to Balabac and southern entrance to Palawan Passage.

On 3 February 1945 BARBEL sent a message to TUNA, BLACKFIN and GABILAN reporting numerous aircraft contacts daily. BARBEL had been attacked by aircraft three times with depth charges, and would transmit a message "tomorrow night" giving information. This was the last contact with BARBEL. TUNA reported on 6 February 1945 that she had been unable to contact BARBEL for 48 hours, and that she had ordered her to rendezvous at 7°-30'N, 115°-30'E on 7 February. The rendezvous was not accomplished and TUNA reported her search unsuccessful on 7 February 1945.

Japanese records indicate that on 4 February 1945 a plane attacked a submarine in position 7°-49.5' N, 116°-47.5' E scoring one hit near the bridge with one of two bombs dropped. It appears almost certain that this attack sank BARBEL.

C.L. Raguet

BARBEL sank 10 ships for 55,200 tons and damaged two ships for 14,000 tons during her three completed patrols. Her first was made in the Nansei Shoto chain. She sank three medium freighters, a large freighter of 19,600 tons, and a large tanker. In the same area on her second patrol, BARBEL sank a freighter and two escort vessels. She also damaged another freighter and a tanker. During her third patrol, conducted in the South China Sea, BARBEL sank two medium freighters.

USS Barbel, down the ways

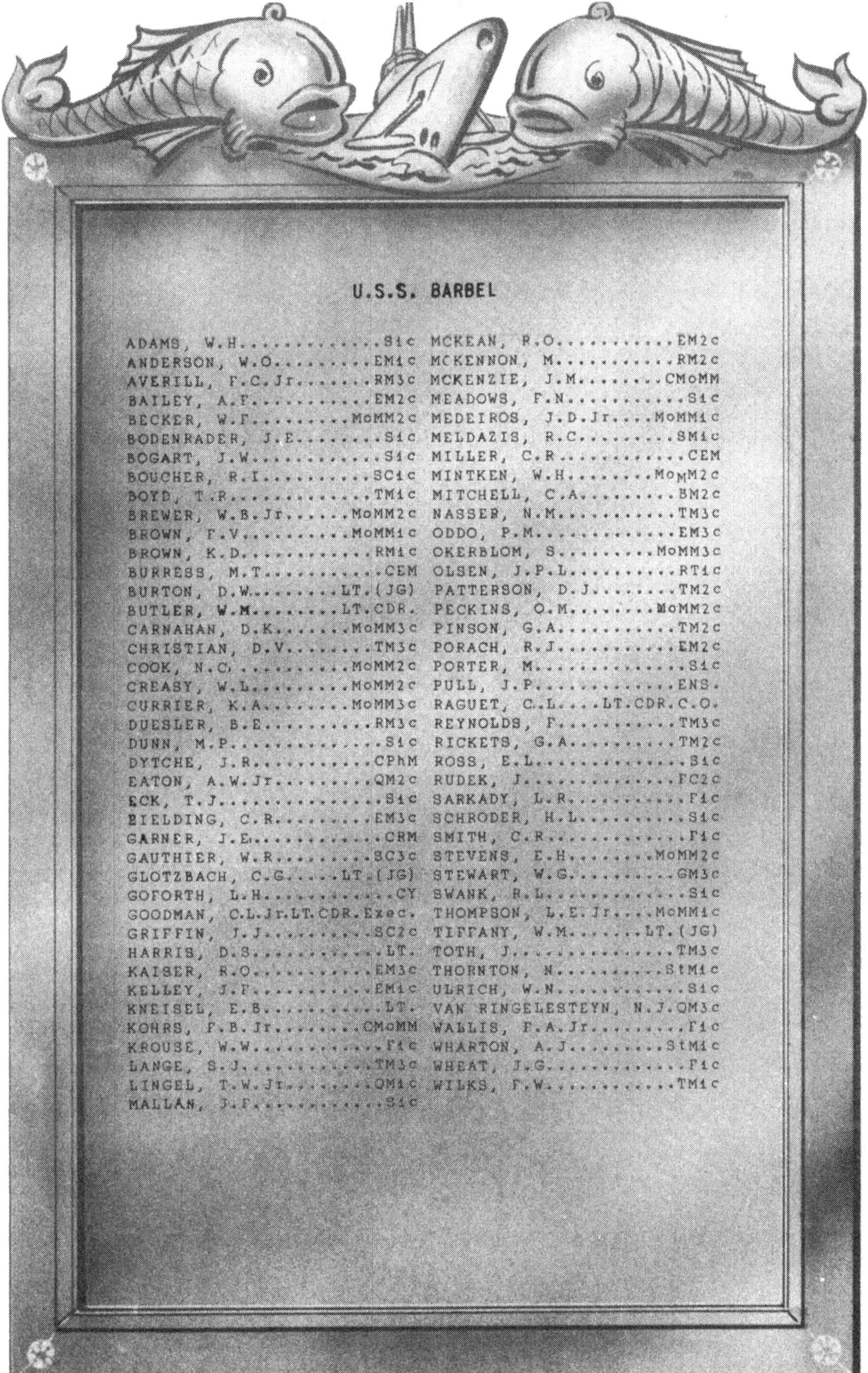

U.S.S. BARBEL

ADAMS, W.H.............S1c
ANDERSON, W.O..........EM1c
AVERILL, F.C.Jr........RM3c
BAILEY, A.F............EM2c
BECKER, W.F.........MoMM2c
BODENRADER, J.E.........S1c
BOGART, J.W.............S1c
BOUCHER, R.I...........SC1c
BOYD, T.R..............TM1c
BREWER, W.B.Jr......MoMM2c
BROWN, F.V..........MoMM1c
BROWN, K.D.............RM1c
BURRESS, M.T............CEM
BURTON, D.W.........LT.(JG)
BUTLER, W.M.........LT.CDR.
CARNAHAN, D.K.......MoMM3c
CHRISTIAN, D.V.........TM3c
COOK, N.C...........MoMM2c
CREASY, W.L.........MoMM2c
CURRIER, K.A........MoMM3c
DUESLER, B.E...........RM3c
DUNN, M.P...............S1c
DYTCHE, J.R............CPhM
EATON, A.W.Jr..........QM2c
ECK, T.J................S1c
FIELDING, C.R..........EM3c
GARNER, J.E.............CRM
GAUTHIER, W.R..........SC3c
GLOTZBACH, C.G......LT.(JG)
GOFORTH, L.H.............CY
GOODMAN, C.L.Jr.LT.CDR.Exec.
GRIFFIN, J.J...........SC2c
HARRIS, D.S.............LT.
KAISER, R.O............EM3c
KELLEY, J.F............EM1c
KNEISEL, E.B............LT.
KOHRS, F.B.Jr..........CMoMM
KROUSE, W.W.............F1c
LANGE, S.J.............TM3c
LINGEL, T.W.Jr.........QM1c
MALLAN, J.F.............S1c

MCKEAN, R.O............EM2c
MCKENNON, M............RM2c
MCKENZIE, J.M.........CMoMM
MEADOWS, F.N............S1c
MEDEIROS, J.D.Jr....MoMM1c
MELDAZIS, R.C..........SM1c
MILLER, C.R.............CEM
MINTKEN, W.H........MoMM2c
MITCHELL, C.A..........BM2c
NASSER, N.M............TM3c
ODDO, P.M..............EM3c
OKERBLOM, S.........MoMM3c
OLSEN, J.P.L...........RT1c
PATTERSON, D.J.........TM2c
PECKINS, O.M........MoMM2c
PINSON, G.A............TM2c
PORACH, R.J............EM2c
PORTER, M...............S1c
PULL, J.P...............ENS.
RAGUET, C.L....LT.CDR.C.O.
REYNOLDS, F............TM3c
RICKETS, G.A...........TM2c
ROSS, E.L...............S1c
RUDEK, J...............FC2c
SARKADY, L.R............F1c
SCHRODER, H.L...........S1c
SMITH, C.R..............F1c
STEVENS, E.H........MoMM2c
STEWART, W.G...........GM3c
SWANK, R.L..............S1c
THOMPSON, L.E.Jr....MoMM1c
TIFFANY, W.M........LT.(JG)
TOTH, J................TM3c
THORNTON, N...........StM1c
ULRICH, W.N.............S1c
VAN RINGELESTEYN, N.J.QM3c
WALLIS, F.A.Jr..........F1c
WHARTON, A.J..........StM1c
WHEAT, J.G..............F1c
WILKS, F.W.............TM1c

Air-Sea Rescue - Painting by Vandis

KETE (SS369)

Departing Guam on 1 March 1945, KETE (Lt. Cdr. Edward Ackerman) headed for her second patrol in the vicinity of the Nansei Shoto Island Chain. In addition to performing a normal patrol, KETE had orders to submit special weather reports, and to carry out rescue service during an air strike by carrier based planes.

On the night of 10 March 1945, KETE reported having sunk three medium sized freighters on the previous night. She reported on the night of 14 March that she had fired four torpedoes which missed a small enemy cable laying vessel, and that she had only three torpedoes remaining aboard. In view of the small number of torpedoes left, KETE was directed to depart her area on 20 March, and proceed to Pearl for refit, stopping at Midway enroute for fuel. On 19 March, she acknowledged receipt of these orders. On 20 march she sent in a special weather report from position latitude 29°-38'N, longitude 130°-02'E. This was the last message received from her. At normal cruising speed she should have arrived at Midway about 31 March 1945. When she was neither sighted nor heard from by 16 April 1945, she was reported as presumed lost.

Japanese information concerning anti-submarine attacks gained since the end of the war gives no positive evidence to what happened to KETE; none of the attacks on U. S. submarines occurring within the period from 20 March to 31 March 1945, was made in a position in which KETE was likely to be.

There were a few minelines in the Nansei Shoto Chain, but since KETE was already east of the islands at the time of her last message on 20 March and was heading home, loss through a mine is considered highly improbable. It is now known that a number of enemy submarines were in the area through which KETE was required to pass enroute to Midway. RO-41 was sunk east of Okinawa by a U. S. destroyer on 31 March 1945, and two other Japanese submarines were sunk southeast of Okinawa near this date. Conditions attendant to KETE's loss suggest the likehood that one of these submarines might have torpedoed and sunk her and been unable to report the attack before being sunk. Thus, KETE must be considered probably a loss due to an unreported enemy attack. She is credited with sending three medium freighters, totaling 12,000 tons, to the bottom on this last patrol. During her first patrol, conducted in the East China Sea, KETE encountered no enemy eargets.

U.S.S. KETE

ABTS, L.A.............EM2c
ACKERMAN, E.......LT.CDR.
ADAMS, J.C.Jr.... LT.(JG)
APKING, J.D...........S1c
BERGADINE, D.L........F1c
BLODGETT, L.E.........S1c
BRANIGER, F.W.......CMoMM
BROOKS, C............QM2c
BURNSIDE, W.H.Jr...LT.(JG)
CALLAHAN, P.C.........F1c
COBRIN, B............EM3c
COOPER, E............EM2c
CROWLEY, R.W.........RM2c
COLE, H.M............RM3c
CRUTCHFIELD, C.R.Jr.LT.(JG)
DAWSON, W.H..........CK3c
DEININGER, F.R........F1c
DERRAH, H.W...........Y1c
DIETRICH, H.O.........CCS
DORTCHE, C.F........StM1c
DRAKE, K.L............LT.
DUL, W...............TM3c
EFFERSON, M.L.........S1c
EDGEN, D.P............S1c
FENTON, D.G.......LT.(JG)
FRENCH, H..........CMoMM
FRIESEN, B.........CMoMM
FULLER, R.W...........F1c
GLYNN, J.F.Jr.........S1c
GRISWOLD, F.J.........S1c
GUNZINGER, J.H.......RT2c
GWINN, E.E.Jr........EM3c
HAAG, B.H............ENS.
HART, R.A.............S1c
HARTBANK, G.E......MoMM3c
HAYDEN, P.O..........TM1c
HENDERSON, E..........S1c
HINES, J.L...........TM3c
HOLSHOUSER, J.R.......CTM
HOOPER, S.L..........RM3c
KATZ, A.J............EM2c
KELLY, N.W...........EM3c
KENSLER, E.N.........TM3c
KRAUT, R.P...........EM2c
LASITER, J.L.......MoMM3c
LITZENBURGER, F.Jr....GM3c
LOGSDON, E..........Bkr1c
LOWERY, B.B........MoMM3c
LYNN, C.W.Jr.......MoMM2c
MALKO, G.R............S1c
MARSICO, A.T..........F1c
MARTINI, F............CSM
MC LENDON, B.E.....MoMM2c
MESSENGER, G.R........S1c
MOORE, C.L............S1c
MOCCABEE, S.A........SC2c
MORRISON, H.F......MoMM1c
NEWTON, A.V........MoMM1c
O'BRIEN, J.A..........CBM
O'CONNOR, M.A.........F1c
PAGE, G.T..........MoMM1c
PETERSON, C.Jr........S1c
PIPER, I.V.........MoMM3c
PRICE, G.O.........MoMM2c
PUSHEE, D.C..........QM3c
RACER, R.R............S1c
REIMERS, F.F..........LT.
RICHARDS, F.A........GM2c
SCHEMM, G.J..........QM3c
SCHENABAR, M.D.....MoMM2c
SCHUMACHER, P.F......EM1c
SIMPSON, O.H.........CPhM
SNYDER, J.I..........EM2c
SPIKES, R.H.......LT.Exec.
STARR, J.G.Jr......MoMM1c
THOMAS, F.L.Jr........CRM
THOMPSON, G.R.........S1c
THORN, K.............GM3c
VAN DAM, P.V.........TM2c
VILLALBA, S.H.........F1c
WAGGONER, J.S.........CEM
WALLICK, R.A.........TM2c
WALLING, F.S.........TM2c
WESTPHALL, J.A........LT.
WILSON, G.W..........TM1c
WOODWARD, G.I........RT2c

TRIGGER (SS 237)

Departing Guam on 11 March 1945, TRIGGER, under the command of Cdr. D. R. Connole, headed for the Nansei Shoto area to conduct her twelfth war patrol. She was to provide rescue services for carrier based aircraft, as well as to carry out a normal offensive patrol.

After having sent several routine messages enroute to her area, TRIGGER reported her first action on 18 March. She stated that she had made a seven hour end around on a convoy she had previously reported, and had attacked. She sank one freighter and damaged another. The other two merchantmen of the convoy and four escorts proceeded west.

For some time, allied forces had been aware of a large Japanese restricted area west of the Nansei Shoto in the East China Sea. The area had been marked "restricted" in captured enemy notices to mariners, and allied forces were obliged to accept that the area was mined, and to keep out of it. Submarines had been warned of its presence and given its position, and were in the habit of proceeding around it to the north when patrolling the Formosa Strait and the adjacent China Coast. The convoy which had been attacked by TRIGGER was heading for this restricted area. It had always been strongly suspected that there were gaps in the minelines, since the area was too big to be at once completely and effectively mined.

Immediately after receipt of TRIGGER's report of the attack she had made, ComSubPac told her to give as much information as possible concerning the subsequent movements of the convoy, in order to help establish the existence of a safe passage through the restricted area. On 20 March TRIGGER reported that the attack she had made on the convoy had taken place at 28°-05'N, 126°-44E, and that she had been held down for three hours by escorts following the attack. When last seen or heard the convoy was heading for the restricted area, but TRIGGER had been unable to regain contact when she was able to surface.

On 24 March, TRIGGER was given further orders. On 25 March she was to move west and patrol between 29°N and 31°N west of the Nansei Shoto chain, remaining clear of restricted areas and outside the 100 fathom curve.

On 26 March TRIGGER was told to proceed at best speed to 31°N, 132°E, to form a coordinated attack group, known as Earl's Eliminators, with SEADOG and THREADFIN. The group was to be commanded by Cdr. E. T. Hydeman in SEADOG. This message to TRIGGER required an acknowledgement, but on the same day she sent a weather report which did not contain an acknowledgement, and she never was heard from again. On 28 March, SEADOG reported that she had been unable to communicate with TRIGGER since the formation of the wolfpack. To clarify the situation for the other submarines, TRIGGER was given

another assignment and told to acknowledge, and the wolfpack was disbanded on 30 March.

After many attempts to contact her by radio had failed, TRIGGER was ordered on 4 April to proceed to Midway. When she failed to arrive by 1 May 1945, she was reported as presumed lost in enemy water on her twelfth patrol, after a long and illustrious career.

Since she knew the position of the enemy restricted area containing mines, and had been told to keep clear of it, it is extremely doubtful that TRIGGER's loss was due to a mine. On the afternoon of 28 March a two hour long depth charge attack was conducted by Japanese planes in cooperation with ships in 32°-16'N, 132°-05'E. SILVERSIDES, HACKLEBACK, SEADOG and THREADFIN, all near the area, heard the attack. THREADFIN obtained two torpedo hits on a DE in 31°-49.5'N, 131°-44'E, and she was depth charged by accompanying escort vessels. Eighteen charges were dropped on her, none particularly close, but she reported that the charges were set for 450 feet, which made them much more dangerous than the usual run of depth charges. An hour later, THREADFIN reports, "Many distant strings of depth charges and several heavy explosions heard from what was believed to be the eastward. (In the opposite

direction from the location of our attacks). It sounded as though someone was getting quite a drubbing." No other submarine in the vicinity reported having been attacked, although all reported hearing many explosions.

The Japanese report of the above attack states, "Detected a submarine over eight times and bombed it. Ships also detected it-depth charged. Found oil pool of 1 x 5 miles in size the following day." Since it is extremely doubtful that THREADFIN received sufficient damage to have left the oil pool described by the Japanese, it must be presumed that TRIGGER was lost in this action. That it occurred two days after TRIGGER had been told to acknowledge a message, and none was ever received is not considered unusual. Conditions often forced submarines to delay transmissions for considerable periods of time.

TRIGGER is credited with one freighter sunk and another damaged on her final patrol. This makes a total of 27 ships sunk, for 180,600 tons, and 13 ships damaged, for 102,900 tons, during the ship's entire career. Her first patrol was in the Aleutians, but no attacks were made, since no worthy targets were contacted. Going to the Empire in the area south of Honshu for her second patrol, TRIGGER sent a freighter to the bottom, and damaged two large tankers and a freighter. TRIGGER's third patrol was a mining mission as well as an offensive

patrol; it, too, was in the Empire. She saw a large freighter blow up and sink when it hit a mine she had laid, and also sank two freighters by torpedo attacks. Also on 10 January 1943, TRIGGER torpedoed and sank the Japanese destroyer OKIKAZE near Honshu. TRIGGER covered the Palau-Wewak (New Guinea) traffic lanes on her fourth patrol and succeeded in sinking one freighter and damaging two more. Again in the area south of Honshu, TRIGGER on her fifth patrol sank a large freighter and damaged an aircraft carrier and a tanker.

Her sixth and seventh patrols were in the East China Sea. On her sixth she sank three good sized tankers and a freighter, doing damage to another freighter. Her seventh resulted in the sinking of four good sized freighters, one tanker, and one large transport. The eighth patrol of this vessel was made in the Carolines on the Truk-Guam route, and she sank a large freighter-transport and an escort vessel. She sank four freighter-transports as well as a patrol vessel near Palau on her ninth patrol; she also damaged a large tanker, two freighters and a sampan. TRIGGER's tenth patrol, as her last did, covered the northern Nansei Shoto area. She received partial credit for sinking a small tanker, which was sunk co-operatively with SALMON. TRIGGER's eleventh patrol was in the Empire, but resulted in disappointingly few enemy contacts and no attack apportunities. This ship was awarded the Presidential Unit Citation for her fifth, sixth and seventh patrols.

U.S.S. TRIGGER

ABSHER, N.A............FC3c
ARSENAULT, E.A.........S1c
BACKER, D.G.Jr.........EM3c
BALL, R.B...........MoMM1c
BARRY, J.V.............F1c
BERANEK, R.C..........EM3c
BIRD, J.B...........MoMM1c
BOEDING, J.M..........TM3c
BOLZ, K.W.............SM2c
BUTTS, H...............S1c
CAIN, B.W..............F1c
CARTER, A.J..........StM1c
COLES, H............MoMM1c
CONNOLE, D.R......CDR.C.O.
CRAIG, W.C.Jr.......MoMM3c
CRUTCHER, B.E..........F1c
CURRY, P.P............TM1c
DE LONE, M.V........MoMM3c
DERRICK, C.A..........GM3c
DODANE, R.L........LT.CDR.
DORRIES, R.J...........F1c
DOW, W.E...............S1c
DUNNAM, J.W..........FCS2c
DUSKO, J.P...........Bkr2c
EMMONS, W.L.Jr.........S1c
ENGLE, R.E............EM3c
FISHER, J.P...........EM3c
FISTE, H.L.............CEM
FOSTER, R.M...........TM3c
FRANKS, J.A.........MoMM3c
GLEASON, H.R.......LT.(JG)
GREENWELL, R.H..........LT.
HAMBRIGHT, R.E.Jr...MoMM2c
HAMPTON, G.T...........F1c
HARRISON, R.J.........RT2c
HOUSEHOLDER, J.R......EM1c
IOVINO, V.T...........EM3c
IRISH, C.B..............LT.
JOHANSON, L.A.........RT2c
JOHNSON, S.G...........ENS.
JOHNSTON, R.F.........TM2c
KELLY, R.M............EM2c
KEMARSKY, R.N.........RT1c
KIMMEL, M..............S1c
LIVINGSTON, K.A.......EM3c
MABEN, C.G............RM2c
MC HUGH, L.J.Jr.......TM3c
MAC VANE, A.L.........SM2c
MELTON, R.H..........CMoMM
MISNER, D.E.............LT.
MORGAN, H.P............S1c
MORIN, R.C.............F1c
MURRAY, R.W............S1c
NILES, F.L.............F1c
OLSON, D.T.............Y1c
OSTER, L..............SC1c
PALMER, G.E...........TM2c
PAYNE, L.R............TM1c
POLLACK, R.C..........EM2c
PROSS, J.S............QM1c
RAE, W.H..............TM3c
REED, J.A...........MoMM1c
ROBERTS, C.J.......LT.(JG)
ROBERTSON, C.C......MoMM1c
RONDEAU, N.N..........RM2c
SCHEIDEGGER, C.O......QM3c
SCHENCK, C.E........MoMM2c
SHEPHERD, J.E.III..LT.CDR.
SINCAVICH, J.W..........LT.
SMITH, D.L.............S1c
STAKICH, D.R........MoMM2c
STEWART, J.N..........EM1c
STOCK, M.N.............S1c
TARGOSZ, G.S..........GM3c
THOMPSON, N.E.........CK2c
THOMPSON, W.C.........EM2c
THORNBERRY, C.G........S1c
TURNER, H.J...........EM2c
WATSON, B.J...........SC3c
WEEKS, J.R.............CTM
WELCH, C.A..........MoMM2c
WIDDEKIND, F.H.........F1c
WILDEY, J.T...........GM1c
WILKINS, D.L...........S1c
WILKINS, L.W...........S1c
WILLIAMS, C.A........CMoMM
WORRELLS, C.M.Jr....MoMM2c
ZUGECIC, W.M..........CPhM

Ships Company USS Trigger at Guam

SNOOK (SS279)

SNOOK (Cdr. J. F. Walling) departed Guam on 25 March 1945 in company with BURRFISH (SS312) and BANG (SS385) to carry out a coordinated patrol with Commander Walling commanding the group. They were to patrol Luzon Strait, the south coast of China, and the east coast of Hainan, and to perform lifeguard duties if so directed by despatch. SNOOK returned to Guam for emergency repairs on 27 March, and departed on 28 March to rejoin her group. The patrol was SNOOK's ninth.

In accordance with her orders, weather reports were received daily from SNOOK as she proceeded westward until 1 April, when she was told to discontinue making them. On the same date, SNOOK was directed to proceed westward to join a coordinated attack group under Comander Cassedy in TIGRONE. BANG and BURRFISH already had been assigned lifeguard stations, and were not available for the attack group as originally planned.

Although the last message received from SNOOK by shore bases was on 1 April, TIGRONE was in contact with her until 8 April, at which time SNOOK's position was 18°-40'N, 111°-39'E. On 9 April TIGRONE was unable to raise her by radio, nor was she ever able to afterwards. TIGRONE being unable to raise her may be explained by the fact that on 10 April SNOOK was directed to move eastward toward Luzon Strait, and on 12 April she was ordered to lifeguard duty for British carrier based air strikes. Her position for this duty was in the vicinity of Sakeshima Gunto, about 200 miles east of northern Formosa. No acknowledgement for these orders was required. On 20 April the Commander of a British carrier task force reported he had a plane down in SNOOK's vicinity, but could not contact her by radio. SNOOK was ordered to search the area and to acknowledge these orders. When she failed to make a transmission, BANG was sent to make the search

J. F. Walling

and to rendezvous with SNOOK. Although BANG arrived on the scene and rescued three aviators, she saw nothing of SNOOK. When SNOOK had not appeared or been heard from by 16 May, she was reported as presumed lost on her ninth patrol.

Japanese anti-submarine attack reports available at this time give no information of an attack which might have been on SNOOK. There were mines in the vicinity of Sakeshima Gunto, but SNOOK had information of these which had been gained from captured enemy documents. It is improbable that she would have gone into the minefields unless intentionally to rescue a downed aviator. She was not asked to penetrate any minefield in effecting any rescue.

A number of enemy submarine contacts were reported in the vicinity of SNOOK's lifeguard station during the period in which her loss occurred. During April and May 1945, five Japanese submarines were sunk in the Nansei Shoto chain. The curcumstances surrounding SNOOK's loss suggest the possibility that one of these lost submarines may have torpedoed her while she was surfaced during her lifeguard duties and it was not reported. It is known that such tactics were suggested to Japanese submarine commanders by their superiors.

No attacks had been reported by SNOOK prior to her loss on this patrol. She was, however, responsible for sinking 22 enemy ships, totaling 123,600 tons and damaging 10 ships, for 63,200 tons, on her eight patrols prior to her loss. Her first patrol was from mid-April to the latter part of May 1943, along the China Coast from Formosa to the Empire. She sank four freighters, a patrol craft, a sampan and a trawler. In her second patrol, SNOOK covered the East China Sea area. She sank two freighters and damaged two tankers, one of the latter being a very large ship. During her third patrol, SNOOK covered areas in both the Yellow and East China Seas, and sank a transport and freighter, and damaged a sub chaser. Her fourth patrol was along the Empire trade routes to the south. Here she sank two freighters and damaged three more.

SNOOK went to the East China Sea again on her fifth patrol, and sank four freighters and a freighter-transport, while she damaged a fifth freighter. In the same area on her sixth patrol, SNOOK damaged one freighter. Her seventh patrol was in the Luzon Strait area and the northern South China Sea. She sank three freighters and damaged a fourth freighter and an unidentified vessel. SNOOK patrolled the Kurile region north of Japan on her eighth patrol, but contacted only three ships. Two were Russian and the other was not able to be attacked.

U.S.S. SNOOK

ADAMS, R.B..........CMoMM
BAGBY, E.E.J.........TM2c
BAUM, R.L............RT2c
BILLINGSLEY, R.S....MoMM3c
BOLGER, K.P...........F1c
BRANUM, B.A...........RM3c
BROWNING, N.E......MoMM3c
BROWNSTEIN, S.........EM3c
BURDICK, R.K..........RT1c
BURGER, L............PhM1c
BUSBY, C.R.........LT.(JG)
BYRON, D.A.............F1c
CAVE, J.E..............F1c
CESARE, B.A...........EM2c
CHOATE, S.D...........QM1c
CLARK, E.P.II......LT.(JG)
CRAWFORD, D.L.........GM1c
CRAWFORD, G.L..........F1c
CROSS, J.A.............F1c
DOLPH, W.L............RM1c
ECKENRODE, C.J.........S1c
EDMUNDS, C.F...........S1c
ELLIS, W.P............EM2c
ETKIN, H.R.Jr.........EM2c
FARREL, W.S.......LT.Exec.
FELABON, J.C.......MoMM3c
FRY, D.W..............EM3c
GAMBARDELLA, A.........S1c
GARDNER, S.P............LT.
GLASS, J.J.............F1c
GREGORINI, V.........Bkr2c
GRINDZAK, A............F1c
GROAT, J.E.........MoMM1c
GRUPP, P.H.........MoMM1c
GUTHRIE, A.T..........TM3c
HUGHES, R.L............Y2c
HURLEY, D.J............CEM
INGRAM, R.R............S1c
JOHNSON, H.M.........CMoMM
JOHNSTON, J.Jr........SC2c
JULIAN, H.F...........TM3c
KEISER, P.F............S2c
KELLOGG, W.E..........TM1c
KLOSTERMAN, F.J........F1c
KRAMER, N.T...........TM3c
LAMONT, T.W.II.........S1c
LANG, W.T..........MoMM1c
LUNDGREN, L.W..........S1c
LUNKEN, J.I........MoMM2c
MANEY, F.R.............F2c
MANLEY, J.G...........EM3c
MC ENTYER, O.W.........S1c
MC GAHAN, J.E.........QM3c
MC GUIRE, R.M..........F1c
MC NEILL, D.J......LT.(JG)
MLYNEK, V.P...........QM3c
MORGAN, C..........MoMM2c
MORGAN, J.K...........GM3c
OLSON, G.C.............S1c
PAGE, G.C.............TM1c
PARKER, J.S...........RM3c
PHILLIPS, N............S1c
REGAN, J.B.............F1c
REGISTER, M.L.........EM1c
REHBIT, W.J........MoMM2c
RODNEY, W.J..........StM1c
RUSSELL, A.M.Jr.......TM2c
SCHOEN, R.L...........EM3c
SCHRAMM, W.C..........FC3c
SCULLY, J.F...........TM3c
SCHWENDEMANN, R.L..LT.(JG)
SHELTON, W.E..........St3c
SILVIA, B.............SC1c
SLOAN, J.C.............S1c
SPENCE, E.L............S1c
SUKOLO, R R...........RT3c
TOULSON, H.T...........F1c
WAGNER, H.K...........EM2c
WALLING, J.F......CDR.C.O.
WELCH, A.W.Jr......LT.(JG)
WILL, J.A..........MoMM1c
WOOD, R.E.Jr.........FCS2c
WOOD, R.E..............F1c
WRIGHT, J.N...........ENS.

USS Snook - Award Ceremony

LAGARTO (SS 371)

LAGARTO, under Cdr. F. D. Latta, departed Subic Bay, P. I., on 12 April 1945, for her second patrol in the South China Sea. On 27 April, she was directed to the outer part of Siam Gulf.

LAGARTO contacted BAYA, already patrolling in Siam Gulf on 2 May 1945, and exchanged calls with her by SJ radar. Later that day BAYA sent LAGARTO a contact report on a convoy she had contacted consisting of one tanker, one auxiliary and two destroyers. LAGARTO soon reported being in contact with the convoy, and began coming in for an attack with BAYA. However the enemy escorts were equipped with 10cm radar, and detected BAYA and drove her off with gunfire, whereupon the two submarines decided to wait and plan a subsequent attack.

Early on the morning of 3 May 1945, LAGARTO and BAYA made a rendezvous at about 7°-55'N, 102°-18'E and discussed plans. LAGARTO was to dive on the convoy's track to make a contact at 1400, while BAYA was to be ten to fifteen miles further along the track. During the day, numerous contacts reports were exchanged. At 0010 on 4 May after a prolonged but unsuccessful attack, BAYA was finally driven off by the alert escorts, and no further contact of any kind was ever made with LAGARTO.

Japanese information available now records an attack on a U. S. submarine made by the Minelayer HATSUTAKA, believed to be one of the two radar-equipped escorts of the convoy attacked. The attack was made at 7°-55'N, 102°-00'E in about 30 fathoms of water, and in view of the information presented above, the attack here described must be presumed to be the one which sank LAGARTO.

This vessel's first patrol was in the Nansei Shoto chain as part of an anti picket boat sweep made by submarines to aid Admiral Halsey's Task Force 38 in getting carrier planes to Japan undetected. She sank the Japanese submarine RO-49 on 24 February 1945, and participated in several surface gun attacks with HADDOCK and SENNET. Two small vessels were sunk and two more damaged in these attacks, and LAGARTO shared credit for the results with these submarines. Commander Latta had previously made seven patrols as Commanding Officer of NARWHAL. Every patrol made by this officer was designated successful for the award of combat insignia, a record surpassed by no commanding officer in the Submarine Force.

F. D. Latta

U.S.S. LAGARTO - Launching at Manitowoc, Wisconsin

U.S.S. LAGARTO

ANDREWS, H.D. ....CTM
ANKER, C. ....CMoMM
AUCHARD, F.L. ......LT.(JG)
BJORNSON, C.H. F1c
BREITHAUOT, C.W.Jr. Y2c
BRITAIN, W.L. ....CRM
BROCK, A. S2c
BYRER, C.R. F1c
CARLETON, W.E. RM1c
CATOZZI, S.G. QM3c
CATHEY, L.T. MoMM3c
CLOUSE, G.E. TM2c
COOK, C.T. MoMM1c
DAVIS, J.E.Jr. TM2c
DOUD, L.M. RM2c
ENNS, A.H. TM3c
FISHER, R.L. MoMM1c
FRANTZ, J.J. S1c
FRASCH, O.R. MoMM1c
GERLACH, J.N. F1c
GRACE, R.F. ....
GRAVES, W. QM1c
GRAY, D.J. EM2c
GREEN, R. StM2c
GREGORICK, R.L. EM1c
GREGORY, J.P. S2c
HALSTEAD, G.E. RM3c
HARDGREE, T.L. MoMM1c
HARRINGTON, G.C. ...MoMM3c
HARRINGTON, T.J. ...MoMM2c
HARRIS, J.B. S1c
HARRISON, J.C. MoMM3c
HINKEN, W.R. TM3c
HONAKER, W.F. EM3c
IRVING, L.G. ....LT.
JEFFERSON, H. S1c
JOBE, J. ....CEM
JOHNSON, F. S1c
JOHNSON, J.R. ....CEM
JORDAN, W.H.Jr. S1c
KEENEY, A.H.Jr. ....LT.
KIMBALL, F.M. RT1c
KIRTLEY, A. StM1c
KNEIDL, J.W. MoMM2c
LATTA, F.D. ........CDR.C.O.
LEE, N.B.Jr. S1c
LEWIS, R.J. MoNM2c
LYNCH, L.J. F1c
MABIN, W.T. SM1c
MARRIOTT, J.M.Jr. S1c
MC DONALD, J.H. SC3c
MC GEE, J.M. TM2c
MENDENHALL, W.H. .....LT.Exec.
MOORE, W.L. F1c
MOSS, W.G. S1c
O'HARA, L.R. RT2c
ORTEGA, H.E. F1c
PAPER, D.M. S1c
PASH, J.S. ....LT.(JG)
PATTERSON, R.R. RM3c
PERRY, R.C. F1c
PETERSON, J.W. TM3c
PETERSON, R.F. QM3c
PHELPS, W.B. ....LT.(JG)
PLUSHNIK, H.R. F1c
PRICE, G.A. ....CMoMM
REEVES, M.D. EM2c
REICHERT, R.E. F1c
ROBINSON, T.T. BM1c
ROOT, J.H. MoMM1c
RUBLE, H.T. ....LT.
RUTLEDGE, W.I. S1c
SHACKELFORD, W.C. SM2c
SIMMERMAN, R.F. TM2c
SPALDING, R.B. ....CPhM
STEHN, J.E. GM2c
STIEGLER, D.G. EM2c
ST. JOHN, C.M.Jr. EM3c
TAIT, F. MoMM2c
TODD, H.A.Jr. ....LT.(JG)
TURNER, F.D. ....CGM
WADE, A.M. S1c
WARNICK, W.C. S1c
WICKLANDER, M.M. MoMM2c
WILLIAMS, J.L. S1c

BATTLE SURFACE - Painting By Vandis

BONEFISH (SS223)

In company with TUNNY and SKATE, BONEFISH (SS223), commanded by Cdr. L. L. Edge, departed Guam on 28 May 1945 to conduct her eighth war patrol. This coordinated attack group under Commander G. W. Pierce in TUNNY, which was one of three groups then penetrating the Japan Sea, was ordered to transit Tsushima Strait on 5 June 1945, and to conduct offensive patrol in the Sea of Japan off the west central coast of Honshu. This area was further subdivided, with BONEFISH assigned to patrol the northern portion.

BONEFISH successfully transited Tsushima Strait, and made rendezvous with TUNNY on 16 June 1945, in position 36°-40'N, 135°-24'E. Commander Edge reported he had sunk one large transport and one medium freighter to date. On the morning of 18 June, TUNNY and BONEFISH rendezvoused in the vicinity of 38°-15'N, 138°-24'E. BONEFISH asked permission to conduct a submerged daylight patrol in Toyama Wan, in the mid part of western Honshu, and having received it, departed for Suzo Misaki. She was never seen or heard from again.

L. L. Edge

BONEFISH, in accordance with the operation order, was to renezvous with the other eight submarines of the three groups, in latitude 46°-50'N, longitude 140°-00E at sunset on 23 June 1945, in preparation for the transit on 24 June of La Perouse Strait. BONEFISH did not make this rendezvous, and after the other eight vessels had successfully transited La Perouse Strait, TUNNY on 25 and 26 June waited off the entrance to the strait and unsuccessfully tried to contact BONEFISH.

Rear Admiral Christie Greets Crew at P l Harbor December 1943

Provision was made in the operation order governing this patrol group for submarines in case of necessity to proceed to Russian waters to claim a 24 hour haven, or to submit to internment in extreme need, or for them to make their exit from the Japan Sea prior to or after 24 June. When all of these possibilities had been examined, and she had not been seen or heard from by 30 July 1945, BONEFISH was reported as presumed lost.

Japanese records of anti-submarine attacks mention an attack made on 18 June 1945, at 37°-18′N, 137°-25′E in Toyama Wan. A great many depth charges were dropped, and wood chips and oil were observed. This undoubtedly was the attack which sank BONEFISH.

In total, this vessel sank 31 enemy vessels, for a total tonnage of 158,500, and damaged 7, for 42,000 tons. She began her career as an active member of the Submarine Force with a patrol in the South China Sea in September and October 1943. She sank three freighters, two transports, a tanker and a schooner, and damaged a fourth freighter. On her second war patrol, conducted in the Celebes sea and near Borneo, BONEFISH sank two freighters and an escort vessel, and damaged a minelayer. Again in the South China Sea on her third patrol, BONEFISH sank a very large tanker, a medium freighter and a schooner, and damaged a second large tanker. This ship went to the Celebes and Sulu Seas for her fourth patrol and sank two freighters, a transport and a tanker, while she damaged a sub chaser. Post war information also reveals that on 14 May 1944, while firing at the large tanker which she sank, BONEFISH hit and sank the Japanese destroyer INAZUMI.

This vessel's fifth patrol was in the same area as her fourth, and she sank two small freighters, a large tanker and five miscellaneous small craft, while she damaged a second tanker. BONEFISH covered a South China Sea area in her sixth patrol, and sank two large tankers and a freighter during September and October 1944. She also damaged two medium freighters. Then, after a thorough overhaul and the installation of much new equipment in San Francisco, BONEFISH made her seventh patrol in the East China Sea. She had only one attack opportunity and did no damage. However, she took two Japanese prisoners from a downed enemy plane, and performed reconnaissance work on the southern end of Korea. BONEFISH was awarded the Navy Unit Commendation for the period of her first and third through sixth patrols.

U.S.S. BONEFISH

ABEL, D.Z..............ENS.
ADAMS, T.B..............Y3c
ADAMS, W.S............Bkr3c
AMBURGEY, L.M......LT.(JG)
ANDERSON, G.I.Jr....MoMM3c
AURELI, S.J............S1c
BECK, M.L.............GM2c
BROWN, R.W.............F1c
BROWNING, J.A.........EM1c
BURDICK, G.A........MoMM2c
CANFIELD, K.T.......MoMM2c
COLEMAN, J.A..........RM3c
COOLEY, Q.L...........StM2c
DANIELSON, O.C........SC2c
DUNN, D.H..............ENS.
EDGE, L.L.........CDR.C.O.
ENOS, E.R..............F1c
EPPS, W.H.Jr..........StM2c
FELD, P.F..............F1c
FOX, D.C..............RM2c
FRANK, R.E...........CMoMM
FUGETT, M.A...........QM2c
FULLER, G.N..........CMoMM
HACKSTAFF, H.J........RM2c
HARMAN, G.O...........TM1c
HASIAK, J.J...........TM3c
HESS, R.D..............S1c
HOUGHTON, W.S.........TM1c
JENKINS, R.W..........EM1c
JOHNSON, J.C..........RT1c
JOHNSON, S.E.Jr.........CQM
JOHNSTON, T.M......LT.(JG)
KALINOFF, M.W..........F1c
KARR, W.G.............RM2c
KEEFER, R.T............S1c
KERN, F.B..............ENS.
KING, E.W.............EM2c
KISSANE, J.E...........S2c
KNIGHT, F.S...LT.CDR.Exec.
LAMOTHE, J.L...........Cox
LARACY, J.J.Jr........EM3c
LEWIS, J.A.............CGM
LOCKWOOD, T.G.......PhoM3c
LYNCH, J.F............TM2c
MAGHAN, A.G............F1c
MARKLE, J.E...........EM2c
MC BRIDE, R.J.......MoMM2c
MILES, H.V.Jr.......MoMM1c
NESTER, S.A...........EM3c
NEWBERRY, J.R..........F1c
OLSON, D.H..........MoMM2c
O'TOOLE, W.P..........EM3c
PARTON, J.F...........EM3c
PAULEY, G.W...........RM3c
PASKIN, T.............RT2c
PHENICIE, J.E.......MoMM3c
PRIMAVERA, L.J.... .MoMM1c
PRUNIER, G.A..........EM3c
QUENETT, C.F..........TM2c
RALEY, C.H.............F1c
RAY, R.C.Jr...........SM1c
RAYNES, J.A...........EM1c
RHANOR, C.J............S1c
REID, J.A..............F1c
RICE, R.P..............S1c
ROSE, R.A.II...........ENS.
SCHILLER, R.G..........F1c
SCHMIDLING, C.J......FCS1c
SCHWEYER, R.H.........RT2c
SLATER, R.E........LT.(JG)
SMITH, L.C.Jr......LT.(JG)
SNODGRASS, R.L.........Y1c
STAMM, R.S............SC1c
SURBER, R.M...........EM2c
TIERNEY, D.R........MoMM1c
VELIE, R.C...........TME2c
VINCENT, T.F.Jr........S1c
WHITRIGHT, W..........TM2c
WILSON, J.R............F1c
WILLIAMS, J.J.......MoMM2c
WILLIAMS, J.R.Jr......FC3c
WILLIAMS, T.F..........F1c
WINEGAR, C.D..........TM3c
WOLFE, L.E............TM3c
WRIGHT, G.W..........PhM1c

BONEFISH Arriving at Pearl Harbor

BULLHEAD (SS332)

Departing Fremantle for her third war patrol, BULLHEAD (Lt. Cdr. E. R. Holt, Jr.) on 31 July 1945, started for her area (from 110°-00'E to 115°-30'E, in the Java Sea). She was to leave her patrol area at dark on 5 September and head for Subic Bay, P.I. CAPITAINE and PUFFER were also to patrol in the Java Sea area, as were the British submarines TACITURN and THOROUGH.

BULLHEAD arrived in area on 6 August, but CAPITAINE did not arrive until 13 August. On 12 August, CAPITAINE ordered BULLHEAD to take position the following day in a scouting line with CAPITAINE and PUFFER. There was no reply and on 15 August, CAPITAINE reported, "Have been unable to contact BULLHEAD by any means since arriving in area."

Since those submarines named above were in the same general area as BULLHEAD, and COD and CHUB passed through in transit at various times, it is difficult to point to one Japanese anti-submarine attack as the one which sank BULLHEAD. However, the most likely one occurred on 6 August 1945, when an enemy army plane attacked with depth charges in position 8°-20'S, 115°-42'E. It claimed two direct hits, and for ten minutes thereafter, there was a great amount of gushing oil and air bubbles rising in the water. Since the position given is very near the Bali coast, it is presumed that the proximity of mountain peaks shortened BULLHEAD's radar range and prevented her receiving a warning of the plane's approach.

BULLHEAD sank four enemy ships, totalling 1,800 tons, and damaged three ships, for 1,300 tons, in her first two patrols. Her first patrol was made in the South China Sea from the latter part of March to the end of April 1945. No enemy contacts were made, but on 31 March and again on 24 April BULLHEAD bombarded Pratas Island with her five inch gun. She also rescued three airmen from a downed B-29 following an air strike on the China Coast. In May and June 1945 BULLHEAD patrolled the Gulf of Siam and the South China Sea during her second patrol. Here she sank two small freighters, a schooner and a sub chaser, and damaged two more sub chasers and another small freighter, all in gun actions.

U.S.S. BULLHEAD

AIPLE, A.Jr............QM2c
ANDERSON, H.A...........Y2c
BARRINGER, R.H..........S1c
BELL, G.L............MoMM1c
BENNER, J.D.............S1c
BERTRAM, W.D.........MoMM2c
BRIDGSTOCK, H.R........RT2c
BRUME, R.M...........MoMM2c
BUCZEK, K.J............TM2c
BURNS, R.B..............CTM
CHURCH, R.W..........MoMM1c
COLLINS, J.F...........EM3c
CRANDALL, H.E........MoMM3c
DAHL, E.M............MoMM3c
DAVIDSON, G.M...........F1c
DAVIDSON, J.K........MoMM2c
DAY, C.J...............EM2c
DOUGHTERTY, C.W........SC1c
ENGEBRETSEN, E.M........CQM
FAHEY, J.P.............RM3c
FOSTER, R.G.............F1c
FOUST, K.E.............QM3c
FRITZ, F.C.............RM2c
GAY, C.W...............EM3c
GILHEANY, J.F.Jr.......RM3c
GOSSETT, P.S.......LT.(JG)
GRAVES, C.M.............S1c
GREAVES, W.F...........EM3c
HACKETT, H.B..........StM2c
HACKMAN, E.D.Jr.........LT.
HANCOCK, J.L...........GM2c
HARRIS, J.J............QM3c
HAWKINS, W.P...........BM2c
HEATON, G.V..........MoMM2c
HELFERICH, T.P........CMoMM
HENRIKSEN, D.O.....LT.(JG)
HOLT, E.R.Jr...LT.CDR.C.O.
HUISMAN, L.W............S1c
IRELAND, W.............TM2c
JENKINS, L.L...........EM2c
JENSEN, J.R............EM3c
JEWELL, F.J............QM2c

JOHNSON, P.Jr.........StM1c
JONES, J.W..............CEM
KEISTER, R.A...........RT3c
KOPF, J.J..............EM3c
KULCZYCKI, W.A..........ENS.
MANNAS, O.V............TM2c
MARIN, H.K...........MoMM2c
MARKHAM J.P............TM3c
MCDERMOTT, H.A.......MoMM3c
MORGAN, G.P............TM3c
OLSON, P.W..............S1c
OVEFBEEK, P.F...........S1c
PALMER; R.W.............F1c
PARKS, W.J.............GM1c
PARPAL, J.J........LT.(JG)
PATTENGALE, R.M........TM3c
PATTERSON, R.S........SoM2c
PEART, W.M.............EM1c
PERRY, R.J...........MoMM1c
PHILLIPS, K.R.......LT. Exec
PLATT, C.W.............SC3c
PINDER, R.A...........CMoMM
RALSTON, W.J.Jr........TM3c
RITCHIE, R.J...........EM3c
ROBERTS, J.A...........EM1c
SANDOVAL, J.............S1c
SCHLEGEL, L.A...........F1c
SCHMIDT, O.G.H..........F1c
SHORT, W.E.............TM1c
SHEUY, B.Jr............SC3c
SIEFKEN, D.M..........FCS2c
SIMMS, J.II........LT.(JG)
SMIDA, E."M"..........PhM1c
SMITH, C.J..............CRM
SMITH, W.M..............CEM
STIFTER, F.T...........RT2c
STRASSLE, R.W......LT.(JG)
TAYLOR, C.H.............S1c
TOBIAS, M............MoMM3c
WATSON, A.T...........CMoMM
WEBB, L.L...............S1c
WIERSMA, E.J............F1c

No thought of flight, none of retreat, no unbecoming deed that argued fear; each on himself relied, as only in his arm the moment lay of victory.

Milton: Paradise Lost

Printed by Fourteenth Naval District
Publications and Printing Office
Pearl Harbor, T. H.

www.ingramcontent.com/pod-product-compliance
Ingram Content Group UK Ltd.
Pitfield, Milton Keynes, MK11 3LW, UK
UKHW061831190726
13855UKWH00006B/1755